# An Uncommon Truth

## A story of friendship and the search for Truth.

# Jesse MacDonald
# Rene Sanchez

# Volume 1: Getting to Jesus

Why a book (mac):

What am I doing writing a book? Even attempting to seems crazy, maybe even arrogant. It's easy to say in a way, I'm being called to. Jesus wants me to. Not just me, but my friend as well. Both of us need to write this book, we need to tell a story, a very particular story of our friendship and our journey. He as a guide and I as an eager, but reluctant student. Well not quite. I thought that I was the teacher, and that he was the lost student, at least for awhile, a long while. Eventually though, I realized the truth, which was that I was lost and searching, while he was standing on solid ground patiently watching me flail around, fighting my way to the truth, or maybe more honestly, fighting against it. It was a long journey 8 to 10 years worth of close, intimate conversations, with a background as simple as a cafe, or as extraordinary as remote mountain wilderness. The journey is still continuing, but I hope it's more as equals, than of a lost arrogant soul and his friend who watches with humble concern. This is really a story of truth of finding God and of reaching Jesus. But it's unique, at least it's our own and personal, but maybe it's quite normal. It's not all faith and all miracles, though I think in the end it is a miracle and faith was definitely involved. You see I am a person who gets possessed by ideas and takes them to their end. I live them out. I don't really think them through completely. I just say to myself, "that sounds right or true, lets see if it works." I do that until I realize it doesn't. I sort of, really, only learn the hard way. I really try though, I argue it, I believe it, and I live it. I'm not bragging about this, i'm just telling you how I operate. I don't even know why I'm like this, but i've been this way for pretty much my entire adult life. I was actually a way more stable child and adolescent then I have been as an adult. My guess is that as a child I didn't bear the responsibility of my free will nearly as much as I do as an adult, and I wasn't searching, I was completely naive and ignorant, and therefore temporarily blissful. The good news is that I live life and I learn, but I'm restless, I'm always digging at something. Well not always, but I am working at an idea or solution to life, to psychic boredom or existential boredom, and I'm willing to admit when it isn't working, or when it's not worth it, or when it made things worse, or sometimes makes things better. Like right now, writing this book while having my kids distract me, ask for snacks, play with a loud spiderman doll, ask for a bottle, fight with each other over the spider man. It's not working, so I need to stop. Good bye.

Why Me? Why Mac? (sanchez):

At first glance, Mac and I seem an odd pair. It has been laughable the looks we get in public because he's a tall white dude with tattoos and I'm a short, stocky, brown dude. The beginning of our journey is equally odd. I think God in his infinite wisdom even used my sinful nature to begin our friendship so Mac could see that I was honest in my quest for big "T" Truth. I have been a believer since I was 12 years old. I know this sounds weird and you're thinking, "Oh, well...he just doesn't know what else is out there and; therefore, I don't' have to listen to him." You are right and wrong. You are wrong that I do not know what else is out there. Very early on, I asked myself the big questions, "Do I just believe this because it's what I was 'raised' with? Is there something else out there MORE true? How can I be sure that God is the answer?" I have spent my life pursuing and refining these questions and the answers to them. You are also right...you don't have to listen to me. You don't have to listen to anyone. You don't even have to listen to the Absolute Power trying to speak to you through the universe, your relationships, your heart, and the Holy Spirit. The absolute power of the universe has given you the power to ignore Him...so what chance do I have against an unwilling heart? None. This is all to point out why Mac and I became best friends and travelers on this strange and dangerous path. Every person looks back at themselves and thinks, "Oh man...I was such a goober (or some version of that)". I will say that for Mac this was not the case. As I was called to minister to him and to serve him, I remember being floored by his ability to follow his beliefs. I had become used to people saying one thing and living a completely different way. Yet, here was a guy that lived what he believed. I could see hope here. I could see that if his vision was calibrated correctly, then he would be a powerful ally. I had lived for so long alone because eventually the falseness of beliefs would drive a wedge between myself and "friends". Here was a guy that if you could point out his flaw logically...he would change! Just like that. What I had come to believe was only practiced by myself and authors long dead was now in front of me. As radically different as we seemed on the outside, here was a guy that was just like me in his heart. He wanted truth desperately. He was willing to lay aside long held beliefs if he was wrong. He was intelligent and reasonable and still listened to his heart. I imagine it is a lot like someone who is an expert in a field being at a party where people try and and impress him with the little knowledge they have of his field and he begins to predict how each conversation will begin and end. Suddenly, here is someone that is an expert in another field that seems unrelated but because both people have sacrificed, studied, and searched; they are instantly joined in the knowledge of what it is like to struggle for new heights, new truths, and a willingness to change how they have been doing something because there is a better way. This is what it was like to meet Mac. He had a mind like Aristotle...like C.S. Lewis...he was a rare man of principals and action. So began our long journey. We had an unspoken commitment to being honest, patient, kind, forgiving, and adventurous. It was a mixture of climbing Mount Everest and exploring outer space. We weren't sure what we would find or how hard it would be, but we were committed to reaching the top...from there we would fly.

**Difficulty in writing the book (mac):**

Another attempt at this book. We struggle with getting what we do down. We are trying to put down what we know to be true. We are trying to write about our journey. It is way harder than anticipated. Stumbling around in darkness comes to mind. We think we have something to say. Something to add. We don't know how to say it exactly, in what way, or what medium to say it in. I think I need to write, just for myself to at least eliminate from a possible way out of our current occupation. High school teachers, ugh, I don't even want to explain. So I won't not right now. I need to focus on this, I so desperately am running from mediocrity. I have been for some time. Accepting a small existence of struggle and pain seems out of the question. At least to struggle at something that seems worthwhile or meaningful seems appropriate. How do you find meaning in a situation that seems like a trap. Seems like a giant chinese handcuff, where the harder the struggle, the more ensnared you become. Looking back, at first glance, there seem to be some choices and actions that are regrettable, some big decisions that were wrong and only if I could go back and make a different choice things would be fine now.  But then upon further examination those choices are built upon other less significant or at least seemingly less weighted choices and actions, and those branch back to a time where I don't know how conscious or mature or awake I was to have made any other choice. So at some point it's all an interesting entanglement of free will and then my not so free nature and circumstances my father and mothers sins, my neighborhood, schools, teachers, friends and their sins and all of their good as well to get me here today. Still doubting if this is what I ought to be doing with the little time we are given on this earth and in this life.

The process or method of seeking truth (mac):

Back to what we do, we being my best friend and I, Sanchez. What we do and what we have been doing is talking, but it's not just your average conversation. It has been a continuous conversation about the nature of us, us as humans and the world we live in. It isn't a lofty philosophical debate, that we treat as a game and then actually don't apply. It's more like a continuous therapeutic session of real discovery and growth. We go, this seems right and true and real, now let me try it out in the world and see if it works. Then it does, or it doesn't, and based on the working or not, we continue it or give it up. Well kind of. It's not even that easy. It's like observing closely how we actually are, flaws and all, impulses, beliefs, strengths, and weaknesses. Then after observing and examining them, we take them apart, comparing and contrasting until we start to find some nugget of value that we can abstract and make universal or at least rings true. We don't just use ourselves, we sort of use everything, our families, colleagues, movies, books, tv, friends, etc. I'm even reluctant to write friends here because the real is that there is really only one friend that I can speak of, the rest are illusions or fragments of friends, perversions even. This is a hard truth to admit and even harder to actually live. That's exactly what we do we attempt to find and face the truth and in order to do this you have to be willing to look in the dark places the places you want to avoid. We think it the only way to actually learn and discover the real. This temporary sacrifice of discomfort ultimately leads to a deeper comfort and truer existence. This book is maybe an attempt to find more friends. Or at least help others be better friends. The purpose of this book is even a work in progress. I think we're trying to lay out a real journey of both seeking the real true nature of reality, of friendship, to tell an interesting story, all while attempting to help others along the way. We both want to help. We both have applied and continue to apply the lessons that we've learned in our own lives. We both want to know if we're wrong, there is a real possibility that we're in a positive feedback loop, of agreeing because we're friends, of missing key flaws in our thoughts and actions. If we use the pragmatic and practical definition of truth, that is the thing works or doesn't, then from some angles I can argue that we are failing in our path. In that, we have no other friends, and very few people around us that seem to understand what we're up to, or if they do, are willing or able to play along, or even follow along. We want to know if we are flawed in our beliefs and/ or reasoning, or that the people who come into contact with us and that ultimately choose to walk away are wrong, or I suppose some other option that we haven't considered. Such as, we're both wrong or nobody is. To add to it we haven't taken our path lightly nor our beliefs nor our actions or thoughts for that matter. We have bet our life on it, but we both, I think are willing to accept the possibility of being wrong and looking as squarely as possible at our own reflection and accompanying shadow and admit defeat, walk back in shame to a more stable position. We aren't going to just roll over, but the possibility of being wrong, or off in our journey is an open door, as a matter of fact for me, I'm even partly hoping I am, my life isn't perfect and if my aim is off I want to know I really do. I think we both do. The person reading this we ask to do the same otherwise you're just wasting your time and I'm wasting my life pouring it out on these pages in the these words and sentences.

How can we tell it's working? (mac):

One indicator that I'm on the right track is that I'm in way less psychic pain now than I once was. I'm in less despair and discomfort. My life has more meaning now than it used to. I could just chalk it up to age, but that wouldn't be an honest analysis. I observed long ago that older isn't better it doesn't mean you have more figured out. It always seemed like it should but it seemed it was rarely the case, or rather it is rarely the case. So just because im not young anymore isn't a good enough reason to give that fact credit for a better life. Another way to tell is that I've been doing the above for years and years that is seeking for a way, the way, the truth, the light, the answer, something, anything that actually works. Whatever I had wasn't working it was weak and caused harm to myself and to others. So I know what I have now is significantly better than what I once had. In that fact, there is no doubt. Anything that did work before such as being honest isn't thrown out with this new and better way, it simply gets put into its proper place or highlighted in a way that makes its importance more clear, more relevant, and more true. So I guess the inner terrain of my conscious, the deepened calmness in my soul, my understanding my individual psyche, my improved levels of pain, guilt, and desperation, all the negative emotions are so much less and I understand them so much better, that it's almost incomprehensible. And therefore one such proof of the validity of our discovered method and claim.

My relationships with others, the ones that have stuck around, are better, deeper, truer, built upon a more solid foundation than before. Amazingly so, having a clearer grasp on the nature of reality and our place in it, allows me to interact with others in the proper way with the proper rhythm. The ones that aren't around, though extremely hurtful and missed, I can clearly see the flaw. I can clearly see that I stayed and they walked away. I can clearly see how off they are. I would even venture to say that they would admit it was they that left and it was by their own admission of guilt, cowardice, flaws, weakness, running from truth and seeking shallow comfort. Some have admitted it, while others I can just see it.

The other place to judge the validity our way is through observation of the lives of the surrounding community. We have the ability, using an objective standard, to see the fatal flaws in others ideas actions and words. We can see from their less true, more off  ideologies, and their idol worshipping, their false absolutes, their placing themselves too high or too low, and their placing their attributes, skills, and talents too high or too low, we can see them stumble, just I did and do. The stumblings in life that are inevitable when your aim is off, that I couldn't even see are now lit up as to see their real danger and therefore the real ability to avoid them. (there is some truth to once an alcoholic always an alcoholic, more precisely though the root of the demons that possess us aren't easily eradicated but tend to remain lurking and hiding until our pride and arrogance proclaims its victory over evil it's then that the spark is lit and life is given to the flame of death) Only through the awareness of my own filth can I see the same in others, and only through Grace can I attempt to manage my own filth and attempt to help another.

Yet another indicator of the validity of the way we have yet to lay out is its sound logical structure. Its wide ranging application its historical accuracy. The universality of it from the dawn of time to present. The lateral and vertical application of it, the accessibility of different levels of intelligence and maturity to it. There are echos of it everywhere we look; literature, movies, tv shows, the news, art, philosophy, and science, and even random encounters. It explains so much, fits so well, is often unexpected, and not necessarily what we would have wanted or chosen. The other is that we haven't met a formidable opponent, other variation, or more applicable way. No matter where we've looked. And we ve looked and looked and continue to look. The strange thing is, the more we look the more evidence appears to support not contradict our claim. At every turn every small truth or new fact they all point in the same direction, they all fit in to the same puzzle. It's as if we have found a map and all of the landmarks, street signs, hazards, amusements, rest stops, and watering holes all make sense, you suddenly know where you are and where you are headed. You now know where you've been and where you got lost. When the map is correct the adventure is manageable, when your map is wrong or compass broken then the terrain is deadly.

Everything Matters (mac):

This matters, we matter, and I matter. We are important, this is important, what we say and do matters. When I tried to live as if it didn't, as if they didn't, things quickly fell apart. It's pretty easy to see that when I pretend it doesn't matter and that I willfully or unknowingly meet pain either giving or receiving, the weight of meaning pours forth so unstoppable and unavoidable that we quickly move to minimize it, remove it, or escape it. Even taking our very existence into our own hands, or worse others. Less dramatically we take measures to mask or suppress the pain. This does nothing but admit pain is real meaningful and significance. Fear is a motivator, but pain reigns supreme. Just think of the man jumping out of a skyscraper window to avoid the pain of fire, facing his fear of certain death by falling to the ground from hundreds of feet in the air. I wanted pain not to matter, I wanted my words to not matter or at least at times, I wanted desperately for words and actions of others not to cause me pain. I wondered honestly if I was just too sensitive for this world. I wanted things to matter only when they were beneficial to me, or helped me move through the world unharmed. But when they did harm me or somebody else I wanted to claim, even desperately, that it didn't matter, that none of it does. Sticks and stones will break my bones but words will never hurt me. This bothered me, because the pain of words have always hurt far deeper than the physical pain of a stick. This is a best wishful thinking at worse a deeply misguided bit of advice we tell children to further harm them with a blatant lie. To tell them that the pain they are feeling from their mean friend isn't real sets the stage to have the child think the fault is in them rather than the one that through the insult. This line of thinking is the beginning of nihilism, because if the words use to harm don't matter, then the words I cry for help don't matter either. This then implies the breaking of my bones is somehow separate from my spirit but if my heart doesn't matter then why should my body. So in the end nothing matters. Then we have reached nihilism and it's cold deadly attractiveness. I see the glimmer of complete chaos and the familiar sense of "fuck it" "i don't care" "screw it" "what does it matter anyway" So I tiptoe closer and closer to it, wanting to sip its power and claim its throne in my life. Then the logic that got me there begins to whisper, wait a minute, if nothing matters, and you yourself used your pride and arrogant intellect to get here you must abandon it, for it too falls into the abyss of no significance. I cannot claim nothing matter makes sense, if sense itself doesn't matter. Then the real lie is exposed, immediately and fiercely, you only want the nihilistic view to be applied sometimes, and you want somethings to matter, and other things to not, you want to decide yourself, you want to proclaim good and evil in accordance with your own center of the universe selfish disgust, you want to be God. You want to use logic when she suits you, but treat her as a mistress, in the true non committed sense, of using her when it pleases you. And like all good mistresses, she demands more of you, she begs you to leave your true commitments your other idols your other ideas that go against her. I shall commit to nothing and everything depending on my mood. Again leaving logic aside for a rationalist approach. I never commit and therefore never admit to anything and quietly because I will never admit to this right here. Nobody will know. I will build a mask and I will always hide my true intentions, and I will win and gain supremacy. I am perfect, and if I'm not, my mask is, so who will know the difference? For acting in a truly nihilistic way, for even a moment, brings forth such destruction and chaos, that I can't say that I have ever actually attempted it. Only have I pretended to, or danced near the fire, threatening to throw myself in, but never having the courage or stupidity to follow through. I actually think it impossible to remain Nihilistic in any real sense. Even in small seemingly trivial situations the horror of nihilism screams to stop.

Once I let go of the silliness of wanting things not to matter and accept that they do, then comes the enormous burden, the facing of the terribly enormous burden that everything does in fact matter. Not only does everyone and everything matter, but specifically I matter. What I do matters. Why I do what I do matters. What I say and think matters. What's in my heart and mind matters, And all of them matter, whether I want it to or not. As if this burden wasn't big enough, there's more, and that is that I can't even judge the significance, or the depth or breadth of how much they matter. Once this colossal truth presents itself, then the enormous responsibility weighs down upon your soul. Its stunningly difficult to do anything at all, to move, or think, or feel, or say anything, for there are trappings in every direction. But then you realize that doing nothing is something and it too has the same infinitely important weight behind its choice. So from here where do we go? We go carefully trying to figure out the correct path forward because if there is a way then I need to know it for each step I take has the weight of the universe behind it. Then the journey toward the knowable unknown begins. The questions roll out in order, how do we know what's real or not, what's true or not, how do we know what is good and how do we maximize the good and minimize the bad. Do some things matter more than others? Is there a right way a particular path or are there many? Is it finite, or infinite? Who else has figured it out? Where do I find answers? Where do we begin?

Where did my beliefs come from? (mac):

It's strange to think of how my beliefs were formed. It's also strange to think of how they evolved and changed. There is a sort of magic to it. The idea that everything is relative or interpretive, and that there are no absolutes is a big idea, with huge implications. When I acted upon them life got crazy. I'm still paying the price for believing in such nonsense. But where did I get those ideas, I certainly didn't just make them up. I was more, observing how everyone acted, trying to fit in I guess, and it just became obvious that this is what everyone was doing. The implied rules of not really committing to any belief. The committing to not committing. My beliefs came from the world. They came from the tribe I was apart of. They came from what the collective of people said and did around me, including anyone who's voice or actions entered into my conscious or subconscious.

Sunflower (sanchez):

The sunflower is one of the only plants on the planet that can actually track the sun daily. It senses the light and turns to gather in as much as possible. I am not sure if God in his wisdom made this our first meeting place or if it is just serendipitous. Either way, our first conversation was at a vegetarian restaurant called "The Sunflower". Here was a guy that had found, objectively, one of the best milkshakes in all of Sacramento, but claimed there was no such thing as objectivity. It intrigued me because I did not sense falseness in his belief. He really held these two opposing beliefs simultaneously. I could see the path to God through this milkshake, but the call was to wait...almost 8 years before putting it to him so directly. I obeyed and began the conversation with the idea that there must be SOME things that are better than others. I don't even mean in the same category as milkshakes. I mean with the most basic concept that to exist is better than to not exist.

Here, some might jump light years ahead and point out the painful and torturous lives some have been forced to live and how those individuals would have preferred non existence to existence. However, the call here is to tell the journey of Mac and me, so you will have to wait for part two. Even then, I will say that this is so often an objection that I will leave you with this. If I could answer this objection with reason and certainty, would you come to believe? If you are honest, you will find that your objection is not to any one moral question, but rather that you don't want this to be true...the way. We would have to meet and talk. It might take 8 years. We might have to go to the Sunflower.

Why it took so long (mac):
This is a good place to jump in. There is a reason why this journey took so long. I had a philosophical, psychological, and strong emotional block against the idea of religion, God, or gods, Jesus, or anything else rendered Christianity or faith. I will go

into why later, but just trust that they were there. So part of why this had to take so long is that I had to face myself, my own misguided chains of a life unexamined or rather unexamined in the proper way. I had been examining but without the proper tools or the proper knowledge on how to examine. I also didn't fully trust my examining ability nor did I trust anybody else's. It was examining the universe with the end in mind instead of being generally open to any answer. It was like exploring arithmetic without proper tools and more importantly with the firm assumption whatever was the answer, it could not be that 2+2 was indeed 4. To add to this I was not fully aware of my blunder, I thought I had honestly dismissed it. I thought the evidence against it was clear. I thought I had successfully ruled out a theory, or that there was no way to really be sure anyway so why even really try. It was all a waste of time. Even writing this I'm aware of the contradiction in my old beliefs. How could I have been absolutely certain I had ruled it out, and absolutely certain there was no way that anyone could rule it out. This is exactly the point Sanchez is making. That I was using my free will to only rebel, even illogically and irrationally, against an age old answer to all my questions, mishaps, brokenness, confusion, and aimless existence. Another equally important part of the why the length of journey took so long, is that I had to learn to trust Sanchez himself. I honestly thought he was the one misguided and lost. I honestly thought I would be the one showing him the way or least showing him the falsity of his way. For us even to have a coherent discussion I had to first come to understand that some things actually existed. Then that there were some things that were better than others. I wasn't even going to concede that the conversation we were having was real, or that life was real. I don't know why, but I wasn't going to just give away ground. I was going to play devil's advocate and make him work for everything. Surprisingly to me and maybe even him, over the next 13 years it was I who worked stubbornly to defend my positions, and he who held the the steady line of truth in almost every encounter. In case I haven't made my point, let me put it more directly. If he would have said what he said above to me, that I just wasn't ready or I just didn't want to know the truth. The Sunflower Cafe would have quite possibly been our last meet up. I would have dismissed him so quickly, and so aggressively, we might have never hung out again. At the very least it would have set us back. I wasn't ready. He was right, but I wasn't even ready to hear I wasn't ready because that truth I needed to face myself.

(sanchez):

So we started with existence. I remember Mac physically squirming. He turned in his chair sideways. He became frustrated. He said, "You can't say just say that" to each and every answer to each and every question and objection he had. It was difficult to watch because I was afraid of losing the first potential like minded person I had met in a long time. I will confess that I was tempted to let it go...to hide my faith. I felt the temptation of two roads laid out. One where Mac is driven away from the Truth, and me as Its messenger, as so many before him had been or one where our relationship would be built on falseness and then would eventually crumble under the weight of trying to live REAL life. This was my human reasoning. I never imagined what God had in store. A man sitting across from me that would go home, wrestle with the Truth, and come back the next time with more questions. God is infinite in his wisdom and grace.

I am thankful.

Let me be clear. I am no saint. If we gathered all the sinners on the planet into one place, they would call me chief. I have failed God, my family, my best friend, myself, and many others. I am the last person on this planet I thought He would call to help others. I am unworthy, unfit, and unreliable; but I have nowhere else to go. He is the Truth, the Way, and the Life.

It's all relative (mac):
This for me is where Sanchez comes in, even getting to this point in articulated form is from our conversations. Up until him the conversations I had were of the form of implied non conflict, or more like if we have a conflict we will preserve each other and allow there to always be a way out, or by simply dismissing anything truly to the contrary. In other words, the thing that everybody around me, and including myself would do, and that society on a whole was doing and still is doing, is not being honest with where they stand. Maybe even claiming that we

don't really stand anywhere at all. Much later in this journey I find out that there is a name for it, postmodernism, or the idea that everything is relative and that there is no right way to be, no true or correct way to live life.  The idea that there is an infinite amount of interpretations of the world, and therefore there is no one correct way or path but many, or rather infinitely many. SInce there is no absolute meaning or significance to life anybody gets to choose their own. You can pick it up or not, you can shift at any moment. If one of them catches you up, just claim a different one. There no longer is anything that is true or factual, there is only opinion, and by the way they are all equally valid, or equally not. The term, "live your truth" gets thrown around as if we can all have our own facts. Even our words are now subjective, there are no objective meanings of words. You get to choose their meaning. The dictionary well those are only words that oppressors chose. The powerful wealthy few have placed their own truth above yours. This of course is complete nonsense in its truest form, there exists contradictions throughout, and contradictions are the tools of reason to let you know she isn't pleased. More on words later.

Let's take the word example and watch what happens. So we are a tribe of people that all need to communicate with each other to survive. Technically and literally we need to talk to each other to survive. Like, "look out for that snake." Now, if we were able to all choose our own words for objects by choosing our own definitions of the words then I would quite literally not know what you meant by the words you said. I would have different words and meanings to them than you. It seems obvious that we all must agree on what words we use for each thing. So we have to agree on the object being the determinant of the meaning and the word itself. That way when we say rock we can all agree what one is and what one isn't. We have to do this with each word, let the object decide, we name things and we all remember the name we call it and now we can communicate. Once we can communicate then we can survive. Not only survive the snake but survive the confusion and chaos of a meaningless world or meaningless words.

Here is another way to look at it. We all know there are different languages on the earth. We also see that we could learn another language or two. We are impressed when anyone masters more than three. Now imagine that each person had their own language, literally billions of languages, imagine the confusion. How would you teach a child to speak? They would automatically mimic you and then choose your language in order for them to survive. But then they grow and we somehow convince them to rename everything on the planet or at least in their existence, and start anew. The loneliness of each of us having our own words would be unbearable. The world wouldn't work. No relationships would be formed, everyone would find themselves isolated, no books would exist, what would be the point, nobody but you could read it. Ok enough of this I hope from this we can see that we need objectivity.

It turns out in my own journey that coming to this conclusion or rather discovery of this rather obvious truth and its weight, is and was important. This in fact is where we began. Understanding that there is such a thing as truth that is objective. Discovering that there must be a reality that is there whether I am or not, a truth that depends not on my interpretation or creation, but simply on my discovery and observation. There are in fact things in this world that do not depend on one's opinion or perspective. That there is a truth in the thing itself, in the object, that depends not on the one interpreting it, not on the subject viewing the object. This is where sanchez and I began. We were the subjects and we were using objective meanings of words to discover the truth of the universe the cosmos life and our place in it. But before we could go any further, we had to start somewhere, opera music is where he lead me.

A Night at the Opera (sanchez):

Understanding the term of Objective and Subjective is difficult. It's made difficult by the fact that we are subjective beings interpreting an objective world through senses that are fallible. Add to the mix Pride and you have the perfect storm. Anything that offends me, pushes me, or makes me uncomfortable can be dismissed by my subjective perspective as irrelevant or untrue...for me. The closest I can get to explaining how this works is opera music. I love music. I listen to all kinds of music...except opera. Now, if I were to simply use my subjective reasoning I might think and say things like, "Opera sucks" or "It's not as good as mid 90's reggae rock". The problem is that opera music is objectively better. It has stood the test of time. It is revered by those much smarter and more experienced than me. It is complicated on levels that I can not understand. These praises of opera are not the same as loving the newest boyband or insta-famous social media star. In fact, it's the opposite. It has been studied for hundreds of years by billions of humans and found worthy all over the planet by countless listeners. The flaw is in me. I may never come to appreciate opera, but I can not reasonably find the fault in opera. I must look inward and admit I am too lazy or not intelligent enough to understand its worth. The good news is that there is enough good music in this world that I could live my whole life never really understanding or appreciating opera and I could live a good life. Opera music is not the absolute Truth of the universe; therefore, in the end, it can be categorized as subjective. In fact, all things when held individually up as an absolute fail. Nothing can survive when lifted to the level of absolute because the structural integrity of it will fail when the weight of all meaning and truth are placed upon it. There is only one thing all the known and unknown realms of reality that can...but that is for part two. In the meantime, we can find small examples of objectivity that continuously point to a more absolute reality.

The flaw is in me (mac):

Well said Sanchez. There is however a place where I get stuck or at least I did when I first heard it. The flaw is most definitely in me, and others might get stuck in the same way. I got stuck then, and it still gives me pause now, so let me try and explain. It has to do with the lower case objectivity versus upper case Objectivity. When we are talking about judging ice skating let's say figure skating in particular. The judges use an objective standard or rubric to judge the quality of performance. They have in their mind the perfect performance and then go down a checklist of criteria to see where this particular performance falls. Now obviously there is some human subjectivity in the judging, but we have multiple judges to help compensate for an individuals bias and human error. We could, if we had the time and resources, add more professional judges to the panel, and then the objectivity of the judging would increase. The point here is that with many things in the world, if we have an objective standard we can judge within that particular realm its objective value compared to other objects in the same realm. We can even at times come up with a set of objective criteria to judge one realm versus another realm. Like objectively playing badminton is a better hobby than smoking cigarettes. We can say that it's objectively healthier, more fun, more interactive, sustainable, and just overall objectively better to play badminton with your time than it is to smoke. However when we look closer at this example we still, in the end, would have to reserve judgement, and say, well it depends. The reason I think, and this is where things get a bit complicated, is because in relation to capital 'O', Objectivity, the activity in which we choose to spend our time matters in a different way based on a different criteria than our own. We now get into the idea of a lateral move relative to the Absolute and a vertical move relative to the Absolute. If we put the Absolute in His proper place at the top of everything else, and He is the source and creator of the Objective Good, then no matter what our human criteria are for what is objectively good or bad or better or worse becomes obsolete (or subjective) when comparing it to what the Absolute says is Good. When I was first learning this from Sanchez, he used ice cream flavors to depict a lateral move. Meaning; that no matter what flavor of ice cream you choose you can't say one flavor is objectively better than the other. In general we can say that your choice moves you laterally in relation to Good or Bad. In other words neither choice of ice cream, vanilla or chocolate, will get you a better or worse life. Where as telling the truth versus lying would be a vertical move. Telling the truth moves you up the vertical scale closer to the Absolute Good and therefore a better life, and lying moves you down the scale further away from a better life or the Absolute Good. Let me for the sake of us all get back to our specific example of smoking cigarettes versus playing badminton. If let's say I were smoking a cigarette with a man who had just lost his wife in a tragic accident, and I was there smoking with him to comfort him, and to help him through a tragic time, with a heart of selfless service, instead of going to my weekly badminton game with my mistress, then we could say that even though lower case objectively smoking cigarettes is a worse pastime then badminton, upper case Objectively we could say that I was doing the higher Good. This is what Sanchez is saying when he says, "therefore, in the end, it can be categorized as subjective". He is speaking about opera music, but he means EVERYTHING, every activity, every pastime, every choice, every decision, every thought, and every feeling, EVERYTHING. To be considered big 'O' Objectively Good we must compare it with the Absolute Truth's Ultimate Will. His will, in the end, is the only thing that matters.

Importance of Objectivity (mac):

It's hard to overemphasize the importance that this new found understanding of objective reality versus subjective reality played in my understanding of the world and my place in it. It's as if up until then, I couldn't really trust realty. I couldn't really trust anything to actually be real. I couldn't trust that there were some things that were more right than other things. It was unsettling to say the least. Once I realized that Sanchez was right, that we could discover an objective standard in which to judge things like music and movies, the world opened up in a way that made so much more sense than before. It was almost magical. Let's just say it was magical. Things that I knew to be true in my body, but couldn't really articulate or trust, began to be objectively true. I could now see why they were true and that they were in fact true, regardless of how I felt about them, but more importantly regardless what anyone felt about them, thought about them, said about them, or opinion they had on them. It was and still is overwhelmingly powerful.

We started with movies, because we both liked movies, and we were able to now discuss them with an objective criteria of what made a movie good and what made a movie bad. We were able to objectively come up with the criteria! It was no longer, let's just stop and 'agree to disagree', like so many conversations with so many others in my past had gone. The allowing and accepting unreasonable and irrational arguments and beliefs was no longer the only option. Nobody could say, "well that's just your opinion" and have it carry any real weight. I understood what they meant, that is, the conversation is done, or "I can no longer make any sound arguments", or "I don't really care what you say" or "no matter what you say I'm not changing".  Once I understood there is in fact a reality, it was no longer about winning in an argument. Arguments became powerful tools or vehicles to get to the actual nature of reality. In fact an argument become fun, in a way hadn't experienced. It wasn't a way to defeat the other person, it became with Sanchez, a way to discover the objective reality of whatever topic we were talking about. We stayed with more shallow, less important topics for years. We still do from time to time. Back then, it was as if I needed to get to know the process. I needed to see it played out and feel its results in things that seemed insignificant compared to the big picture. Eventually though, we had to circle back, it was inevitable, because that's what I was really searching for, the Answer, the Absolute, or the Objective reality. Becoming a movie critic passed through my mind, but I knew intuitively and objectively, that, that couldn't be it. It was at least little 'o' objectively worse than scrambling (A discovering of mine, in my pursuit of the very best exercise, stemmed from running to trail running to off trail running, to scrambling- river bed rock hopping, climbing, swimming, tiptoeing adventure into the unknown). I wasn't just testing out objectivity to see if it could support my smaller questions, and therefore support the larger ones, though I was definitely doing that. I was also testing its use in other relationships with other people in my life, but more importantly I was testing out Sanchez. Was this just some fancy trick in language he was playing on me? Was he just saying this stuff or was he living it? Well over time it became clear he was not only living it, but that he had been living it, and he had staked his life on it. Others weren't everyone else was doing some at best lukewarm version of it, or really just picking up and putting down objectivity as if it were a tool of convenience, rather than what I had come to discover, which was that it was one of the most important and reasonable tools I had ever encountered in my entire life

Once I really trusted this method of looking at the world in a more objective and mathematical way, I could use reasoning in the right way to reason through things. I mean it wasn't as if I wasn't using reasoning before Sanchez, it's just that without an objective standard, how could I or anyone trust anything. If the goal posts were always moving or the rules always shifting, then what use was playing the game properly? Wasn't it better just to move the goal posts and change the rules too, until they lined up with what you already wanted? So as I began to trust and put more weight onto this way of thinking, I also began to expand this new way onto more important and far reaching topics.  As I began to aim the tools on less on random chance or really arbitrary personal taste, I began to not only see the flaws in my taste, but also where I had gotten it right. The key here is that in fact I was able to see it! This was so huge, so gigantic, so refreshing that I could see why one burger was better than another. I could see why one song, was better than another, why one artist better, than another, one idea better, than another, and one truth more true than another. Sanchez and I began investigating not only movies and TV, (though that hasn't really stopped.) We began exploring everything we found interest in, shoot, we even started exploring how objective our own interests were or weren't. At some point along the way, Sanchez introduced me to CS Lewis an author that helped changed his life and that would eventually help to change mine. (I am skipping ahead here, but it's relevant and important.) The first book I read, was called "Mere Christianity." The first time I read it, the clarity of speech, of thought, and idea were astonishing. The well reasoned position was stunning. I had now after years of training with Sanchez and then on my own come to understand good thinking vs. bad. Or at least I began to throw out poor thinking. CS Lewis was seeking like we were, he was reasoning like we had, he was exploring and dropping truth like we had. It was exploding from the pages, it was magical, shoot it was magic. CS Lewis begins the book with a beautifully written chapter on the truth of objective moral values and what that implies. I read the whole book, but was only able to really trust or accept his very first arguments or chapters. I wasn't ready yet, but this was the first time anyone outside of Sanchez had shown me clear thinking. Objectively good thinking and insight. I was floored, I was astonished. I began to trust Sanchez even more. There is something in the power of multiple sources saying the same thing. Not only was I able to view and live in the world better than before, with a real sense of the objective reality, not only was my best friend able to use and apply sound reasoning and logic, but also this dead man who wrote children's stories was saying the exact same thing that we had been discussing, in a slightly different and definitely eloquent, beautiful, and clear, stunningly clear way, an Objectively clear way.

So let me sum it up at this point. I became wickedly good at applying objective reasoning to everything in specific detail in my life. I wasn't ready yet, but closer than I thought to applying that same tool to bigger more abstract principles. Sanchez was applying objective reasoning everywhere. By the way, we weren't always in agreement about what movies or food or clothes or subjects or activities were better than others. But we both were in agreement on the process by which we could obtain a well reasoned view and perspective on those topics. We would argue for hours, even days, weeks, months, or years on the same subjects. We were conceding where we were found to be wrong, and welcoming each other to the new truer ground with open arms. We didn't just play in the sphere of mental theory. We would embody and act out or really live what we found to be true. We would hypothesis and experiment. We would go test our theories and come back with results and adjust when needed and put it to bed when we were satisfied. We even attempted to find the best liquor, the objectively best adult beverage. We worked our way through lots of top shelf drinks to find them. I don't know that we ever found the top exactly in that realm, and might need to return to that one. It was fun, it was adventurous, and it was meaningful. I was beginning to climb the ladder of objectivity into the more important, life changing subjects such as morality. We battled on this front too, but eventually with the help of reasoning, and CS Lewis, my own experience and obviously sanchez, I was able to eventually see the truth. That is, there is a moral law that weighs on us all, and it has been consistent over space and time throughout history and civilization. If in fact this is true, then doesn't that mean there must be a lawmaker? This newly found objectivity was crucial, there must be a standard to judge all things, ideas, art, music, movies, food, goodness or badness, rightness or wrongness, and well life. That standard must be objective, we couldn't have made it up. It became blaringly true that no matter what the masses said, or the generations have hollered, or sophisticated sophists and philosophers have written, that this standard that we can use to measure reality must be Objective. This standard then in turn must have a source. Who was the author of this standard? Who created reasoning, math, logic, beauty, goodness, rightness, and lightness, who or what? Man, I found that I wasn't in the uncertain ground of relativism any more, but dang it, I had found myself in a completely new and strange land. I was no longer in the safety of what everyone else had always done, where exactly was I, how did I get here? The problem is, I knew exactly how I got here, I could no longer plead ignorance. There was something refreshing about the new solid ground I was standing on, the new planks and hull in my boat were solid, they were built by me, not by myself of course, but I built it I knew how and where they came from I knew how to take it apart and how to put it back together. There was also something scary, I was getting into deep water here, no longer could I honestly go back, I was out there, out here in reality and it was different than I had expected. It was more real than I had previously known, and there was clearly a true way and that meant there were clearly many false ways. Steering was way easier now and I was making clear progress, in theory and in life, in depth of understanding and in actual application of principle, but the sea was getting rough and the current speeding up.

The problem becomes enormous and confusing, the problem is huge, it doesn't work. It isn't logical and it has fatal flaws. First being that there are not an infinite amount of viable interpretations of the world, and that even if there are more than one, it doesn't mean they are all equal in there validity and truthfulness. Before Sanchez, I was living in this inconsistent and incoherent world view. I was under the impression that everything was grey or rather relative. That there were no absolutes. That everything depended on your perspective. It's a very convenient way to operate. Or at least seemingly convenient. Anytime somebody claims you wronged them you get to say that's just your opinion. Or you get to say, "from your perspective it looks that way, but from over here I'm innocent." When somebody wronged or harmed me, however I got to cry foul, and explain vehemently that they were wrong. I was inconsistent, looking back I wanted to have my cake and eat it too. I was a hypocrite, so was everybody else who I interacted with in general, from professors, friends, family, acquaintances, colleagues, students, neighbors, tv personalities, to artists. I mean everyone, I was just articulating it, and I was also struggling in life. I became king of rationalizing, of arguing whatever viewpoint and perspective I had. It wasn't working. What I mean by wasn't working, is that it left me feeling tired and guilty, and blaming everyone for my issues. It was causing harm to others, I could feel it. I acted it out, did what I wanted, and tried to do as much damage control as I felt necessary, after my ways didn't work. I was king of reality. Right and wrong, good and evil didn't exist, just a bunch of opinions bumping into each other. Deep internal conflict, with a bright smile outwardly. My mask was wearing thin, the games of the world were exhausting. Somehow positive thinking was mixed up into the worldview, which was my world view, but also I can't really take full credit for it because it was given to me by the world. I remember a movie called "What the bleep?!" spoke of quantum physics and showed how reality wasn't static, so that we could manipulate it with positive thinking. Force a smile, put a happy face over the misery and the misery would cease to exist. That didn't work either, but I thought I was just a poor practitioner, it seemed to work for others, at least they claimed it did. Stay shallow, also seemed to work for others. The problem I believed, was the world not me. I was good, that's what we all told each other. I really can't be clear to exactly where I got this idea, looking back it was prevalent among just about everyone, all people I interacted with. It wasn't some deeply researched view point, or even well examined, it was just easy to grab, and the rest of the world was playing along. It's how the world was made up. Like a whole bunch of lost or sick people reaffirming their belief that they were all ok, that we were all healthy, and even thriving. The world was just a big playground with no real consequences. Until there were. Things weren't working anymore. I was lost. I was in deep pain, I was trying different things to fill the gaping hole inside that seemed unfillable. The best I could do was lose focus on it. Get distracted from it.  It didn't stop me from searching. I tried following my passion, falling in love, not caring, caring too much, fighting for a cause, getting political, drinking alcohol, doing drugs, having sex, and abstaining from them all, eating whatever I wanted, eating super healthy, or even not eating. I tried marathoning, ultra marathoning, I tried buying stuff, but I was getting more and more lost and none of the things were working. I think the closest I got was trying to express my darkness through music, art, tattooing, drawing, painting, and playing in a band. I knew interacting with people was better than not. I felt the deep loneliness inside, the guilt and shame, the isolation, I carried them all like heavy bags. The well constructed mask I had constructed, that I was trained to construct and wear, more like to flaunt, was wearing thin. Passions changed, the best I could hope for was pain distraction, but the abyss lurked just beneath. I wanted to run. I was ready. I always wanted to run. I had a son. I was 24. I wasn't ready to settle down. I rationalized leaving his mom and staying a father. Nobody advised me not to. Actually one guy an acquaintance gave me pause, he warned me as gently as he could, but my mind was made up. My son ended up being my tether, the thing that made me begin to face my demons. Therapists and psychiatrists with different techniques, none of them provided answers, at least not sufficient ones. Some of my darkest moments were when the initial realization happened that the freedom I so desperately sought, ran right in direct conflict with being a good dad. Seeking true love might have been a mistake, and the deep lonely game that I had been playing, that of relativism, wasn't working. Real thoughts of suicide, of my son, and family being better off without me were coming to me in my darkest hours. The deep depression was real. The mask was wearing extremely thin.

1st things 1st (sanchez):

A concept that came up very early on in our exploring was 1st things 1st. This is powerful because Mac wanted the "answer" immediately. I wanted to give the "answer" immediately; however, this was not the call from God and I imagine it would have been like trying to drink from a fire hose on full blast. It would have been too much at once. I learned a long time ago that you have to put 1st things 1st. If you try and put 2nd things first, you start to upset the order of the universe and yourself. It sounds silly, but if you put 2nd things 1st, things don't work. Often times, we don't see when we're putting 1st things 1st, but we definitely see when we try putting things out of order. This is why there is a brief moment of confusion when you try opening a door you think is unlocked and it doesn't open. You pause and think, "Wait...what is happening?" Then you realize, "Oh man, I forgot to unlock it" or "What the heck? Someone locked it.". Notice here, that it doesn't matter whether or not you were the cause of the locking of the door...the result is that you can't unlock it unless you have the key. (Yes, you could break in, but this is a metaphor and; therefore, eventually breaks down as a tool to explain things).

This was a hard lesson for Mac. He was starting with "There is no God" or "It's highly unlikely there is a God and; even if there was one, He's done such a bad job, I don't want to know him". You see? He was starting with the end result instead of putting 1st things 1st. The arguments will be spelled later, but I will show you how I helped him to understand this concept. This leads back to objectivity and subjectivity. If everything is subjective, then nothing is objective. This can't be true because this is an objective statement. It's like saying, "There are absolutely no absolute statements". You are cutting off the branch on the Tree of Logic on which you are sitting. You are no longer connected to reason. We can provide proofs and reason to convince a reasonable person of Truth, but no amount of proof and reason can convince an unreasonable person of Truth.

Where does this leave us? Well, there must be at least one absolute in the universe or we could not even perceive the universe or the "right and wrong" of the universe. And this is where I leave you. It is mind shattering to have to rip that first plank off your lifeboat that separates you from the ocean of madness and chaos you can hear slapping at the boards. However, to build a ship worthy of exploring the deep waters...you must. You must replace the hull of subjectivism with a hull of absolute Truth. It's the only way.

Everything is not relative (mac):

Ok. This is important. So let's just pause for a minute. I was in the habit of saying "Everything is relative." It seems obvious now, but back then it was so strange, and difficult, and weird to have Sanchez point out the flaw here. It took me a lot longer to really get, than it seems like it ought to, but it did. When I say "everything is relative" what I am doing is saying, ALL things in the universe are suspect to multiple interpretations, or no one way is more valid than another, and therefore NOTHING can be trusted or known. The thing that Sanchez would seemingly with ease point out, is that using my own words and logic, the sentence "everything is relative" is itself relative. "Everything is relative" is in the set of ALL things in the universe, so it to

CANNOT be trusted. Mind blown. I thought it a trick at first. Like fancy talk or rhetoric. I felt like I had just witnessed an elaborate card trick. How in the heck did he do that? This was me sawing off the branch I was sitting on. How was it that I had never heard of this? How could I not have seen this? I did not make this relative crap up, I just used it like everyone else I knew. Nobody pointed this out ever. Why didn't anybody in school, in any of the years I attended, point this out? What kind of freak was this Sanchez anyway? How could he do that so easily? It took a long time to really knaw on all these questions. I think I knew it immediately, but it took me along time to really accept it, the sinking in was slow. Once I understood then, I begin to apply it. Then the thing happened that happens when you buy a yellow car, you begin to notice all the other yellow cars in the world. You had no idea how many yellow cars there had been, until you yourself owned one. This is exactly what happened to me, with this idea, this truth. It was like everywhere I looked people were walking around saying there are absolutely no absolutes! I was in awe, like everyone, I mean everyone was sitting high up in the trees and all of them in unison were sawing off the very branches that they themselves were so firmly planted. It was strange, it still is but less so, just because I'm so used to it now. Eventually I was convinced by the truth, that there had to be some things that were absolute, like at least one, it was the only way reason would allow. This realization woke me up in a way that is hard to describe. It gave me for the first time, something solid to sit on, that I had actually discovered and tested and now knew to be true, like really knew it and could defend it. I knew exactly how I got here, and how dangerous the mush I had been caught in actually was, and eventually with help, dredged out of.

The beginning of the beginning (mac):

Around this time in my life Sanchez and I became friends. He worked at the same high school as an english teacher and I a math teacher. We were both relatively new to the profession, and eventually we started to talk and hang out at school. Our friendship eventually became such that we met outside of school. Our first meet up outside of school was at lunch, at a little vegetarian restaurant called the Sunflower Cafe. We sat outside at a picnic table. I'm not sure on all the details of how the conversation started, but I remember my arrogance. I remember him saying "I've studied what the greatest thinkers of all time have said on the subject" and I was like "me too" and he was like, "oh ok well then let's talk." Challenge accepted. That conversation happened 12 or 13 years ago and it hasn't really stopped. I have to admit something here. I hadn't studied. I wasn't lying precisely It was more ignorance as to what studying meant. I thought I had studied for some reason, probably because I was or am a prideful and arrogant person, who up until that point had argued with people, talked to people, and nobody had anything to say to me that was contrary to my point. They couldn't argue their point, I at least was trying to argue mine, so I went around unchallenged. The other phenomenon that I think was happening, was that the people I was talking to were equally lost and so there was an implicit agreement that we would not really disagree on anything or they simply agreed with me. Even though I was craving it, needed it, wanted it, I couldn't find in person anyone to challenge me. I didn't even think to look in books or on Youtube or the internet, I didn't think studying was valuable. School was a place to jump through hoops, and I was good at it, but it wasn't a place to learn and apply anything that mattered or that was relevant to my actual life. Beyond making friends and impressing teachers. It was as if all of the relationships I had, were built on some other principal, other than being completely honest or real, or at least attempting to. It's as if we were all protecting each other from the lie we were all living. The lie being, that we were good, that everything was relative, especially morality, that there was no God, and if there were, He would agree with me and love everything that I was doing. That He couldn't be the God of the Bible, that the Bible was obviously not literal, and therefore untrue, that science and reasoning reigned supreme, and that there were no ultimate authorities or absolutes. So we could all be gods, do what we wanted, when we wanted it, until of course it would end in bitter conflict and betrayal. It's not as if any of this were in the clear view, it only is looking back from a different viewpoint that I can see it.

So this conversation at the Sunflower Cafe, was me representing that viewpoint, because in effect I was most qualified to represent our lonely, yet popular, lost tribe. While

Sanchez was to represent the oppressed and mindless church goers, or so I thought. So I was going to bring him up to speed so that he could join the club. It's scarily funny, in a dark way, that I wanted to inflict in him the pain I was in. Only in my lostness, I was honestly trying to help. My thoughts were something like, it's better to suffer in reality, then to remain ignorant in bliss. Which I actually still think it right and true. This story that we are going to tell started on that day and hasn't stopped. In no way did I predict its outcome or realize what Sanchez was up to. Or more accurately what God was up to. Right here and now as write this years later, I reflect with a swollen grateful heart with tears in my eyes, blurring the keys that I type, as I humbly say thank you to my dear friend Sanchez for helping me find my way, and to God for waiting patiently looking over the both of us. I fought long and hard for the opposition, but ultimately had to take my pride and my loss, and ultimately realize the ground I was standing on wasn't solid, it wasn't even ground, it was death and decay, and I was drowning in it, and so was our whole tribe.

These conversations with Sanchez were varied and wide ranging. They took place over many years and adventures. I don't know why we were both willing and able to reason, but I think we both thought we were right, but the key is we were willing to concede a point, if the other person showed their position to be more right. It wasn't just reasoning though. At points along the journey, I was sure it was, but there was and is something else going on during these conversations. There is an observation of the other person's actions, body language during the conversations, and real life going on along with the conversations. A trust and bond are being formed, a real relationship, based on the grounds of what was actually working in his life, and what was actually working in my own life. We were, I think, both watching what each other were doing, and then we were openly and honestly discussing our lives. We still do. He would come to me for advice and I to him. Each of us was from the beginning good listeners. We also actually believed in what we were saying, and acted it out in our actual lives. So even though this is a story of seeking and finding truth. It is also a real journey where the messiness and complexity of the individuals, and of a friendship are at play. Real emotions, real time, real distractions, real blind spots, real flaws and real triumphs. We used intuition and feelings to guide us, not logic in a vacuum. Though there was and is plenty of reasoning, pure Reasoning needs to be considered along with the unknown the mysterious the supernatural. We would say, "that make sense" or "that feels right" or "that has a ring of truth" to indicate agreement and something that clicked. There is something in mind, body, and spirit that begins to shift and change. It is a moving of planks, in the boat of belief. If we imagine our underlying beliefs and structures as a wooden boat that collectively keeps our worldview a float, we can then see the importance of each plank in order to hold our psyche together. We can't just demolish or dismantle the boat too quickly without replacing it with something else. It would cause a violent reaction and feeling of drowning a neurosis, or mental breakdown. It's something that we have to keep afloat while we are building replacing and repairing and shifting the structure. We deeply know this and fight desperately to keep anything to stay afloat on. The abyss is way too dangerous, scary, and harmful for us to let go. Whether we know it or not, whether we have examined it or not, we all have such a boat, and we all protect its ability to float. When we really learn something new we can feel those planks shifting.

Nothing comes from nothing (sanchez):

It took 2 years for me to explain and for Mac to understand this next concept. This was the idea that other experts; far more well known than us and a vast majority of the human race that have contemplated the origins of everything, have come to the realization that the universe had to come from somewhere. There are two major ideas and one minor idea when it comes to everything. One is that the universe always existed and therefore needed no creator. Science has shown us that energy is decaying which means it can not be infinite in the past. The second is that the universe had a beginning; therefore it must have a power source outside of physical nature. This would be the idea of a god (notice the little G). The third is a vastly inferior and very rarely held position that none of this is real. Variations include this all being a dream or virtual reality or illusion. I have never met someone that has held this belief to its true end and in its entirety. For Mac, he struggled with the idea of the Virgin Birth. I remember saying to him, "Wait, you mean to tell me the miracle of the Virgin Birth messes with your mind, but the ENTIRE universe coming from nothing doesn't?" I remember him staring at me and blinking for a couple of seconds. I could see that he had never considered what this meant to his world view. He could see that objections he had held his whole life were not really examined. He began to consider that perhaps he held his objections with the end in mind rather than honestly. He began to look into the most common objections to Truth on wikipedia and other open sources. He would come to me at times and say things like, "Have you seen the list of Theist vs Atheist online?" I could see that he was stunned that this was not more common knowledge. He began to see that there seemed to be an agreed upon understanding in the world to not 'dig deep' into the most common obstacles to Truth. I am not sure why this is. As a child, it was fascinating to no end to study what the great minds of the ages had thought of the idea of the Absolute or Truth.

The craziness of reality (mac):

The Virgin Birth and in general miracles were a sticking point for me. (more on miracle later) What I want to discuss here the nature of reality. I don't exactly remember where this revelation came from or when, but I definitely remember the stunning clarity of the insight. It had to do with the entire New Testament and in particular Jesus and all that goes along with it. The Resurrection, the miracles, the God/man person, The Savior of the world, the fulfilling of the prophecy and God's plan, the timing of the events, the specific location, and just the singularity of the moment and how much rested upon it seemed so impossibly strange. The stunning moment came when someone (either Sanchez or CS Lewis or both) pointed out how strange all of existence was. We are floating (FLOATING!) through space on this very unique meteor. We are these strange creatures who are part beast and part something else. We are conscious. We know we're going to die. There is a variety in us and on this planet that seems infinite while at the exact same time there is a commonality that makes it all seem like we're really just alike. Then they pointed out (paraphrasing someone with whom I can't recall, so obviously I can't remember exactly what was said, but nonetheless...) "just look at the procreation of our species. How strange is the reality of sexual reproduction of humans? The whole thing I wouldn't have guessed, it's startling and spectacularly strange from top to bottom!" And it is! The whole thing is so ridiculous and so weird and so different than anything I or any human would have guessed or invented. I will spare you all the salacious details but just stop and think, really look at how wonderfully unique and real the whole thing is. All of reality is this way, I think sex and birth, the mixture of pleasure and pain, the strangeness of the human anatomy, arousal itself, nakedness, and vulnerability, is an example that particularly highlights just how crazy reality really is. When I really looked at this, I had a very similar reaction to what Sanchez is describing when he explained the idea that I had a problem with the Virgin Birth, but not the Origin of everything. Blink, blink, uuuh... wow. When I finally really, honestly, looked at reality I was stunned. Why should I NOT have a problem with the strangeness of how God had made sexual reproduction, but shake my head in stubborn defiance and disbelief of the story of

Jesus. They both in fact, have this unique style, the spectacular strangeness, and infinite wonder of the same Author. I had no problem whatever on the fact that I indeed had a soul. And I had not an ounce of doubt, that it was strangely and deeply important. Yet I had complete and utter doubt and disbelief on anyone explaining the point or method in saving the darn thing.

Seeking (mac):

The other thing, when looking back I noticed, is that when you really seek, you will find, and when you begin to concede territory over to what is real and true the path narrows, and the escapes are fewer and farther between. The forward momentum begins to carry you, until one day you're faced with a choice, to bail off the journey and remain a coward, or to continue forward even though it's not what was expected, or wanted, or thought in your wildest dreams. It isn't clear when beginning your pursuit of mathematics, that you will reach calculus or even higher more abstract mathematics. You just begin with simple arithmetic, and it makes sense, and works. So if inclined to continue your journey, the path forward has already been walked along, and set out, and no matter what else you want it to be, you don't get to decide or choose, all you can do is stop studying get fed up or distracted. We don't reach calculus in math, not because it isn't real or that it doesn't exist, or that we can't. We don't reach calculus because we don't want to, it takes too much energy, and we quit, or really we never even begin. That doesn't however stop us from participating in the benefits of mathematics, when our houses don't fall down, and our electronics work, and our vehicles stop when we want them to, etc. It does stop us from understanding the world we live in.

A word about emotions (mac):
Emotions don't seem to be in us for no reason, they don't exist to simply foul us up. They are more like indicators. Flashing lights when things are working or when they're not. Now along the way we have discovered that a negative emotion doesn't tell us where the broken parts are located. They tell us simply that something is wrong, and our naive pride points the finger outward when we have a false belief of goodness. That all that we do is not at all bad but rather misunderstood. Once we figured out that the emotion is specific with who is at fault, then further investigation has to happen to sift out the broken parts

from the non broken. We use the analogy of a man pointing his finger all around at different people situations places symbols and objects. If in fact each object is causing pain in his finger he has one of 2 options. To blame everything that he is touching as painful and wrong or to realize his finger is broken and that he should stop touching those things and realize it is his own flaws and brokenness that hurt not the outer things. Once you realize this is a real option then the emotions are showing you your own flaws not everyone else's you can observe and watch and discuss what it is you are actually feeling and examine the validity of your claim that something else is broken or that you are. We can if not examined miss the mark in either direction either too hard on ourselves or not hard enough. This lesson for me has proven to be invaluable. It gives a pause when you have to question an emotion before acting upon it. It makes the emotionless pressing in most cases or perhaps more organized or at the very least less surprising when you can point to the cause of the emotion. It gives value to the emotions but doesn't let them rule the way forward. We need a finer instrument than that of the loud warning system of emotions to plot our way forward.

Back to the reasoning as not the only way to truth. The heart and mind must be at work, the emotions and intuition need to be at play especially once you trust either of them. A willingness to critique honestly anything any action any intention any feeling or otherwise thought that flies into your conscious is an important part of this journey. All of the tools at our disposal turned out to be important, when moving to a closer more real understanding of the world and who we are in it. The mind and body connection the oneness of the human and the complexity of things we trust and have faith in come into play.

A word on seriousness (mac):

We take our conversations seriously, we are really trying to figure it out. We both are laying it on the line. That's not to say that we don't have fun, or that it we are all somber and stoic. We laugh and joke plenty, and we often take seriously, that part too. At times it is light and at times its heavy. We don't employ others in our search unless we feel it correct. We often dig at a concept for hours or days, but then just as often put the concepts down and let them digest in the unconscious, subconscious, or ether of spirit in the universe and then let the magic and mystical experience of time let it work its way deeper into our bones. Until it's time to bring it back up. We are both very serious about this journey. Serious enough to keep a light grip and walk away or change directions if there is a better way.

A word on faith (mac):

Faith the word was taboo for much of the beginning of the conversation there had to be because it brought up an emotional response I had faith that faith was impossible, but I didn't know how much I was enacting on faith. Faith that my reasoning was sound and that I was smart enough to figure this out became clear eventually after years. But at first it wasn't spoke of. Not because of any flaw in faith but seriously a flaw in me. My pride wasn't ready yet and somehow sanchez knew it. So a lot of the slowness of my journey was due to the many emotional hang ups i had demons so to speak of my past upbringing and unexamined parts and pieces of my soul or psyche.Religion God and especially Jesus were simply not real choices though I could freely talk about them not without strong emotional disdain, and at the beginning I was even unaware of the immense intense and irrational roadblock to a large portion of the way forward. Or maybe more like I gated it off in my heart and mind as a viable alternative. So a lot of the beginning work had to do with baby steps toward objective truth reality and the existence of at least one absolute. With those even we had to start with an innocuous example music and movies. Something that sanchez and I had a common experience in enjoyed discussing and most importantly could get me to see my flaw in an area that i wasn't so deeply emotionally against. Its like I had to learn the principles of construction on small meaningless safe pieces of furniture before I could safely build a house. The small projects are where I learned the real principals the basics that allow for me to build a temple or a city. We see that in many areas of learning, we have to be able to try it out on real things but that don't mean life or death. We have to give ourselves room to grow and a safe place to experiment. Without the threat of shame or embarrassment. Learning a musical instrument is like this and any tool we can relate that once we have the practical experience of the tools we are more and more comfortable and trust the tool as well as our ability to use the tool in more and more complex situations. The tools of truth are this way, there is really no difference. The same tools we use to analyze and critique a child's behavior are the same methods used to analyse and critique an adults or a families or community or country or world the stakes get higher and the complexities get more but the tools remain the same.

Pain (mac):

I wish I could speak of my journey as a wonderful trip through awe and joy and the miraculous revelation of life and existence itself. It wouldn't be true though, still sadly my biggest motivators are pain and fear but mostly pain. To this day I struggle with the pain of existence. The pain of my past. The pain of loss and of lost potential. The pain of betrayal. Pain is what got me changing seeking and searching in the first place. It is what drew me to music and art. Not as a fan but as a demon killer or at least a demon exhauster. Or maybe even a place to rest my demons. All that is to say a place to heal the pain, to get in tune to it. The feeling of what is the point what is the meaning and purpose why am I here at all, what good am I. I had no answers but my childhood and adolescent mode of being had ran me directly into pain. When things aren't working the pain begins, the questions begin, when things are difficult beyond comprehension and reason and cause are no match for the scream of pain. It is what drives me, even as I write this it feels weak but it is true. It was never the search for glory or fame that I was running toward, those motivators those carrots were never appealing enough to get me moving, but that stick, not even the threat of the stick for I am or was or both too arrogant to care about the threat, the actual pain of the stick or whip is what got me or gets me. Its as if I could feel a bit of risk before I chose the wrong but until the consequence of my action was in full view and the pain of the wrong decision was at my door  I would continue down my rotten path until the pit of despair was in my gut. The wrath of guilt or the realization life was changed because of me forever. Only this got me moving and move I did. Sometimes the pain would be immediate and I could feel the pain of my decision right away and no what not to do. Other times it would take years to manifest just how wrong I was and then getting out of the trap I set for myself was near impossible or just impossible. Then the realization that the pain was going to linger for much longer. When we take pain as in physical, we quickly see that this pain is exactly the kind that if severe enough will get us to seek help or treatment or medication, it will get us into the doctor. Even then however we might not go until it is too late or the problem has gotten way worse. Imagine if you will that you don't believe in doctors or the institution of medicine or science or the medical profession or institution in general. What do you turn to. Everything and anything is the answer. Do they work these alternative pain relievers these so called natural remedies? Well maybe but maybe not and maybe they work partially or the placebo effect takes hold and you think they work for awhile. You end up following fringe methods and false authorities. Taking snake oil to cure all sorts of ailments. This is me in the realm of spiritual, mental emotional and psychic help. That is where my pain always came from at least the kind of pain that made me need to search out a remedy. But stubbornly and as ignorantly as possible I tried all the alternative new age modern methods first. Never looking at tradition or ancestry or what has worked for thousands of years. So when I say I was really looking to find the answer to my suffering, I was but only insofar as religion stayed far away. I wasn't seeking Nirvana or Heaven I was running from hell. A hell that I had gotten myself into and couldn't even comprehend how deep that hell was. I didn't even know to what extent the brokeness and pain was my fault and how much was my lack of foundation my lack of reasoning, the lack of society my stupidity in following the falsity of the world. I still don't know how much was me and how much was everything else, but that matters less, once you realize they key to it is in your own hands then you have enough to take action. I still suffer, but less, the pain is not as acute. I still am lost but less, I still struggle with existence. I still have pain of betrayal and confusion of results. It isn't the type of pain that I cannot bare or stand it's something that I can face without wanting to escape it or take drugs or alcohol to numb it. It's not even something that I need distraction from. So the truth will set you free is the claim and I am still not free from pain, but I am in my pursuit of truth and application of it vastly freer than I once was and for that I am eternally grateful.

Rationalization versus reason (mac):

I became or was taught or both how to rationalize. I was never taught how to reason. Not in any real way. The lessons of reasoning came through these conversations with sanchez. To clarify what I mean by rationalize its to have an end in mind then make up reasons in order for that end to be validated excused or justified. Where as reason will point you to the truth whether you like it or not. Reason is more mathematical in that it only works one way and one way only it is either is or it isn't true or false. Reason cannot contradict reason is the judge of thought. What i was doing up until I met sanchez was rationalizing, I was perverting reason to my own aim rather than its aim or her aim if we speak of Mother Reason. In math the subject I was trained reason held supreme, but in real life I would leave reason in the world of math and pick up the deceitful rationalization. I was able to argue or persuade myself and others to opposing points on the same subject, or at least I thought I could. I could argue the benefits of monogamy or polygamy or the value of marriage or the horrors of this old institution. Through my rationalizing I would act it out and live whatever it is that I wanted the truth to be for in rationalizing there are multiple variations of truth whatever flavor was mine at the time I would aim my twisted hunched over second cousin of reason at it and away we'd go. There is something in the air here that seems necessary to speak on. That is reasoning is clearly is uncomplicated its pure its honest so it doesn't need to hide in overly complicated treatise. Where as the falsifier and the liar especially the intellectual kind uses the house of mirrors to jumble up the truth so far that it's hard to see exactly where they stand. The rationalizer will never get stuck in one place for when the foundation begins to slip and slide and shift under their feet they just move to another faulty position. Its tiring being a rationalizer. Where as reason is more calm building itself on firm ground and slaying the rationalizations with ease. In my experience the lesser perverted rationalizer and their over inflated ego of intellect, is overconfident in their abilities. I know that I was. Since they are built on false grounds once Mother Reason comes into play and examine the smaller more feeble rationalizer she easily finds the fatal flaw in her opponents ways and can quickly make the mask fall. I wouldn't even say that her counterpart is an opponent more like a disease of the intellect or an annoying insect to an elephant. For whatever the rationalist builds since they are perverting reason, reason will always find the defect and point it out. Often the rationalist has built a fairly tall and sophisticated and even nuance structure of seemingly logical and reasonable strength but when the reason for building such a thing is to deceive or to enable a wrong path or to hide true intent it is pure reason that will flesh it out. The entire structure will tumble from the slightest push from the easy gust of reasons breath.

The first real lesson in our conversations that seem entirely obvious now is the existence of an objective truth. When I was living in confusion and falsity of the kind of the people around me it was the idea that each of us had our own truth and that each of our opinions were equal and that truth was dependent on your perspective. There were no real victims or criminals just different perspectives. In fact the criminal could very well be just as much a victim as the victim and the victim just as much the criminal. Why not? This would account wholly for the greyness of reality. The overarching well it depends. What's good for me isn't necessarily good for you and vice versa. And like all good lies there is some truth mixed in with the poison. Perspective, opinion, and subjectivism are real and they do matter. And the differences in them are colorful and even desired on a good many topics, but taking these to an absolute level becomes absurd. Sanchez' s first lesson to me was about opera music, ice cream, and movies. Little did I know how profound subjective versus objective was. Even once I had it down I was entirely reluctant to begin applying it to more abstract and meaningful places in my own life. It changes music, ice cream, and movies forever. I could no longer look at them the same or even experience them the same. I knew intuitively I think that if they changed those in such a dramatic way what would they do to the rest of my life. The ship of rationalization that I had built my existence upon was beginning to shift sway and flex under the weight of truth. I was not going to let it crumble or sink in an easy way.

Old books vs new books (sanchez):
Use the Holy Spirit to guide you. If you're not a believer; if it ever happens, remember this part. If it doesn't, just take my

word for it. It's funny that I knew how to use a library to find books on Aristotle, Socrates, St. Augustine, and other great thinkers, but I didn't know how to fill out a library card application. While I waited for my grandmother or mom to come get me, I would sit for hours and read philosophy/religious books and memoirs of great thinkers. I know this is not normal. As I grew older, it surprised me that others had not read these books. In fact, most of the time the average person would express a very odd sentiment...they felt unsure or unworthy of reading the great books of human existence. A person would imagine they were unable to understand Aristotle even though they had never read his works. They would disqualify themselves before they had even tried. I have found that the works are not as hard to understand as most would believe. The sign of an intelligent human is being able to take a complex concept and then explain it in such a way that it can be understood. I am not saying there won't be difficult parts, but with a little determination, anyone can use reason and logic to understand. If I was forced to recommend either a new book on philosophy/religion or an old book on the same subject, I would recommend the old book. It has stood the test of time. It has retained value even when the society or culture has changed or is completely different than the one in which it was written. This is how we find universal truths. They are true across time and space.

Looking beyond myself (mac):

Looking beyond myself and those around me for truth, advice, reality or any other actually valuable information was not something I did. Sanchez for some reason was able to be humble in his journey early on, and he trusted his ability to read or search or analyze others logic. I wasn't. The reasons are not entirely clear. However I think I have an idea why I wasn't.

First, I was good at school. Everyone told me I was smart. I got good grades with ease. School was not a place to really learn, school was, and has always been a place to get good grades and move on. It was an elaborate hoop jumping game. I was naturally really good at that game. I mean reading, writing, and arithmetic, I learned, but everything else was to just please the teacher, not to apply to my life. Once school was out, I didn't care to discuss, or apply anything that was spit out of a teacher's mouth. They were more like an adult, I wanted to please, not a person that was trying to help me understand the world.

Second, nobody I knew read for knowledge, everybody read for pleasure. Reading was just like watching a movie or tv or playing video games. It wasn't a tool to actually do anything. I only remember going to the library to get one book to help me repair my car's clutch ever, but we went to the library all the time as kids. I had always been told reading was good, and I was good at it from a young age, but nobody ever told me exactly why it was good for me, other than to do well in school, but the point of school was to have a good life or career or something, not to learn anything. Anything that I did need to learn or that was actually useful, I would learn by doing, or by watching someone in real life do. I would never have guessed to read about it. So by the time I reached Sanchez I had only ever learned anything about real life just by living and trying things out, I was pretty fearless and open to just attacking any issues or problems on my own. I was then able to rule things out or affirm their worth, by experience, this was really the only way that worked for me. So when Sanchez was talking about the greatest thinkers or scientists of all time, I was like so what? It was actually a feeling of indifference. I had put all authority in the category of useless, I mean it was fine to admire the great artists musicians etc, but not to learn from them. The last reason for not searching outside of my own experience was simply pride. My arrogance was such that I was convinced that I was smart enough to figure this out. If some other human had figured it out, well then I could too. When I mean figure it, out I mean anything big or small. I got this from my dad I think. He thinks this way to this day and he was constantly telling me this growing up. He would say, "you can do anything you put your mind to" "You're no better or worse than anybody out there." I just believed him. I think he was right to a point, but wrong in the absolute nature of his comment. I took it literally. It is a good characteristic to get things done and to learn,  it's completely arrogant and foolish to take it to an absolute. To say I will never get help, is ridiculous. My dad was willing to get help but only if he had tried and failed first. I was too, but I was even more reluctant. The other thing pride did, is it made me not want to feel stupid. Going to experts for help almost always made me feel stupid. The corrupting nature of authority shows its ugly head here, in that when someone knows more in a particular field than you, they often get haughty. Once their pride gets the best of them, they can't help but make you feel stupid for even asking. Screw that. I had experienced that enough in life to not even want to ask. So it was a combination of ignorance, being cocky, being prideful, and being afraid to be made to feel stupid. What an awesome combination I had to not seek help from books or authority. Now Sanchez was almost the complete opposite, he was eager to learn from others, and willing to ask questions that made him feel inferior, and he was fearless in his pursuit. He would watch Youtube videos, go onto forums, read books, and generally ask anybody anything in order to figure something out. He would almost assume ignorance as a default, even if he wasn't. He would learn as much as possible and then trust his ability to sift out the garbage. He said many times, "I can't be the only one in the history of humanity to ever have struggled at this problem." Where as I would be like, I don't care what anybody else has figured out, I will just attack this head on regardless of others and figure this out my damn self. I wanted I thought to recreate the wheel because it was fun to invent something new. Which again has worked out well in many areas for me, and his method has worked out well for him. I think a flaw in his method is that he lacked confidence in himself. Where as in my method, I lacked humility. So once he started talking about the universe's beginning, I decided to look it up. I was so clueless to this subject that he sort of forced my hand. In general I began to use Youtube, forums, the internet, books, and Wikipedia as tools to learn. I began to look outside myself for knowledge and information about life in general and in smaller more specific things like how to cut down a tree. Again my mind was blown. There was so much information out there, and I was beginning to trust my ability to decipher the good from the bad. I was able to objectively rate good youtubers, from the bad. More importantly I was able to objectively rate good information from bad. The good science from the bad, the good reasoning from the bad all were becoming easier to distinguish. Also if an appliance broke at my house I could fix it without as much frustration, if my car broke I could learn to fix it quickly. Having that objective standard was paying huge dividends. The combination of my fearless approach to things, and Sanchezes approach in studying multiple sources and sifting was working really well. I was growing and learning way more than I ever had about everything I ran across. My pride would get knocked, my humility was being forcibly expanded, but the results were clear. I was getting better and faster at a lot of things. I was learning way more than I ever had in all my previous years. I was learning way more, than i ever did in school, and I finally was using the tools of experience reasoning reading and writing in practical meaningful ways. And oh yeah, Sanchez turned out to be right about the universe. The theories were not as varied or complex as I might have thought. The universe had to have come from something. Nothing from nothing is the same crazy nonsense that made me stumble before. It was easier to accept this time, because one, I didn't hold any belief of the entire universe. And two, I had already learned the lesson of logic, that there are in fact absolutes. The universe coming from something was logically sound, whereas everything from coming from nothing was not.

**When in Rome (sanchez):**

Over my lifetime, I have been led by the Holy Spirit to minister to people by meeting them where they are at. This has meant picking up hobbies that I would not have necessarily have picked on my own. I have gone places and met people that I would never have met without the prompting of ministry. Some of the calls have been awesome and fun, others have been difficult and lame. I have had to change the way I dress, the foods I eat, and the people with whom I 'hang out'. Through all this, I have had to try and keep my heart and mind focused on God while trying to help the people I have been called to minister to. I do not recommend this for the faint of heart. I do not get to pick and choose where I am called. I have been uncomfortable, hungry, hurt, and tempted. I have also been taken care of, fed, rested, and joyous in my service. For Mac, the call was to be in his world without being a part of it. I believe this was what most convinced him of the Truth. He was able to see me be there without being part of it. Now, our lives have changed and his world looks more like mine than mine like his. It's filled with family, God, and work. This may be the biggest irony. All along, a part of Mac believed he was helping to change me, but it was actually the other way around. I was not being deceitful, but it was not the call to announce that my real mission was to help him find God. In the end, I benefitted as much if not more from my friendship and ministry with Mac. I learned how to check my heart for my 'real' intentions. I learned how to take risks in life that I would not normally take. Having Mac as my best friend has been like having a workout partner that is just as strong and motivated. It pushes you to be better.

We are all called to be fishers of men, yet some are not willing to go to the lake and possibly get wet. We must be desperate to help others, to dive head first into the raging waters to catch even one.

**Self taught (sanchez):**
Learning how to think and reading the greats was a strange and difficult journey. However, like all great journeys, it was the experience that made it worth it. I will condense the formula here. Imagine I was reading some "great" book from human history. Plato, Socrates, C.S. Lewis, or watching a video of a

debate between William Lane Craig and Christopher Hutchinson. First, I read the book in its entirety at a pretty good pace. This means I find time...I steal time. If you wait to study the greats until you have 'time', you'll never get started. Truth is found in the hard to reach places and at the most inconvenient times. You must want Truth more than you want comfort (at least temporarily...in the end, Truth brings a joy that surpasses understanding). I read the book without stopping. This means that when I have questions or there is a part I do not understand...I keep going. I don't stop to take notes. I don't stop to look up words. I keep going. It's when you are desperate to get to your destination that you drive a little faster and ignore all the little errands that creep into your mind. After I have finished, I write down concepts, words, and try to map out the arguments as I can remember them. Now, I begin to read or watch again. This time I take my time. At each point that my brain says, "wait...what?" I research until I figure it out. By the way, in this process so far I have not decided whether I agree or disagree wholeheartedly. I'm not at that point yet. How can I agree or disagree when there may be some pivotal point that I do not fully understand yet and, when I finally do clarify, I may disagree with the entire premise? I do not hand over my assent unless I am confident it is correct. So I read or watch carefully; I research opposing views and I check if the argument is a relatively old one just addressed in a new way. You will be surprised how many "new" ideas are really just repackaged old ideas that have already been affirmed or refuted. When I get done a second time, I decide which parts have stood up to scrutiny. There is usually something to learn from almost every good book. Again, it is rare to agree 100%, but it is common to find one that I can agree with somewhere in the 80th percentile. Once I have finished the second time, I read it once more. This time it is a conversation with the author. I either take mental notes or write down physical notes of parts I enjoy or find fascinating. This last read through may not be necessary and may just be my inner nerd. With G.K. Chesterton, C.S. Lewis, William Lane Craig, and Oswald Chambers; I find myself rereading for shear joy. They are unique minds that express Truth in an enjoyable way. I recommend them to you.

A disclaimer (mac):

This might be the wrong spot for this, but I think it needs to be said somewhere. It also relates to the process Sanchez has just laid out. It is about the nature of truth and the process of discovering it versus creating it. We both have read GK Chesterton, CS Lewis, the Bible, Oswald Chambers, and watched William Lane Craig. (Sanchez more than me, more thoroughly, and for longer part of his life) We in no way are trying to copy or imitate any one of them in particular. We aren't even trying to be original in the way that an artist would normally be; creating a piece of art. What we are claiming to attempt here is more as a miner searches for gold, than as a painter paints. We are removing the less valuable dirt and stones from the most precious ones. Just as a miner doesn't claim to be the source of the gold he has found, we are not claiming to be the source of any of what we have discovered. We are willing to find gold or truth in any nook and cranny of either of our collective experience or conscious. The sources we have mentioned above have proven to be rich in precious truth, than the vast majority of others we have 'mined'. We are only trying to be another source for another miner along their own path. There is only one

Source of either gold or Truth and anyone who has sought His Wisdom is bound to discover similar pieces of Him. As miners of truth we are proud to find the purest forms and deepest most universal truths but are just as happy with the smaller flakes and dust we receive. We are not jewelry makers, we want your focus to be an the raw form of what we discovered, not be distracted by 'our' form of it. Our goal is to seek His Kingdom, and to share whatever it is we find. For our eyes are drawn to the brilliance of the gold, not the dirt and grime of the miner.

A word on math (mac):

Math was used as analogy in a good many of our discussions. The idea that 2+2=4 is true regardless of what I or anybody else wants, is and was a powerful fact. Also the way math is accessible to many levels of interest and intelligence is powerful and awe inspiring. The fact that the basics of mathematical principles when understood and followed correctly are enough to lead you to the complexities of the real world and the very highest most complicated mathematics is important and useful to how the world is set up in general. The inarguable truth in mathematics regardless of the practitioner, regardless if the majority of people are poor at math, regardless if everybody says that 2+2=5, its inescapable conclusions against the grain of any human authority. Truth and Math are the authority over man and nature, not the other way around. I have come to be not only grateful to math and it's pure reasoning and trap in the ending of her story, but more convinced in the mathematical structure in most of reality. I'm in no way implying that math is the creator of anything, but rather the underlying language and structure, that not only speaks to how the physical world is made, but also to how the rest of the world is. Reasoning and logic, right and wrong, good and bad, justice and fairness, art and music, patterns of speech, the economy, psychiatry, martial arts, engineering, construction, and ethics and morality all seem to possess an underlying mathematical structure. I'm not saying that the world is purely mathematics whatsoever. Let's leave room for miracle, creativity, for almost perfect, for inspiration, for getting away with things, for luck, for randomness and arbitrariness, for an outlier, for an anomaly, for Grace, for a pardon, for subtleness, and nuance, and for a Divine Will. What I am saying is that the way in which math works, with a certainty in structure, and a particular path to discovery, this way of a fundamental structure of reality, exists in other places besides the material world. It exists in the softer places in the human experience. Mathematical and logical structures exist in the immaterial world, the place where things matter, in meaning itself. Math exists in the human psyche, in human behavior, in the poets poem, and the artist's mind. The underlying structure shows itself in rules and laws and rules of thumbs and karma and growth and decay and movement and space and time.

When you go against the deep underlying mathematical fabric of our reality, it doesn't just give way, in fact it stays constant and firm. The one who chooses to pretend the structure isn't serious, is inasmuch danger as the one who chooses to pretend they can fly. There is something transcendent, powerful and important about mathematics that gets lost. RIght here is where a warning is needed. I think that the flaw in most of us, definitely in me, was not taking the fundamental structure of reality, of the cosmos, on the micro level serious enough. Playing too loosely with the math of life, morality, free will and the Divine Will, has proven a regrettable and painful mistake. I also want to say that holding on too tightly to pure Reason is at your peril. Pure Reason is not the Father, logic is not the Absolute. In fact, Reason, Pain, Objectivity, Math, Art, Music, Love, Good, Evil, and Emotion are all tools not to be worshipped in place of what deserves worship. The trap is that we get the tool confused with the tools creator. If we stop too early in our quest, or rather mistake the tool for the creator, we will ruin the tool, and more importantly harm ourselves and others, for it was not meant to sustain us or even to be worshipped by us, a tool was only made to be used for a purpose. Using them wrong is deadly. Getting to the tools purpose is the aim here, and anything else is blasphemy.

A word on conversion (mac):

One of the points of emphasis along this journey is that of conversion. I had to look up the definition because I never felt nor do I feel that I was converted. I think this an important point. One that speaks to the character and insight of my friend Sanchez and also to the nature of the process. The implied sentiment behind the word conversion is that of persuasion in the sinister hidden sense. That I want you join something or other. Misery loves company so please convert to whatever my viewpoint is. I think a good many a sandwich board guys are of this mindset or the door to door sales people or the missionaries going to "help" the poor people while the intent of the trip is to seek converts. Sort of the more the merrier and volume counts so let us infect the weakest among us. Something like this sentiment and negative emotion is invoked even in the word conversion. What this process is that we speak of and our journey in particular was more like well a journey that we were on together. It was a sharing of ideas beliefs and more importantly of lives of actual actions and words that we both meant. Sanchez wasn't into volume. He was there as a friend, and he was willing to learn from me where I had discovered my little truths. He did not act as an authority or an expert, he acted as a man who was living what he had discovered to be true, and was simply sharing as friends do or at least as they ought to. In this way it worked well it was a give and take. Looking back he gave me more or had the big Truth and Absolute firmly in his grasp but I had no idea and he was willing to lay his cards out and open and not only that, but also examine each individually or together, also admitting if one of them was flawed, or weaker than another or even give credit as to not the originator of the card. Which is another part of this journey that is worth mentioning. That we must use the discoveries of our ancestors before we can create or discover anything anew. Any new discovery without investigation into the past leaves room the error in the idea that it is in fact something new that was discovered. Its new to you who has discovered it but it isn't new to humanity. So reading, listening, watching, and researching those who came before is important. Some of them deserve special mention on my particular journey. CS Lewis and william lane craig in particular, but more on them later. To get back to my point on Sanchez and the way to my ultimate conversion. To speak of it as a manipulated trick entirely misses the mark. There was no manipulation no aha I got you no initiation into some secret brotherhood. If there was ever a hint of that I would have used it against him and his entire world view in the quickest of moments. One truth about me is that I am not a joiner. I belong to no affiliations no tribes no clubs no groups etc. It is difficult to place me with any group that I have chosen, because i just haven't chosen to be a part of anything, not because I am against groups or tribes (if you remember a reason for this book is in partial reason to find a tribe) it is simply because i have found one that suits me. Or I haven't been suited for any of them, for it is entirely possible that I am the issue and not the boy scouts of america. So instead of thinking of any of this as some sort of conversion, it's much more like we both had buildings we were living in and we decided to share how it is we built ours. And upon further examination even though there were some parts of my building that he thought I did better along the way. In the end he helped to show me the flaws of my foundation and process by which I went about building it were flawed and that there was and in fact there is a better way to build it to withstand the test of time and keep it from falling down and crushing me along with all of its inhabitants. He did this not by burning my house down he did this by showing me his foundation and then comparing it to mine. He asked me to inspect his for cracks and breaks and structural weakness, while

I did the same to him. He didn't just come bulldoze my house down. He helped me to replace each nail each board relay the foundation and ultimately show me a better more solid lot to place my home. And again without him and of course Him I cannot say what would have happened but I know the catastrophe was already well under way and the home I had built was already infested with disaster and things were steadily falling apart regardless of how hard I tried to prevent it.

Knowing what it isn't (mac):

A lesson, in the process, that has proven to be valuable, is the figuring out what doesn't work, which way is not the way. Discovering what is false, even though it can be cumbersome, is often the only way forward. It reminds me of how the great sculptors, who sculpted out of stone would think, they would say we are removing the parts that are not part of the end result. We are erasing the bits of marble that don't belong to the finished piece of work. Instead of like clay sculpture where they are building and sculpting something from nothing. Which is a valid approach, both approaches are needed. The ability to build from nothing in the case of seeking truth has proven for me to be more difficult. The ability to point to something and clearly see its stupidity or its falsity or its lack of value and that it ought to be discarded has helped me tremendously. I almost don't trust myself otherwise. I'm more like Sanchez pointed out, a bowling ball that needs bumpers to make its way to the pins. I need the negative push back, the pain of failure or the embarrassment of stupidity to show me the way. Like a fridge that is full of both healthy and valuable food and also rotten and unhealthy food. Sometimes the first step is to simply remove all of the bad food from the fridge so you have a clearer picture of what you do have to eat and maybe more importantly what is lacking so that you can go and fill the fridge with necessary food items. This process is precisely how we moved forward in our search, or at least I did, especially early on. We first figured out what a friend wasn't before we could say what it was or is. Once we know it's easier then to realize just how rare they are, and how few we actually have, or that in some cases how poor you, yourself are at being a friend.


A word on best friends (mac):

When I was young I was in search of a best friend. I had one he still is my friend but he is no longer my best friend. Once I got to adolescence I was exposed to more and more people of my same age and more friendships were formed. Then into high school I developed a different best friend but it was never said. I think however it was there and implied. That friend ended up being killed and that friendship was cut short, so the word best friend never developed. Around this time when my conscious attempt at life began, my conscious attempt at searching for meaning was in its infancy, the idea of best friend seemed immature and irrelevant. It even seemed wrong in this adult relativistic world for how could we even distinguish between friend which was best it was all a matter of opinion and who was to say which friend was better than the other. Because immediately when you call something best you call the other things not best not as good. And when you aren't the best or in that sphere or club its an awful feeling. I knew this intuitively when Someone would ask my favorite food or my favorite color my answer became it depends, it depends on my mood the situation the circumstances and also more accurately i didn't have a favorite because I loved them all equally. It was like asking which child I have is my favorite. On one hand that is absurd, on the other hand well it depends but really it's how dare you imply i have a favorite (its my daughter by the way. haha Anyway this is what I didn't want to do. I didn't want to make my other friends jealous or angry or hurt by excluding them from the best. So i would say one of my friends or my friend, or one of my dear friends. Once objective truth came into focus it changed the game. Because once I defined objective criteria of what made a good friend. It became very clear that I had a best one of those and over the years it's become clear that I have just one of those. So he is my best and only friend. We actually would like more friends but our attempts have proven fruitless. In every case when the topics of this book were brought up they eventually proved too much for them to bare. They all ultimately left of their own free will. The process that has proven so generous insightful fruitful important and ultimately necessary to Sanchez and I, has proven too much for the others.

A word on real talk (mac):

Along this journey, I had the displeasure of finding myself in an anger management course. There was lots of learning involved, hard, painful, real learning. One of the most fruitful, yet most dangerous places of learning was found in this court "recommended", 6 month, anger management course. The course was in a rough part of town, in a nondescript, industrial, office building. The first peculiarity, was that the way they determined how much your payment was, was through a sliding scale, based on income. So if you made over a certain amount, you had to pay more, and the less money you made, you paid less. All the way to zero. This is only important in that I paid the max (the scale was skewed and broken down into various levels of poverty, basically if you weren't poor you paid the max), which among the other patrons, was rare. So there was financial reason to keep me in the program. The way it worked, was there was this one fairly large conference room with white, plastic, cheap, outdoor furniture, you know yard chairs lined along the entirety of the wall, next to each other, to form a big circle. Well almost circle, because in the front of the room there was a whiteboard and a stool. The woman running the whole program was a small woman of about fifty years of age. The way the class was run, on the first day, and everyday thereafter was as follows: She would, what seemingly was at random, but clearly was not purely at random pick a man out (the classes were all men or all women never both) and ask them why they were there. She would say the same question in several ways, like tell me what you've been up to, or how's it been going with your ex, or your wife, or your girlfriend. Everyone in there with rare exception was in that class because of some domestic violence or spousal abuse. The clients came from all walks of life. There were men with multiple felony convictions, to well to do, affluent men. There was even a local celebrity man in there. The boss lady would give us writing assignments and then make us read them to the class sometimes and others we would just talk and listen. Not everybody spoke everytime, you never knew when your turn we be up. Now here is the tricky thing. She expected full honesty and knew how to get it out of us, using a mixture of logic and reasoning, experience (she had been running these group sessions for 20 plus years at the time), interrogation techniques, and using the group dynamic, basically allowing the group to put pressure on an individual to get to a confession of sorts. The problem is that she was the only one who could clear you to pass the class, what she expected was complete honesty, and if she judged you as unfit she would not pass you. If you didn't pass, then you were to remain in the class. The conflict comes from the fact that she had a financial interest to keep you in class. So passing was tough, the more money you paid, the more incentive she had to keep you. And Lastly the honesty part of the equation, since she was the judge, the jury, and the executioner, if you were honest with let's say disagreeing with her, then she could easily say, "well he didn't have his breakthrough yet" or "he doesn't get it" or "he is incompetent" or "he is still a danger to society" etc. So she could keep you in the program longer, if she cared to. She also was connected to local law enforcement and the local court system, so her words carried real weight. She was that awful type of authority, self-righteous and shrewd. From her own word, I learned that the system was unfair, and unjust, it was best for all of us was just stay out of it. Her advice was ironic, in that her own system was unfair and unjust, but we were trapped,with our only escape was perverse honesty. Ok so besides the trappings, the actual way the class was run, ended up working to high degree, and even with all its flaws it actually worked really well. She had a knack for letting us tell our story, and then when something didn't pass the smell test, call us on it, and if we resisted, she would begin the all out attack. Eventually we were all trained in a way, to recognize the sins in each other's words. To not only hear a contradiction or lie, but to also see it. There are many clues when you really listen to someone speak, in tone, body language, posture, micro expressions of there face and hands, that give away the truth. These ended up being universal within the group, we could tell when someone started getting red in the face, or shifty in their seat, that there was a tear in their story. We could hear the stuttering in there speech or the confused stammering, and the subsequent back pedaling when pressed with an inescapable question. We could watch them all go from calm cool and collected to flashes of anger or hurt at certain points in the conversation. Then and there in front of us all, she would poke, because there in fact is the thing that needs poking. We all gave ourselves away. No matter how hard we tried to hide, she would always find us out. I was learning watching and observing, I could tell when someone was sincere or not. I could tell when they were hiding the real story or motivation. I was getting it. The way we would all tell stories, in just a certain way, in order to minimize our own faults, and maximize those of the others involved in our lives was a big lesson I learned. There was no montra, or spelled out method, or twelve steps. There was just a lady, her dog, and a room full of men, who had varying degrees of success in the world, and obviously varying degrees of failures. I began to see her techniques, and I was able to apply them in my own life. I began to be able to speak a bit more honestly about my real intent, and heart behind my actions. One of the lessons that stands out, was that of a man telling his story of how he "snapped", and in a fit of rage, broke everything that his fiance owned. With this the boss lady began to work. She goes, "oh really, blind rage blackout hmm? Totally out of control, really? Why didn't you break any of your things, or even harm yourself? If you were out of control, then why wasn't the chaos more arbitrary? Why was it her things only that were destroyed?" And just like that, the trap was set and sprung and he was caught. He had nowhere to go, the truth was right in front of us all. It didn't stop his pouty anger though. It didn't' stop his defiant, child like response. It didn't stop his arms crossed, "well you can't tell me any different!", and "that's my story, i'm sticking to it!" In moments like these, she would turn to the group and tell us all, this is exactly how we all acted, in the exact same set of circumstances, all of us. Just like kids who get caught with the bag in hand, that they were seen to have stolen, they will still look for a way out. We all don't want to admit those ugly hard truths about ourselves. I learned that in those moments over and over. She would also say, as she often did, to the group in moments like these, "notice the way he responds. Does anyone have any help to give him?" A few men would always volunteer to address him (if we didn't she would let us know how cowardly we are.) They would say, "brother i've been there, boss lady is right, you're off, you just wanted to hurt her, you didn't black out, you just gave yourself permission to harm her." We would all nod in agreement. Not in a snobbish better than though sorta way. No, in a, i'm ashamed because I've done the exact same thing kind of way. She then pointed out what actually out of control looks like. "What we call seizure, severe seizure, where the person falls back and writhes uncontrollably on the ground, spazzing out, they lose all faculties and its scary." "That is out of control, not breaking your girlfriends things." "That's just fucked up!" This type of method of letting us talk ourselves into a trap was common, because she knew us right, that we would all lie in some way, we would all want to avoid the truth of our depravity. Another truth I saw happen over and over, was that it was so much easier to see where everyone else was stumbling when they were on the hot seat, than it is when I was in it. When you get put on the hot seat, which I did a few times, it was very difficult, I found myself being interrogated, getting red in the face, stuttering my words, not being able to think clearly, and the guilt and shame of being publicly caught in painting different picture of what actually happened, one that of course painted me in a fairer light than deserved, was almost unbearable. The men in the group did well, turning to me and telling me where I was off, and from those sessions I left changed. I was raw, but a part of me had died. Something had shifted. I had learned what I had done and looked closer at my real motivations. Now they weren't as sinister as she made them out to be, but they weren't as pure and innocent as I made myself or others believe. I did all the things I saw in others do, I lied by omission, my face betrayed my inner thoughts and feelings, in the form of what she called a smile of recognition. As she described multiple times, a smile of recognition is that little smile, the micro expression that we all do when we get caught. She used the example of a kid with their hand in the cookie jar or with one behind their back. You ask them if they have a cookie behind their back and before their words can tell a lie theri face cracks a small quick smile betraying themselves to the truth. Another lesson I learned from her was that she had her own demons, and her own axe to grind. She was sexually assaulted while pregnant and it left a deep psychological wound her psyche. Looking back I think she had a deep seated hatred for men and that I was no exception. It was scary. I learned that even though she had a very good system worked out, and it did a lot of good. That because her heart was not pure, that in fact she was taking her revenge out on the lot of us and therefore, she did a lot of damage. It was a clear example that the one trying to help, must first seek help themselves. The boss lady should have not only been the boss, but she should have joined the band and faced her own music. She should have been a member of her own class. By not, by staying removed, she fell victim to the pride of power and avoided the benefits of her very own methods. Having her very own hidden motivations and evilness of the heart, she harmed herself and many others along the way. She was never in the hot seat, and she should have been. Another example of the corrupting nature of power and authority was thrown into my field of experience. Another difficult lesson of how not to be was born.

A word on the corrupting nature of authority (mac):
Little "a" authority is corrupting by nature. This goes for all types of authority where one person has the power of authority over another either in physical dominance or mental dominance or age and maturity or through systematic means. Institutionalized power such as but not limited to the following: Priest and children, teacher and student, boss and employee, doctor patient, police officers and the public, soldiers and the public, politicians and the public, farmers and animals, pet

owners and pets. Prison guard and prisoner. Adult and child. Groups and the individual. One reason we think that power and authority are corrupt by their very nature is because the people in a position of power are corruptible by nature. Once they have a place to exploit it then they often do. We are not calling this an absolute or even a law, what we are claiming is that the fact that authority corrupts is the rule, not the exception. It takes an exceptional person to battle their fallen nature to rule justly and not abuse their position. It takes an average man to abuse their power even a little bit. To become a tyrant is easy, to stay humble is rare. A leader ought to be a servant, not attempt to be served by their subordinates, but again this is an ought not an is or does. The other is that corruption works, even in simple he said vs she said. The person who carries the position of authority also carries more weight behind their words. So their version of events gets more credit, and both parties know this. Another way that authority corrupts works is the victim of abuse or corruption thinks if only I were to be the leader or the boss or the teacher I would do it better. The person to escape the feeling of powerlessness will work themselves to a position of power for various reasons but ultimately to gain the thing they had not. So the positions of power are filled with people that want the power. Even wanting that much power is the sinful nature at work. Another fundamental cause of authority corrupting is when there is a conflict between the person of power and their subordinate in the end the negotiations lets say are so skewed to the person of power that again both parties know that they get what they want without any good or valid reason. If we view this as a game the person who gets to power understands whatever game they are playing. To be fair here there is a thing called competence and ability to those who rise to the top, but competence at a skill or craft at the bottom of a hierarchy is completely different than the skill or game of exercising authority or of managing people. It's the managing of people where power and authority become corrupt not necessarily power over the paintbrush or computer programming. We mean that the rule is for a constant level of unjust and unfair outcomes whenever there is an interaction with authority and subordinate. We think that within a rank or as peers once the authority is gone or the power equalized pure relationship can occur, for many reasons but mainly because I have no dominion over you and you none over me so everything between us is voluntary. So the inability to voluntarily walk away from a transaction is what makes the authority be able to trap persuade or convince you on weak moral ethical or reasoned grounds to do or not to do a thing. There is also fear presented with authority and if I am afraid of your power that changes the nature of the thing as well. How then does the fact that authority is a corrupting agent tie into our journey or my journey? I had a healthy distrust and disgust with most forms of authority. I had been the victim of abuse of authority from bad bosses to run ins with police to mob violence to bullies to women and the power of their desire or not. I had also abused power. So my trust in authority of religion was only that I trusted them to be wrong. I trusted all authority to be guilty until proven innocent. This made me extremely skeptical of anyone who thought they knew better. I could only listen to someone who was not an authority. So right here in this book I am no authority we are no authority. We have no credentials or degrees or pieces of paper that say we are in anyway an expert at any of this. All we have what everyone has we have our ability to reason and think, we can feel and we have our experience we can read and write and do arithmetic. And we have the time we have spent this far looking at this particular problem. Also Sanchez was and is my friend not my pastor or priest or boss, nor was I physically afraid of him. Quite opposite he earned my trust of the years and many adventures we had. He was willing to lay it all out as a peer as a fellow traveler and man on this planet born into this world with the same awe and vast unknown as i. Nor i to him I carried no extra power or weight in our relationship. This fact that no authority were present allowed an open fluid dialogue to be present it allowed both our guards to be down and an openness to the truth and to the real to happen. There are legitimate authority. There is one legitimate Authority. They have their place in this world. We have authority over others, we try not to abuse it, but sometimes fail. This truth played an important role once I finally was ready and prepared to read the new testament for myself without the fiercely emotional opposition to that book or that way or that solution.

Sanchez and I establish our own real talk in the school (mac):

Throughout the lessons I learned from the group therapy or anger management course, I would talk to Sanchez about them. We would in turn, explore, discuss, and root out the truth and the falsity of her methods and ways. I would tell him the stories from each class, he would listen and then we would try and figure out if the methods were valid. There were again the ring, the sound, the vibe of truth that he or I would pick up on. Eventually, he and I were able to implement our own real talk class at the high school where we now currently work. We took a group of kids after school that were making up credit and put them in a group setting and began to ask questions. We kept in our heart as much as possible that we were there to help kids, not to harm them. I even ran a real talk circle with my AP Economics class, after they took their end of the year exam. In both cases it worked, very well in fact, and if we're honest, looking back, probably too well. The places that we got to with the kids were deep, and a lot of them weren't mature enough or ready enough to face their demons. We were honest them and ourselves, and we were there to help, but the kids were in many ways just too young. We did do good, and we were able to help I think, but it's unclear as to how much success we had. We definitely learned and honed our skills as practitioners of our own brand of real talk methods, analysis, and practice. Most of the kids after the process thanked us for helping them, but looking back, as is always the case, I see where there was success and where there was failure. The intensity and intimacy that we were able to achieve was too intense and too intimate for the particular set of circumstances. Specifically the age, maturity, and location, at a public high school, where not ideal. In my AP Economics class, it was just too much for the high achievers, especially laying their real selves out in the open, in front of their peers. It just got to a point, where I felt the possible damage or harm, I could have accidently caused, was in the end too risky for the definite and purposeful good. So I cut it short. What our programs did though, was to show us, both in the after school real talk, and in my own class, that we were on to something. The combination of our own conversations, our friendship based upon being real and honest with each other, the methods and techniques I had learned and shared from anger management, and finally the actual implementation with the high school students, proved to us the value and power of the path we were on. Not only did we realize that seeking truth as an individual was beneficial, but that when teamed up with another person to not only seek but apply truth, the value grew exponentially, and the potential seemed limitless.

Reflection on my broken self (mac):

From the real talk experiences and the more internal battles and realization of just how blind and hidden I kept the truth out of my consciousness. I began to see more clearly just how broken myself and others were. I still wasn't able to see the full extent of my badness, but it was definitely becoming more focused. We were to a point, where I could now understand, and see the objective truth in the world. I could see and observe the objective badness in myself and others, and I could feel the despair of this world. I began, to at least, put the pursuit of truth together with the awesomeness of reasoning, as valuable, worthwhile, and ultimately necessary. I was also getting to a point where the other pursuits, the pursuits of putting things, ideas, or activities as idols or absolutes were wearing thin.

Nothing was filling the void of existence. I had experienced true love, and now I was married, but after the honeymoon period, the real struggle of battling my own demons, and those of my wife's demons, were growing more and more difficult. We both are passionate, and that would lead us to explode into chaotic fights. The way I was living was still not working, even though I was reasonable, and pursuing truth, I still was lost, and the answers were closer than I realized. I began to feel stuck, once I new the weight of the world and how much everything mattered, the responsibility was crushing me. How could I tell what to do next? How could I weigh each decision, and make the right choice? What if I was wrong again, and ended up waiting my life, or worse leading my family to waste theirs? How could I hope to heal? How could I make sense of the fact that I was born? What was the point? What was my purpose? Was even possible to find one? How did I know what things I chose freely and what things were simply because of my nature or upbringing? How much of me was a product of something else I had no control over, and how much was me? The questions seemed endless, weight seemed unbearable, I couldn't honestly go backwards to my previous ignorance. I couldn't honestly pretend everything was relative. There had to be an Objective reality an Absolute. But how could I find it? There had to be answers, but where?

The problem with religion (mac):
One of the many themes of our conversations was the problem with religion. I ran the gamut on my issues with religious people. The seemingly mindlessness of believers, is one of the top concerns I had. I had never met anyone who had actually thought through their faith. Sanchez had and has. I had a problem with people just having faith and praying instead of possibly taking action to solve their problems. I had a problem with the judgement I had felt throughout my life by believers. I had a problem with the hypocrisy I witnessed from many believers. I had a problem with the fact that religious people didn't seem any better, but rather worse than non believers. I had a problem with the American type of religion that was and is mingled with politics and patriotism. I had a problem with religious people using their religion to do harm (think American

slavery, fundamentalist Islam, hate groups, and the slaughtering of 'savages'). I had a problem with the denial of truth and science and reason. I had a problem with authority and tradition, with torture and wars. I had a problem with the continued conflicts over religious lands in the middle east. I had a problem with the variety of different religions. (I'm using the word 'had' here, but much of this I still 'have' issue with.) I had a problem with religious people that I would argue with dismissing me with a, "you're hopeless" or "you can't stop my faith" or "you're not ready to believe". I had a problem with religious people only using some mystical or personal experience, as some sort of basis for belief. I had a problem with the cult, cultism, and all the religious fanaticism. I had a problem with rules and the arbitrary nature of them. I had a problem with the phony, fake, filth of religious people that would spew religious doctrine and dogma. I had a problem with rigidity. I had problem with the lack of compassion, the lack of humility, the lack of reason, the lack of love, the lack of acceptance, that I had witnessed over and over first hand. I had a visceral, gut, emotional, disgust with all things religious. It all seemed a lie, the biggest disease that had infected humanity ever. It seemed outdated. It seemed ritualistic and primitive. I knew that there was some good done in the name of religion, but it seemed so small compared to the harm it had done and was doing. It seemed made up to get people through the difficult pain and suffering of life, but in the end caused harm like any lie does. It seemed like the most willfully ignorant batch of nonsense ever. It seemed impossibly improbable. It seemed like all the different types of each religion and the constant fracturing and splintering and the varying shades and differences in detail that they all believed, was evidence of a big sham. I am not going to name them all, but simply driving around and observing the vastly different names and types of churches, synagogues, mosques, titles, books, etc. was enough for it all to seem overwhelmingly complex. I couldn't understand if this religious stuff was so good, why then there were so many door to door salespeople? I couldn't understand the seemingly tiny insignificant rule differences, and the vastly different big ones. I couldn't understand the sandwich board guys, the street proclaimers, the tv infomercials, the mega churches, they all left such a bad taste in my mouth. It all seemed entirely too much to overcome, my arguments and observations against religion seemed insurmountable. It took years, but each and every one of my issues were explained in such a thorough way and not simply dismissed, that most if not all of my issues are resolved. I still have issues, but separating religion and people, truth and falsity and the simple idea of baby and bathwater has become clear. It's complicated in detail, but not in concept and detailed problems deserve detailed answers.

Resolving Religion (mac):

This has proven to be a difficult section to write. There is a lot here. Lots of moving parts. There is the complexity of me and my own issues that have tainted my view on religion, which in fact turned out to be wrong. There are however parts of my original sentiments that turned out to be true, and are more true now, being fully backed with experience, reason, and authority. There are also some points that remained muddled grey or unclear as to what exactly the purpose or benefit is of some of the peculiarities within religion. Then there are the practitioners of religion vs. the religion itself, the practitioners often get in the way of seeing the purity of the doctrines. Then there is the vast variety of religious interpretation some subtle and not so subtle differences. Lastly for now the word itself, 'religion' and what exactly we mean by it.

When I look up the word religion, there is a variety in meaning, there is the version of the word that we ascribe to as a system or set of beliefs of the big questions of our existence. The big ones being Christianity, Hinduism, Islam, Judaism, Buddhism, Taoism and I'm sure I've missed some, but this will do for now. Then there is also the word religion that simply means the set of beliefs of an individual and what they place as the supreme importance in their own life. This last point is important in that in one way everyone prescribes in some way to religion. Everyone is operating in this world on some set of beliefs. I was religious in my own relativism, but would have never admitted it. I only used the word religion to mean the first way, which was the 'system' of beliefs, the organized way. I was outside of these great religions, but inside a lesser more perverted version of my own religion. My religion consisted of worshipping myself as the supreme importance and of dismissing any form of formal organized or systematic religion. My religion was hidden from view, it had been given to me by popular and modern influence, and one of the 'gifts' was to keep my dogma hidden. The rebellious independent self importance and worship was going to have the characteristic of never planting me down, never committing, continual movement of positions, and most importantly for this section the anti-religious, religion.

It's not as if I didn't have help with this position. It was easy to find example after example of unreasoned faith, of faith without cause or blind faith. I had come from a Catholic upbringing. It was never personal. It was a thing that my own father did reluctantly out of duty, what always felt like duty to my mother. My mom had faith but she never had reason to back it up, she sent me to church and catechism to be taught that. But there the problem persisted, nobody ever gave reason for why they believed, why faith was a virtue, why the Bible was true. They started with this is true so now lets hear the stories, but that was way too presumptuous of them. Looking back that's like starting with calculus when you haven't learned arithmetic. I needed an explanation of simple sums and they were trying to, unsuccessfully, main line advanced calculus into me. It was like they were in such a hurry to 'save' me they didn't stop to explain why I needed saving, or to explain in real terms how the world was made up. They were literally giving me a fish without any clue on how to catch my own or that I was even hungry. A raw uncooked fish to a fully satisfied child will only begin to stink and rot. That's exactly what happened to me, all the raw fish I had been given only began to rot and stink, eventually I had to throw the whole lot out. I had no idea how to clean and prepare nonetheless cook and eat the thing.

    I had witnessed first hand the lack of faith in my father, the lack of reason from my mother, and the lack of explanation from the church. That was enough for me to seperate myself from it all, all of the organized religions, but especially any version of Christianity. It held a particularly negative spot near my heart. It was the one that infected my family and country the most. It was the one that had proven inadequate and as I got older the most harmful to those around me. It was the most flamboyant and obnoxious, the most arrogant and prideful. What audacity old broken people had to say' "I will pray for you." Who are you to pray for me? What makes you so high and mighty that you think I need prayer? I didn't ask you for advice or help, and now that you said that I never will. This type of attitude turned me off, in fact it does turn me off. I understand now why it did and why it does, but more on that later. The pastor at my friends funeral used the funeral to 'sell' Christianity, instead of honor my fallen friend. It angered me deeply. How dare he bring that rubbage up at a time like this. It was equivalent to going up to make a speech at a wedding and using the time to ask if anyone wanted to 'get in' on this new pyramid scheme. It was trying to make a profit at a time of sacred honor. It was gross, it still is gross. There was also the political mixing with the religion. The loud vocal right wing, tea-party, republican, conservative, christian coalition, patriotic, science denying, overweight, aggressive, anti everything except guns, the flag and Jesus, craziness of my own country. I didn't agree with almost any of their positions, policies, or methods. I still don't. Whatever that crew was with, I was not. It also seemed like the more 'educated' someone was the more suspect they were regarding 'religion'. In fact reasoning and learning seemed to be reserved for the anti-religion crowd, the science minded, the thoughtful, the inquisitive, and the open minded. It was the religious folk that were stopping progress. That is all the way up until I met Sanchez.

The first thing he did was to resolve the conflict I had with the system of religion and the practitioners. First he himself was as thoughtful and as well reasoned of a person as I had met. So him being him made my criticism already less harsh. The other is the clearly reasoned position of the mathematician can very well be flawed but the math can remain pure and perfect. It works in music too that music can be pure but the musician playing can be flawed. Ok good point. How do you explain all the poor practitioners of religion then!? His reply was something like, "In the same way we can explain so many people who suck at math" That is really it. That's all there is. The poor practitioner in no way is equal to the thing he is claiming to represent. In fact, the poor practitioner only highlights the difference in the perfection of art, math, music, or the thing itself and the imperfection of man. We went back, Sanchez and I, to this argument, over and over and over. Almost all of my problems had to do with the people claiming to represent religion, not with the religion itself, and separating the two proved essential in my journey upward.

The variety of religions and religious doctrine isn't as vast and overwhelming as I first thought. In reality what I was doing is using this as an excuse not to really look into any of them. Of course I didn't realize this at the time, like almost everything else I've learned but I can clearly see it now. I didn't do the same thing with things I wanted like ice cream or books or movies and tv or music. The seemingly endless variety of ice cream flavors didn't prevent me from from eating ice cream at all. In fact it excited me. When considering to read I didn't use the overwhelming choice as a means to not read, in fact it was motivation in that realm. The variety was an indicator that there was value in reading. The same goes for sports, tv, movies and music, the variety makes me want to explore not avoid the entire category completely. It's only in the fact that I didn't want to commit or even really want to change my beliefs that I used the same phenomenon of variety that plagues our entire universe and existence as a non starter. This is that inconsistent rationalization, the abusing reason. I could at once use variety as a way out and a way into something, it only depended on what I wanted. The reason I wanted to stay out of religion, is because I wanted to remain in power of my world. I wanted my will to be the ultimate and final say in the universe. I didn't want to answer to some other authority. Again here I was willing to use authority when I agreed with the outcome but not where I didn't. I was willing to use the authority of science to tell me to eat blueberries, but I wasn't about to let the authority of religious doctrine tell me I couldn't have sex with whomever and whenever I pleased. This method of staying out of the realm of traditional religion allowed me to create and invent my own religion. Just like in the story of Frankenstein I could use whatever pieces parts and perversions of traditional religious doctrines to create a hodge podge monster of my own to limp and lumber along through the world. The problem in the actual story of Frankenstein is that the monster became an uncontrollable problem. That is exactly what my religion had become. It was unsustainable, it was gross, it was harmful, it was ugly and guilt ridden, it had a mind of its own, and it was leading me to my own death. It was steadily strangely my soul and darkening my spirit.

So in the end my only two real claims against religion were resolved by reason. The Christian was not Christianity. I could not use the poor practice and habits of mathematicians as an excuse not to do math. The variety of religions was and is a normal and usual part of my everyday experience. Just as I didn't use the variety of food, methods of preparation, and the difference in restaurants as an excuse not to eat, I could no longer use the variety of religious doctrine as a way to not feed my soul. Besides, it had become clearer and more evident as my eyes were opened, that I did in fact have my own religion. We all did and that mine, for all my attempts and efforts at its creation, was simply and truly unable to hold up to real scrutiny. I and everyone else who was relying on their homemade monstrosities and perverted version of their own religion, was heading in one direction; to hell.

Sandwich board (sanchez):

Mac has laid down some deep Truth in the above section. I hope you hear what he's saying. In other parts of this book, he has talked about the gross side of Christianity that has done more harm than good. As 'christians', we must own up to our collective mistakes and be ready to condemn those that harm, whether that harm was in honest or dishonest error. If you run over my foot with your car on accident or on purpose, it still hurts. One is easier to seek forgiveness for. I have spent years talking to 'sandwich board christians'. Some LITERALLY had sandwich boards and others walked around waiting for opportunities to beat someone up with their beliefs. To each kind of person, I would ask a series of questions. 1. Why are you doing this? They would answer with basically two reasons. "God told me to" and "if I help reach even ONE person...it's worth it." Here our conversation would come down to two answers. They hadn't prayed and received this call from God but instead cherry picked one verse out of the Bible to justify their actions. Second, zero people had come to Christ through their ministry. I know some here will claim that in the history of sandwich boards a few people HAD to come to Christ. I am saying that I have never found this to be true and even if it were true...ask yourself this, "how many have been driven away from Christ because of this ministry?" If it's worth it to do this ministry "even if only one person ever comes to Christ because of it"...isn't it more worth it to stop trying to minister this way because of all the people it ACTUALLY drives away???

A lonely road (mac):

As a kid I wasn't lonely. I had a neighborhood full of kids that were of my age, I had siblings, I had school friends, and I was popular. In Highschool I excelled at academics and athletics. I was voted homecoming royalty and had lots of 'friends'. It wasn't until college and beyond where things changed. It seemed like the more I began questioning things, the less people were interested in talking. I remember trying to talk to people about people flaking. I remember realizing how much it hurt to be flaked on. How wrong it felt, for someone to tell me "yes, I will be there", and then not show. I couldn't understand why they would do that, and do it so nonchalantly. The people I talked to weren't interested in the conversation really. When I flaked I felt bad, I had tremendous guilt, and would do my best to say sorry. Those I flaked on would be like, "don't worry about it, no big deal." I began exploring, about the phoniness of people, or about how wrong the world was, nobody seemed interested, at least not like I was. I wanted to talk about the game and people just wanted to play it. It became increasingly lonely, the more real I wanted to be, the less others wanted to interact. It's hard to generalize here, but in general it became harder to make friends. I wasn't able to relate to my childhood friends like I once had. They didn't want to talk about the things I wanted to, or were unable, or both. In general they stayed into the same things they had always been into, that I had always been into. I was the weirdo, I was changing, because I was searching. They weren't. I would think that I found someone to talk to, but then something would come up. They would leave, or wouldn't follow through, or flake. Then I would call them on it and they would fold. Basically I couldn't really find anyone else that was willing to explore the world of ideas and beliefs and truth like I was. I honestly began to think that was in fact mentally ill, or broken or flawed, or born in the wrong space or time. Worse was that I began thinking that maybe I shouldn't have been born. When I met Sanchez, things changed. He was able to, and even seemed willing to, or even more like wanted to, really talk about things. I remember talking to him about the word busy. We talked about how people would say, "oh, I'm busy", as if it were a valid excuse. We dissected the real meaning of 'busy', and the way it was used to realize what was actually meant. What we discovered was that when someone said that they were busy, what they actually meant was that I wasn't their priority. Something or somebody else was. Whenever someone would say, "I'm busy" meant that they were too busy. It was really code for, "I have more important things to do, and by the way, you are not one of them." We realized also that technically everyone is busy at all times. Everyone has the same amount of time in a day, everyone has the same 24 hours as everyone else. Everyone has their own set of priorities. We realized that even if I was taking a nap I was technically 'busy' taking a nap and therefore too busy, for anything or anyone else. And really who was to say how important my nap was compared to your errands that you ran, or the work you did, or the homeless man you saved. It also was related to and becoming increasingly annoying that when I would say, "I'm busy" that some people would want justification with exactly what I was busy with. It was as if they needed to judge my "busy-ness" based on their criteria. Not even even as if, they were trying to determine whether or not I was in fact busy according to them. They weren't using some objective standard of busyness they were only using their own subjective standard of busyness and not allowing me to have my own subjective standard. Instead of trusting that I meant I was busy, based on my own standard. They were literally putting themselves above me. Me and Sanchez figured this out, tested it, and realized it was in fact true. We discovered that we were all busy, and to use this term was a soft way to say this other stuff is more important than the stuff you want me to do.

The other thing that happened was that Sanchez understood my flaking issues, he knew how to flake. He too felt the sting of flaking. We came to the conclusion that in general, it was simply inconsiderate to flake. Literally people weren't considering the fact that we had built our schedules in a very particular way. We had excluded other options to make time for whatever it was we had committed to. We had told others, that in fact we were busy. For someone to then flake in that nonchalant type of way, was just completely selfish and wrong of them. Sanchez has a wife and three boys. They were very young when we first met. He was clear, up front, that his priorities were faith, family, then friends. Not the other way around. We would commit to something and most times he would come through. However there were times that he chose to flake do to family stuff (notice I use he chose, because with every decision there is a choice, I wanted to say, "he was forced to" but that is not the case, that would have been a save). He would say, "sorry, my bad", he would then explain what had happened, and he would say, "let me make it up to you, let me reschedule now, and pay for the next drink or whatever". In other words, it isn't that flaking is absolutely bad, it's just that understanding that you jammed someone else up, and made them sacrifice and lose out on something else for you. He recognized this, and let me know. Then we were good. I wasn't left with the same sting of bitterness, I could honestly mean it when I would say, "don't worry about it." It was easy to understand, because he was clear.

As this journey unfolded less and less people understood where I was coming from, having Sanchez was confirmation that I wasn't crazy. It was just that I was on a different path and I could say honestly that we were progressing. But something happens as you progress to an objective standard. Less and less people are heading in that direction , less and less people are willing and able or want to operate at a different level. Not that we were better than anyone, it was more like we were just exploring reality in way that made it possible to have a clear direction and learn what was actually true, right, and correct, and of course what wasn't. We were willing to share what we had learned, but it seemed like less and less people wanted to hear it. So the path we were and are on became narrower and therefore less traveled. Before Sanchez I was in a dark place, because I was deeply lonely. My so called friends weren't really friends.  Me being honest had left others un willing to join me. So I was in this place where I felt isolated, like nobody understood, and nobody wanted to understand, and I had done it myself. I was able to release my pain in music, because in a song I could say to nobody in particular what was going on. I could talk about deep real issues in a melody, but not in a conversation. That is until Sanchez. The longer we have been on this path less and less people seem to be on it, people still seem to get hung up on simple truths, like flaking and busyness. So the path in a way is very lonely, but there is a deep joy and comfort in knowing where we stand, knowing that we are on solid ground. We can't honestly go onto less solid ground and act as if it were ok, we also have a bond as brothers and fellow travelers, as true friends, and an intimate understanding of what his journey costs.

It's not all earth shattering realizations (sanchez):
This is a good point. In our journey, before Mac became a believer, we would study little things like "flaking". I, too, had struggled with this with others and could never quite figure out why it bothered me. Our friendship has been mutually beneficial and not always about solemn topics. We have searched for the best burger, the best drink at Red Robin, good movies and TV shows, etc. By the way, the times I did "flake", I was being called to serve elsewhere. It's hard to divide what I'm talking about now. You'll see later. Bookmark this. In Mac's eyes, I was

"flaking", and by standards away from the Absolute...I was; however there is a right way to cancel plans. I remember watching an episode of Dr. Phil about chronically late people. It was a light hearted episode for the most part. Dr. Phil looked at the guy and said, "you're doing it on purpose probably most of the time... or you would be on time or early at least once!" The guy was stunned. He had never considered that perhaps deep down he was really being selfish. He believed his time was more valuable than others...that HE was more valuable than others. There is a deep Truth here. Apart from the Absolute...this is what we all think in some way. It's why we pick the way we live. We believe we are right through our own reasoning and understanding, but if all is subjective...how can this be true? Unless deep down I am being selfish against the Absolute.

Big 'T' Truth (mac):

This is a good place to talk about the big 'T' truth. This is the Ultimate Truth that we are searching for. We denote big 'T' truth in such a way as to speak of the Absolute nature of Truth, the source of all other truth. Any time we capitalize a word that isn't normally capitalized, such as in Absolute, Truth, Him, He, It, Reason, Objectivity, Logic all denote the highest level or the source of it. In a word we refer only to God. Another way to think of it is the archetypal Truth, in the Original Maximum sense, or the purest form of it. We search for any small 't' truth, as smaller pieces that fit into the larger source of Truth. This includes any universal truths, any general or specific truths, any little bit of any thing that is actually true. Anything that actually works and is of practical use to help us operate in the world or better understand it, ourselves, and of course ourselves in it. Something happens in the pursuit of big 'T' truth, all of the little 't' truths click into place. On this journey we have found that all of the smaller truths that we have discovered only get highlighted and brought into the correct place in the context of the bigger Truth. None of the lessons I had learned previous to understanding that there was a source of Truth and an Absolute, were for not. They were in fact smaller truths that maybe seemed random or not linked before now were simply pieces that fit into the bigger picture. It was as if I had collected a bunch of seemingly random facts throughout my life that were a confusing bag of random coincidences. Until they weren't. The analogy Sanchez used was that of mathematics. There are a bunch of smaller mathematical truths, such as arithmetic truths, geometric, algebraic etc. The higher up in math we go we don't lose those the smaller earlier mathematical facts that we learned. Instead we gain a new better perspective as to their proper place in relation to all of Mathematics. They all fit precisely into the bigger picture of big 'M' Mathematics. Anything that was true in elementary mathematics, is still true in high level post graduate mathematics. It's just once you are to the higher level you have a better understanding of the power of the seemingly less significant math. The more complex math was built upon the solid foundational simple math. It doesn't negate the applicableness of arithmetic, it just puts arithmetic into its proper place. So everyone who only knows arithmetic can still use it correctly or incorrectly and those of us that know advanced mathematics still need arithmetic and now understand how it is all connected from the bottom to the top. So even though it's more powerful understand and be able to apply higher levels of mathematics, it's also more lonely, because the pool of people that know and understand along with you are more rare. The amount of time, skill, dedication, energy, hard work, and focus automatically excludes others from the conversation. This goes back to the concept of busy, while Sanchez and I have been busy at this, others have chosen to busy at other things. For instance, I couldn't participate in high level physics, nor should I, I haven't done the time. Therefore I can't add anything new or valuable to the conversation. I just don't know enough, I'm unlearned and unpracticed. I'm ignorant. Those who can participate in the conversation at that level are exceedingly rare, because they have done the work and studied. That's how sanchez and I are in this particular field, whatever it is, the discovery and application of Truth I suppose. That's part of the reason for this book. We are looking for others along this path to join the conversation, not that are at a particular level, but that have a particular desire, to learn, and to grow.

The weight of the world (mac):
There is something to be said here about my many attempts at making something small 'g' good into the Ultimate Good. I literally was trying to place a thing in my heart and soul, into the

depths of me, that in the end, was only built for One. It was as if I was looking down at the many worldly things and attempting to lay my life on them. I tried so many things. I began to get stuck, because I had literally tried just about everything that anybody had ever come up with. Nothing fit. The whole time I was looking down, I should've been looking up. It wasn't like I was attempting the obviously bad choices like drugs and alcohol, those I quickly realized, were not the answer. I started with activities, such as music, art, exercise, health, yoga, tattooing, and meditation. These various activities, to put it simply just didn't work. They were all given as viable answers, but when I tried them, none of them worked. They didn't work practically and they didn't hold up to scrutiny philosophically. At the time however, I was more concerned with practicality, and nothing practically speaking, worked. I put my all into each one. I let go and surrendered to whatever 'it' was. Eventually I would know, that for me, I couldn't commit to or build a life around any one of them. They were all weak in that way.

Wholeheartedly (sanchez):

I would like to point out here that Mac is being modest. He didn't just "try" music. He is a very good professional musician. He's an accomplished artist. He has run hundreds of miles at a time and measured his food down to the gram. If you're thinking, "he just didn't try hard enough!" You are dead wrong. I was there for most of his attempts. Another danger here is to think he is saying you can't be an artist and give your life to it. You can. You just can't claim it is the absolute good and that everyone should. It's a gift, but not a destination. Some of the greatest artists have tortured themselves trying to raise art to the absolute, but it is like trying to fill a bucket without a bottom... eventually you are left with nothing. Art, health, etc. are only shadows of the absolute. We can enjoy them, but we can not live on them absolutely.

(mac):

I then moved from activities to the more philosophical realm of platitudes, life lessons, quotes, or sayings, and ideas that I read about, discovered, heard, or saw. I read Gandhi's autobiography, Malcolm X's autobiography, and Bob Marley's Biography. I read The Tao Te Ching, Tuesdays with Morrie, and listened to the Dalai Lama speak. I listened to self help audio books and listened to motivational speakers on CD. All of them had value but none of them were the answer. There was no 'one' that stood out as the answer.  I then decided that if it wasn't one then maybe it was many. So I lifted words, concepts, and quotes up to live by like "love" or "do no harm" or "truth" or "reason" or "do unto others". The problem with these is that they leave out essential details. When exactly to I love? How much and in particular who do I love? In exactly what way? What did I know? Each word or saying left multiple questions that were unanswered. I tried going with the 'flow' or following the 'vibe', but found that some of these worked sometimes,but none of them worked all the time. At times they flat out failed. Besides practically speaking, nothing working all of the time, I could begin to find counterexamples or fatal flaws to any one of them using reasoning. There were times when love seemed inappropriate, or at least in the "peace, love and harmony" kind of way. Or there were times that in order to protect and love some people, I had to harm another.  Everything I held up as an answer would fit the puzzle in one direction sometimes, but then would fail miserably when used in the same direction at a different time or in a different puzzle. It was like everything just became 'rules of thumb'. I became an avid collector of these 'rules of thumb' or these in general do this or that guiding principles. Then came the contradictions. Which 'rule of thumb' reigned supreme? Which ethic was best? Everything became, 'well it depends'. These seemingly simple and generic rules were becoming exceedingly more complex and difficult when trying to apply them in a specific or particular circumstance. For example when walking by a beggar in the street. Is it better to go with, "Don't feed the squirrels" in order to not enable him to continue to beg or is it better to show "compassion." Is it better to teach him "how to fish" or is it better to just give him a fish. Should I stop and help the man and be a "good Sumaritan" or should I shun him and "take care of my own" How exactly am I to tell what in the world to do? This led me back to, well everything can't depend, because the sentence everything depends would depend on something. I was right back to there are absolutely no absolutes. I also confused by the question, "what does it depend on?" Lastly I was just overwhelmed, like dang thats a lot of variables to be calculating. How can anyone actually know what to do with all these rules of life? Anyone of these sayings or rules or guiding principles had a counterexample. A real life example where they didn't just not apply, but that it was wrong to follow at that particular situation. Everyone of them failed at some point. "Be honest" seemed unbreakable, until you realize you shouldn't be honest always. You shouldn't tell everyone all the time how you honestly feel. The fat person shouldn't be hearing, "you're fat all day everyday" even though we all see it. So I was left with if any one of those guides is good but not perfect, then more is better. My list of mantras, sayings, words, principles, or rules was getting out of hand. I had to carry around a giant list in my mind and refer to it depending on the situation. The problem with a rolodex of wisdom is that it's a heavy burden. Choosing which page to flip to in any given situation takes time. One card will say, "those who make quick decisions win the prize", and the one next to it will say, "haste makes waste." Ah! How do you function with such a huge list of contradictions and complexities? Not only that how could I remember? Was I to actually carry a rolodex? Back to that feeling of a deep singular void, that feels as if it should be filled, but that never is, the rolodex of lessons did not work. The huge book of quotes from wise people was ridiculous. These words would also only offer a thin layer of temporary relief of the despair, but the minute I would look directly at it, the veil would break. Worldly wisdom was not it.

Moderation in everything...except moderation (sanchez): You may see Mac's struggle here and think "moderation in everything" that he just "took it too far". You're right...and wrong. Mac definitely took it too far. Remember, he was looking for the absolute...not the subjective. You're wrong when you say "moderation in everything" because this is an absolute statement. You're saying to be moderate in everything EXCEPT moderation. It would be better to say "moderation in most things", but then you're left with what Mac struggled with...how will I know? The source of your "moderation" standard would have to be outside of time and physical space to see all the ramifications of your potential "moderate" choice. Here, we would be forced to give ourselves over wholeheartedly to the Source. We would have to be absolute in our obedience in order for it to work. We would be moderate in all things because we could never commit to any one thing without knowing in our hearts the Source might call us elsewhere. We would have to live absolutely sold out to what we are called to...until we aren't.

(mac):

I tried finding balance, but balance in a complex world is exceedingly difficult. I would be so out of balance trying to find balance, that I would get physically ill from the stress of it. The other thing that happens when focusing on balance is that you lose focus on the things you are trying to balance. Therefore everything doesn't get your full attention because the thing you are worshipping is balance, not the things you value in the first place. There is a diluting effect when dealing with balance. It's like trying to balance salty, sweet, spicy, along with every herb and seasoning in one dish, when preparing a meal. You end up with a thing that is none of them or too much of all of them. Maybe you shouldn't have done them all together for the sake of balance, maybe the big 'B' Balance is that it should've been sweet and not salty at all.

I tried politics. I tried fighting fights that had nothing to do with me, but that I could see and feel the wrongness of them. I would attack the world and try solving its problems. I mean I couldn't solve mine, but maybe it was because the world was broken. So maybe if I fixed the world, then I would fit into it. The problem with changing the world is that it didn't work. Period. I tried changing my workplace. That failed miserably not only that but it made me public enemy number one at work. I tried helping friends and family but my advice was not requested, just my labor. I obviously tried positive thinking, that failed so quickly it's pathetic to even mention. I also tried cynical thinking, neither were sustainable, neither were true always. They were all pretend solutions. Meaning I had to pretend that they worked if I was going to claim that they worked at all. I tried pretending in all sorts of ways. I tried pretending that the deep unsatisfactory feeling of despair wasn't real. Each and every thing I placed at the altar of my life eventually broke down in some major and fundamental way. Each person, each friend, each activity, each philosophy, each self help guru, they all broke down. They didn't fit. My deep void persisted. When each thing eventually failed, my desperation would grow. I was beginning to think the black dog of depression and despair were just going to be part of my life forever. Maybe I ought to try accepting my miserable fate? There was only temporary escape,  moments of flow, deep joy, meaning, love, there were fleeting moments of eternity. Moments of extreme focus, moments of my heart bursting with deep love with my wife and kids, would come and go. Some things fit better than others and some things I would return to, conversations with Sanchez were a source of inspiration, they still are. At least there I felt like I was getting closer to something, figuring something out, really connecting, laying all on the line. There were moments scrambling or motorcycle riding or building and creating something practical and beautiful that would temporarily leave me satisfied. The problem was that I couldn't find enough of those such moments, because not any one of them would sustain meaning, or I couldn't sustain doing them forever. There were things that in a season of life seemed meaningful, like painting, but then would seem meaningless in a flash. It's like the juice of meaning would be completely squeezed out and I would find that painting was now actually revolting or disgusting. It was as if it had stolen enough of me. Then I would try something else that would act in the same way, but eventually those too would fail me. Working out always got to a point of, ok i'm in shape, now what? In shape for what? In shape so I can continue to work out? I would go nah and quit. I tried cooking, getting really into it, but then as usual I couldn't worship cooking. That didn't work, now what? When it came to people even though I love them dearly not any one of them could fill the deep hole, though they seemed to help the most. Connecting with people, serving them in some way, and relating to them in an intimate way seemed to help. My wife and kids all helped, my family, Sanchez all seemed to help but they too weren't perfect, and what right did I have to ask anyone of them to hold the weight of my entire universe? They had their own suffering and weight to bear, they had their own load to carry how could they carry mine too? I was still writhing in my skin and feeling stuck. The longer I would spend with any one thing the less it seemed to provide the depth of meaning I needed to drive on through the misery of existing. Just exactly how damaged and broken was I? How ungrateful and unsettled was

I? How come others seemed to have such peace and tranquility, but not I? I was a broken, desperate man, living in a broken, desperate world. The weight of the world crushed everything, the weight of me crushed everything. Something deep inside seemed to know that there was something to place at the altar of my life, I just seriously could not find it. I seriously was looking, I seriously was looking in the wrong direction. The struggle was making me tired and I was running out of options. Paradoxically, the harder I looked, the worse my despair got, but that only made me struggle harder. Why is it that others didn't seem to struggle like me?

At some point (mac):

At the beginning of our journey, at the beginning of my own journey I would have called my myself an agnostic. I just couldn't tell if there was a God or gods or not. I couldn't know and neither could anyone else. From the time I found out Santa Claus wasn't real, I had lost any child like innocence in belief of anything resembling a supernatural being. I wasn't ready to commit to Atheism, remember I was much more into committing to no commitment. Absolutely no absolutes. I was playing it safe, and reasonable. I was remaining neutral, I would stay neither hot nor cold, I would remain warm. I would remain lost. Years later when reminiscing with Sanchez he said, "You were an agnostic leaning to atheism, now you are an agnostic leaning to theism." That was startling as much as it were true. At some point along the journey toward the latter end, let's say year 7 or 8, the idea that there was a God seemed more plausible and more possible, than the idea that there wasn't. At some point I realized I had changed. At some point I was ready to change and whatever emotional hang ups I had once had were significantly diminished. I had always thought my position was well reasoned, that proved to be just flat out wrong. At every point of contention, Sanchez was able to argue successfully the case for God, and equally as importantly, the case against Atheism. I had spent years trying to convince him otherwise, but inch by inch his side proved more true. No matter what angle I came from there he was with a coherent, clear counter to my objection. He pointed out that I did have faith. I had faith in Reason, in Mathematics, and in Logic. The idea that there must be a source of these brilliant discoveries was more appealing to my sense of Truth than that they themselves were somehow created from nothing. In fact my faith in Reason had grown over the years. He had pointed out that I did in fact believe in the reality of my own existence, and most importantly that belief was a matter of faith. He was right, I didn't believe we were in a matrix or that this life was simply an illusion. I had faith that reality was real. I had become convinced or maybe even just been able to see the truth in an Objective moral standard, and the weight that it carried. The truth that, if there is a Law, then there must be a Law giver. There must be a source of the Law, an Origin to the Objective morality that I had always felt weighing on me deep within. I now saw that there were obviously absolutes in the universe, and that there must be an Absolute, a source of them all. Sanchez had shown me that it was more plausible for the universe to come from Something rather than nothing. It was the most, no only, reasonable explanation I had heard. Way back from our first meeting the idea that there were some things better than others was true. The entire universe was set up this way. It seemed more probable that there must be a Personal God that preferred some things to others, where else does preference come from? The existence of Good and Evil at first glance seemed solid proof that there was no God, for how could a good God allow it? With the help of Sanchez, I was able to see that if in fact God was Good, and that he gave us free will, then we were able must necessarily be able to freely choose to do good or choose to do evil. Even admitting the existence of an objective good and an objective evil was admitting to the existence of a standard. A personal Being that preferred Good to Evil, again seemed to fit better than not. It seemed impossible that evil was relative or subjective. With each point, the idea of a Lawmaker, the source of Goodness and the existence of evil, the source of Reason, the Preferred vs. not preferred nature of reality, the existence of everything, this one unifying theory, that there was Something behind it was reasonably better than the idea that it was all random. How could so much order come from chaos? How could Reason come from random chance?

Trust me...he tried (sanchez):

Here some of you may be thinking, "wait, what about dual, equally powerful gods that created everything?" If the gods are equal and opposite, then surely they would not choose to exist in the same space. Notice, to even picture them, you must sneak into that mental picture the space they share. Neither would have created the other, and yet both find themselves; inexplicably occupying the same existence. This would mean there would have to be a higher power beyond both of them that arranged this equal footing. I also point out that this is exactly what Christianity believes. The devil and the Archangel Michael are equals and find themselves inhabiting the same space and neither want it to be so. Other silly theories like the flying spaghetti monster are logically not good since they are physical beings not of their own cause. Usually, people here end up using words that describe God and then call it something else. They mean an all powerful, all knowing, all present, non physical being that is good. These are the same descriptors of God (there are more but we will look at those later). It's like learning the word spoon in another language. I may not know what you mean at first until you begin to describe it and then I realize you mean "spoon!" Now, we have some grounds to begin understanding each other.

(mac):

I couldn't say that all this had proven anything exactly it, but there again was Sanchez with this: "You love your wife, right?" Yes, of course I do. "Prove it." he said. I couldn't, I immediately knew it . In fact I felt the sting of the question, the wrongness of it. Which by then, I had come to know that sting well, that sting meant that he was onto something. Just because I couldn't prove I loved my wife, in no way meant that I didn't.  Over time, I have come to realize it means the complete opposite. It turned out that the things I knew deeply, but couldn't prove were more real and more true, than anything that I could prove. Any sort of love, any reality, any beauty, or attractiveness, any connection, my self, my spirit, mine and others souls, the depth of love for my wife and kids, all of my feelings, my intuition, my gut, my sense of right and wrong, all of these realities couldn't be proved, but I knew them to be deeply true. There was in a way nothing more real than those unprovable things. I didn't feel the need to prove how much I loved my wife or kids, I needed to express it. And to prove it made me feel indignant. That was that sting, that thing about his question that rubbed me the wrong way. How dare he ask me to prove it. I wasn't upset with Sanchez, because he was making a point. He wasn't actually asking me to prove anything, but even knowing this it still stung. Wow. That was powerful, even as I write this, it is powerful. Maybe that's why there are no proofs of God, maybe He wants us to love Him like we love each other in the purest sense. In that irrational, deep, beautiful way that we love. We fall into it, we let our guard down, we freely choose to open our hearts. Once we do we can't help it. We don't reason to romance, we explode to it. We stumble our way around it with emotions and feelings, but never do we prove it. We certainly must express it.  I can love Reason all I want and proclaim its superiority in its emotionless cold splendor, but if I think even for a moment about my daughter, the warmth of pure love washes through me. Joy comes from nowhere and overwhelms me. Reason begins to look ugly, that cold face, that 'prove it' is the enemy, prove nothing, I just know it. Prove what? Your questions get silence, I'm busy, my heart is bursting, and I need to get it out, Love has come to conquer Reason. Reason is ruining it. Reason is gross in fact, my daughters love and mine for her wants nothing to do with

Reason. We need eternal bliss. I need poetry, I need hugs, I need tenderness, I need to hold onto this. Reason comes in like cold water on a fire, my daughter is like fuel for my soul, she keeps it burning, and I don't care to say why. That question and answer have no place here, all I care to do is express my love for her. Express my Joy for her existence. Express my gratitude for her.

At some point I was ready to look outside of myself, outside of my own experience, outside of my friendship with Sanchez. The evidence was piling up and I was still looking for a way out. I still didn't want the answer to be God. My own questions and oppositions had been answered. I had exhausted my attack. I had done my best to tear down the arguments for God. I had failed. Sanchez had built a strong case. It was time for me to go looking to see if anyone else had had victory over God.

What I found, when I actually looked (mac):
One of the first things I did was look up the great Atheist thinkers of all time versus the great Theist. Up until that point I had been working on the assumption that there were great men on either side of the argument, and since there were equally

great men on both sides, in amount and in quality, then this was further evidence of the correctness of my position: agnostic. I couldn't have been further from the truth. The actual list of great atheist was small. Like very small. The list of great Theistic thinkers was staggeringly long. It really blew me away. Still to this day I remember the feeling of honest surprise. Along with the feeling of surprise, there was the sudden realization that if I were going to use the argument I had been using, then the argument now pointed in the opposite direction. The truth was that what I had thought up until that point was flat out wrong.I was honestly stunned. More of the planks of my boat had been replaced. They had shifted toward truth. Since those first initial lessons, those first planks, that I deliberately and slowly had removed and replaced with wobbly knees, more and more had been replaced. Eventually I had a completely new foundation. Once I had this new foundation the rest of the boat became easier and faster to assemble. Not only that but steering it was easier. My old way of thinking had left me with a pathetic raft stuck in the mud. The speed at which I could remove or add a new plank was faster and easier, I was getting better at seeking and finding truth, it was beginning to get easier to spot danger, to see flaws, to recognize faulty patterns. The pain of change had come to be a welcome sight and feeling. I felt I had successfully been able to build a solid boat that was my own. That didn't come from a hodgepodge of influence, but that was deliberately crafted using the finest materials and built to withstand the torrent of chaos. My foundation was built with reason and reality in conjunction with emotion and experience. I used everything that was at my disposal and I took my time and did it right. None of this weak amateur raft that had left me shipwrecked lost on an island of muck. I finally had a man's vessel that I was building and I was beginning to let the winds of truth take me where she willed.

To be clear, this list of Atheists vs Theists wasn't conclusive. Another point of truth I had learned is that the amount of people that believe it or not doesn't determine its accuracy. Truth doesn't care who believes it or not, truth just is. I learned that it didn't matter that the whole of western society had thought the earth flat at some point, it hadn't changed the reality that it wasn't. 2+2 was 4 no matter how many foolish mathematicians said otherwise. So my argument that the amount of people on either side of an argument somehow determined the validity or worth of an argument wasn't valid, it was however an indicator. Great minds had in fact wrestled with these ideas. The great minds who had really wrestled with the same things I had wrestled with, had by a large majority landed on the side of God,and this was actually shocking. It was as if the experts hadn't agreed completely, but that the majority of them had come to a consensus. This was yet another indicator that my previous ways were false.

When I started looking at the actual arguments for or against God I was this time laughingly tickled and sort of proud of both Sanchez and myself. I had successfully come up with on my own pretty much every argument against God in the history of humanity, and Sanchez had successfully argued the points and given the answers from the pool of humanity's greatest thinkers. We both had done it in such a way that felt authentic, real, independent, and unique. When I actually looked, all the same objections I had were there, and all the same clear answers to them were also there. It seemed like the atheists were spinning around in jetties, purposely doing mental gymnastics to avoid the obviously more clear theory. The truth. It turns out the mental gymnastics I had once done in order to hold the slew of false beliefs in order to deceive myself, were not my own. That is, the fragmented multiple contradicting, not fitting together, mess of a story of the atheist or of the person who is holding tightly to their own version of reality is quite a common occurrence. It is a sure sign of someone trying not to tell the truth. This is true about every type of story, from a little kid telling story to an adult. From a very specific story of a singular event in time to the broader story of the universe and how time began. The truth makes sense. It clicks, it fits, there is a ring to it. The truth has a sound that we can all hear when we tune to it. We can smell the cleanliness of truth, just as we can smell the stank of deceit. When we lay down our own version of things, when we stop trying to bend reality to our own will, when we lay down what we want the truth to be, and we listen we can find the truth. I have witnessed this as a child when being accused of something I didn't do. I witnessed this too as child when I didn't tell the truth, the spinning around of multiple contradicting stories. I witnessed this in anger management, and then in real talk with kids and adults alike. I witnessed it from my wife when there was a lie between us. Whether I was giving it or receiving it, the symptoms of deceit were always there. My own kids have lied plenty, the sting, the hurt, the opposite of truth, the body language the shadiness all present themselves in varying degrees. It was universal, that a lie doesn't work, it screams out at you. The lie leaves a trail, something is wrong, it doesn't add up. Contrast that with the truth. It clicks, it might hurt, but only because the truth exposed the lie. It might be something you dislike, it might be weird and often strange, but it has a deeper calming sense. It works, it plainly works. I was able to tune into the truth and hear the lie. I had gotten good at sniffing out the truth like a detective. Like a dog, I would dig and dig, until I was satisfied. I always had to find the harshness of reality in myself before I could see it in others. Exactly when I did find it in myself is exactly when I could easily find it in others. This is how the atheists were, their arguments didn't line up. They had a way to over complicate their version of events, just as a child telling a lie, they emotionally didn't want the truth, so they spun up these webs of false arguments and lies. It was surprisingly clear.

Actually... (sanchez):

The first time Mac watched William Lane Craig v Hutchinson, he said Craig had "lost". I might need his help here, but I remember having to point out that Hutchinson kept going in circles without resolving any of Craig's arguments. At the same time, Craig dismantled even Hutchinson's sad attempts at reasoning. The only thing Hutchinson did was get SUPER emotional, then quit the debate. It wasn't until later when Mac began to believe that he went back and watched again and could see how wrong he had been. Again, his objective logic had been compromised by his wanting the answer to be what he was already thinking. Later, he could clearly see that it wasn't even close. It's hard to recommend Dr. Craig without having someone there who understands arguments and logic or you too will fall into the trap of finding what you already want to hear.

Another point is that often Dr. Craig's opponents would say things like, "well, you're radically different than most

Christians". On the other hand, sometimes during the audience participation, a "Christian" would assert some false or illogical statement and Dr. Craig would not hesitate to correct them. You see? He's on the side of Truth; not being right or "Christian".

Dang…(mac):

He caught me. I wasn't trying to lie. It wasn't in my heart or mind. I suppose I just lost some credibility here. But maybe as team we gained some. He checked me right out here in the open. Notice how gently he did it. (more on bedside manner later) Sanchez asked for my 'help' and offered a way out, that he was possibly mistaken. He has a real gift to deliver harsh truths in the gentlest, non offensive, and least threatening way that I have ever seen. I wish he was mistaken. He remembers it right though. At least I trust his version of the truth more than mine in this case. I do recall way back watching a debate and maybe not being as impressed with William Lane Craig as I have mentioned here. I think I got caught up in the romantic version of the story. I eventually began to see through the emotion, and eventually was able to, but at first I'm sure Sanchez is right. I stumbled over the emotion, or maybe even got lost in it. I definitely am flawed. My memory is still unclear of some details of our journey and in particular this case. In our defense we are trying our best to tell a story, a true story, but one that captures the essence and the detail in the right way. We aren't trying to sugar coat a thing. I know we both want this to be as real as possible. It's really not even about us. It's about you the reader. We want you to learn from us and get closer to Him. So if it takes me leaving an honest mistake in this story as we stumble along trying to recount something that has been happening over a period of 13 years, then so be it. We are, in fact, 2 normal guys, with normal guy flaws, imperfections abound, and our families and wives will attest. If you ask our colleagues they might be excited to speak on our downfalls. We are fallen without any help, we are trying to lay it down as best we can in our bankrupt state, please excuse the mess.

I began watching debates on Youtube between William Lane Craig and his opponents. Again I was shocked. It wasn't what I had expected. The atheists were weak. Again they used bad tactics and never were able to dismantle any of Mr. Craig's arguments. He was a sort of boring, nerdy speaker but he had truth on his side and stuck to it. Debate after debate he stuck to his five points. He would build his arguments up giving a good sound reason for each and then in turn, knock down his opponents arguments. He would even explain how a debate ought to work. The opponent was to build their own case for atheism, and in turn attempt to dismantle Mr. Craig's arguments. It actually seemed pretty clear, it's exactly how Sanchez and I would operate. We would take each argument and break it down as far as I needed and then I would try and destroy it or find it's flaw. He in turn would do the same to mine. It wasn't done in a formal way or setting, but it was done in a well reasoned way. There was no audience to impress, it was just us trying to get to the bottom of things. The atheists up against Mr. Craig, wouldn't touch his arguments and they wouldn't tear his down either. It was actually bizarre to watch and listen. Instead they used poor reasoning, logical fallacies, emotional claims, and usually in a very arrogant way. They also were surprised it seems that Mr. Craig actually believed what he was saying. They had already formed such a low opinion of believers in God that they had dismissed him and them long before the debate. All of this was eerily familiar, I saw in them all of the flaws I saw in myself. They too were starting from the end. They too were closed to the idea of God. It wasn't a real option, they had chosen freely to not even consider it, not honestly look at it. The truth of my position was weak they used very similar arguments that I had once used. I saw the impolite, flailing, arrogant atheists throwing around small truths mixed in with big Falsities. I saw them picking up and putting down their own logic. They were abusing reason. They weren't really looking, and because I had been there, I could now see the grossness in the position. It was like watching alcoholics make their case not only for alcohol, but for being an alcoholic. I too was an alcoholic, I was now in recovery and sober. Once I was sober I could see how gross it was to live that way and how all the other alcoholics were cheering each other on. Mr. Craig was humble. He was polite, but he was sharp. He stuck with sound reasoning and his arguments. He listened, took notes, and broke down each of his opponents positions. His opponents varied in profession. They varied in age and personality. Often they were better speakers and more entertaining. A lot of them were modern scientists, who were an authority in science, but in no way had a clue in the realm of objective reality or the beginning of the universe, or anything of the sort. They were unexamined, they hadn't actually been challenged in their view, they hadn't sat across from a worthy opponent like I had. They didn't seem like they had really taken their time to get to their position. It was as if they just now found themselves standing across from Mr. Craig. He's basically a stranger, they could easily after a two hour debate simply dismiss, him and anything he said. They were doing it in public. It was embarrassing. I had done a better job, a more thorough job, and had hit these topics. The inevitable conclusions I had discovered weren't being honestly looked at it.

When I went back to Sanchez time and time again after watching these debates he and I were now able to agree on how much more impressive, true, and right Mr. Craig was. Sanchez had seen the same videos and had come to the same conclusions,regarding them. That is specifically that Mr. Craig had won every debate, that the truth was powerful, that the evidence for God was overwhelming greater than that of not.

More planks were torn from my old raft and new planks were added to my new boat. The direction was getting more focused, the path was narrowing and the winds and current were speeding the journey up. It was scary and liberating at the same time. Things made more sense, more than they ever had, but nothing was as I had expected. I was heading in a direction that I did not want to go, but even my resistance was losing its will and its power, I could no longer honestly and vigorously turn away from the possibility of God. If I was honest the path was clear it was only in my lostness and emotional weakness that I was still fighting against it. CS Lewis had made this observation and it had stuck, that only when I was hungry tired and worn down was it that reasoning failed me. It was in the darkness when fear would prevent me from striving for truth. It was in those times i would want to nuzzle up to my old comfortable relativism my old agnostic self. Not that it was better but precisely because it was mine. I was a dog returning to lap up his own vomit. It was only in the mud of falsity that I was able to remain stuck. Once I cleaned my eyes and ears of the gunk and used truth as my guide I could see all to clearly the steps laid out in front of me. I could also the see the way I had come. I wanted to stop. I couldn't though, not yet. I had come this far the only honest way was forward. I remember how excited I was and how I was telling people in my life how far I had come and all that I had learned. Looking back I think they were watching me like they were watching someone on a ledge talking about jumping off. They couldn't help but watch, but it was with apprehension fear and excitement to see me about to see if I could fly. How wrong I had been. How wierd the truth was. I felt like I was on a ledge, that I had over a long time and with great effort had climbed to. I was pausing to look back down from where I had come. It was scary. Looking up was scarier than looking down, it was all so exciting and freaking me out. I couldn't believe where I had ended up. Maybe I would finally find an answer. Maybe I was ready to move on. Part of me wanted to hang out here on this ledge, I could just rest for a while, a long while. Something inside was battling. Part of me was calm and persistent and ready to continue, and part of me was fighting and flailing. I wanted to hold onto who I was. I could still save face here on this ledge. I could still remain agnostic and just lean more toward God. I could still remain uncommitted. The problem was it would have been dishonest. I would have purposely remained ignorant. I knew how to search now, my search wasn't over. I had to muster up my courage and face my pride. I knew now which part of me was good and which part was evil. It was strange to watch,once I saw what my old pride was doing it made me laugh, laugh right at myself. Was I really that scared of the truth? I guess I was, and with that I leapt.

Order matters (mac):

This goes back to what Sanchez said about 1st things 1st. Everybody's journey is different, mine took a long time because I was so reluctant so lost and had such a horrible foundation. So Sanchez had to start from scratch from the very bottom. We've tackled and will tackle all the steps that it took in detail but I want to lay them out in a little more straightforward and simple way. I first had to learn that there was something real that I could trust or had been trusting all along. Then it was onto the fact that reality was objective and that we could use the tools of reason, conversation, reading, and exploring others to find out what that objective reality was. From here Sanchez could then explain that since there was an objective reality, that there were absolutes, there must be a Source of it or them. We could now discuss the Supernatural, the Absolute, the Truth, the Origin of the Universe etc. I was now able to conceptualize God. From God then Sanchez could answer the next logical question. If there is one God why so many religions that claim Him? The answer was simpler than I had expected. It all stemmed around Jesus. If Jesus was in fact who he said He was, then Christianity was the way. If not then we could look into the Jewish Faith, or the Muslim Faith, or some other Eastern religion like Taism, or any other monoTheistic creed. It all stemmed on Jesus, wow! That's it all those years of wrestling with all of these topics, and now it all came down to the gospels in the new testament. I still hadn't read them I still wasn't ready but this was intense. This mattered. There was a lot riding on Him, I honestly didn't know what I would find, I was hesitant. What if I read Him and it didn't seem true or real? Then what? Then I would be a Muslim or something? That would be weird. I could see it though Sanchez the Christian and Mac the Muslim. I think what scared me more though was what if Jesus convinced me? Then what the heck did that mean? That I was an idiot all along, and that some major changes were in store. I had already changed so much over the past 8 years, I didn't know how much more I could handle.

A word on Reason (mac):

We as humans are imperfect individually. That's one reason we cannot attempt alone to reason through important issues. When I first heard Sanchez talk about the simplicity of how we all know what we know I was amazed at the simplicity, clearness, and the ice coldness of it. We only use three things to know all that we know: reason, experience, and authority. It always felt like way more or way more complicated than that, but once I saw it and heard it, I could clearly see the truth in it. It was I the flawed human that used these three tools incorrectly to come up with conclusions about the world that I had wanted to be true. This is extremely common in all men. I know this from my own experience, and from listening to others experience. I know this from reason, I can infer that because of our flawed nature we all must do this. I know this from the authority of CS Lewis, Sanchez, GK Chesterton, and William Lane Craig, in that they all have confirmed this. I take the fact that the earth is round from authority, the authority of pictures and of scientists. I take the fact that I love my wife from experience, the multiple experiences I have with dealing with all people and the recognition that with her my love is unique, deep, and special. I take the Pythagorean Theorem to be true from all three, experience, authority, and reason. For with clear reason I can prove the Pythagorean Theorem true in a multitude of ways. In most of mathematics, since I am somewhat trained in it, I can use reason to do all sorts of fancy proofs and derivations. Our claim is that Reason is from The Source, and that we can't reach pure Reason, but we can and should attempt at it. The way we have learned that works best is to run it by others to check for human error. We do this in science with 'peer reviewed' studies and papers, in math with 'peer reviewed' theorems and proofs. The key is we don't just allow 'anyone' to check our reasoning because not everyone is equipped. A person must be 'trained' in a way, not necessarily formally, but in a way to use reason appropriately. I would say this is another critical reason why this journey took so long. I had to be trained in how to use reason properly. I was abusing reason to gain my own ends, I was also ignorant in Reason's power, and ignorant in my ultimate weakness and flaws. I could reason before Sanchez, but I couldn't reason well. I could rationalize, argue, and battle to win, but I couldn't separate that from the coldness of good reason. I was way too attached to my ends to see through the fog of my emotional hang ups and flat out errors in simple practical reasoning to realize my means were off and confused. I am still marred with my human error, but not nearly to the degree at which I once was. Eventually I became confident in my ability to actually use reason properly, with the carefulness it deserves. This happened through 'real talk' and 'anger management', by reading and exploring what great minds and theories had to offer, and by battling with Sanchez over and over and over again. Once I got the foundation of objective reality properly sorted out, and the subjective poison out of my system, then Sanchez and I could look at our reasoning, evidence, and experience more closely and honestly. Once I removed the subjective ownership of what I believed or what I thought, and moved my position to this is what is or this is where reason takes me, I was much more free to explore without the pain of my planks being ripped from underneath me. It was now more like the planks of the boat of the universe which isn't even mine was being worked on. It was like doing surgery as an unskilled doctor on my own body versus as a skilled surgeon doing surgery on someone else's. The training, the separation, and the fact that it's no longer 'mine' makes all the difference in the world. What Sanchez helped me to do, and that now we help each other to do, is check ourselves. We aim at reality with the tool of reason and we spot each other, correct each other, and push each other to continue to aim. I still at times feel the sting of being wrong when I bring an idea to him and he allows me to finish my thought and then goes, "You know that spot at the beginning that you based this argument on, it doesn't work." Bink, my whole argument is scrapped. I fully appreciate it. It makes me more careful the next time. We both are trying to follow reason to get to pure Reason. We are always refining, this book is a process in refining. We are reading what each other writes with the same scrutiny that we speak and have come to base our relationship on. We are still putting Truth above all else.

Miracles (sanchez):

This book will not be written in chronological order. In fact, I don't know if there is a discernible order other than to say that whatever we are called to talk about next...that's what we will talk about. For me, next is the topic of miracles. Again, Mac struggled with this like most people do. He thought things like "that's not how the universe works!" or "then why doesn't God perform a miracle right now in front of me". The resistant rebel wants the King to meet his demands and perform on demand. He stands on a rock in a relatively life denying universe with reason and logic, love and flowers, and says, "More!!!!".

To the first point. Notice that the idea of miracles really bothers the non-believer. If it bothers you, then I would like to point out that you have put down your belief that the universe is random and has no meaning. You see, if you really believed this, miracles wouldn't offend your sense of reason (actually you would have no reason to trust your reason which is a byproduct of chaos, but that's another point). You of all people should be surprisingly accepting of miracles. If an entire universe could pop into existence uncaused; then why would water into wine bother you? Why would a few fish into many fish bother you? You believe everything came from nothing...at least with the wine we started with water. In fact, these miracles are not so random and unconnected to the universe as you would first think. In the "normal" order of things, rain (water) falls to the ground. Grapevines soak up this water and, with sunshine and nutrients from the Earth, grow. From these grapes, we ferment and get wine. We turn water into wine...just as Jesus did. So here is the Son of the Master of the Universe at a wedding and He does what normally would take time to accomplish and He does it in an instant. He shows that the same Source of rain, sun, earth, and man is in Him. This is what a miracle is. It is the revealing of the Source behind all of our universe in an authoritative way. This is what you are probably really objecting to. You are angry at His authority. Your finite being is meeting a small taste of the Infinite One and it is scary. I agree.

The second point is that many believe that if God were to produce a miracle directly in front of them, they would believe. Are we being honest? Notice that the Bible and history are filled with tales of miracles and divine intervention; and yet, many did/do not believe. If Jesus Himself could not convince everyone who saw His miracles, what makes you think you would come to believe? This is a heart issue. If in your heart you are not sincerely willing to consider you may be wrong about the most important Truth in the universe, then God Himself cannot change your mind.

Resistant Rebel (Mac):
I was and am a resistant rebel. I could not and cannot hold even this attitude and way of being as an absolute. In the end, I had to resist and rebel against me. Against my pride, against my past, against those around me that I had allowed to persuade me. I had to resist and rebel against comfort, against false independence, against false freedom, and against falsity in general. I could no longer rebel and resist truth or reasoning or Authority. I had to submit to something other than my resistance. Here we were again at another topic, at another point

where Sanchez had clear and reasoned answers, where all I had was my bloody knees from falling down the mountain again. Did this stop me? Of course not, I kept fighting, but I was getting better at trusting good reason, and at really looking at my experiences honestly. I could see Sanchez's points. I had lived in the world long enough and seen the miraculous nature of small events like my son being born. I could see that everything, even the fact that I existed, that I had found Sanchez, that we were here and had life in a lifeless universe was all miraculous. I understood that if there was a Source that powered and created all of it, even space and time, then this Source must certainly have the ability to create miracles whenever He pleased. It stood to Reason, that if He created the laws of nature and nature herself, then He perfectly well could break those laws whenever and however He Willed. Who was I indeed to pretend to 'know' otherwise? So even though I had never seen anybody raised from the dead, or witnessed somebody who was blind then see, or knew somebody who could not walk, then get up and walk, I could now at least, open my rebellious, resistant, heart and mind, to the real possibility and even high probability of Miracles.

Children, not robots (sanchez):

Mac also objected to this point. I will say that he got over it faster than most. This is one of the reasons our journey continued. He was willing to change. There were times when he would come back with objection after objection in an attempt to ensure he had not missed a viable alternative, but in the end he would admit when he was wrong and then alter his world view and begin moving forward.

He has spent a lot of time talking about how different and special I am. I would like to take a moment to say that Mac has done the more incredible journey of the two of us. It would be like if we were both about to climb Mount Everest. I would have studied, read, watched videos, talked in person to other climbers, and planned for years to take step one. Mac would be busy falling down the mountain in a bloody, mad scramble to the top. He is bold and determined when it comes to Truth.

So, one day, he brought up the very common objection, "why doesn't God just make us 'good'?". This seems very reasonable from the outside, but it misses the mark. God wants us to love Him freely and choose a relationship with Him. If He wanted mere obedience, He could have made us robots or mind slaves, but this would not have been real love.

There is a scene in the movie "Bruce Almighty" where Jim Carrey's character is talking to Morgan Freeman representing God about free will and Morgan Freeman says,"You can't mess with free will." And Jim Carrey's character says, "Can I ask why?" To which Morgan Freeman grabs him by both shoulders, shakes him and says, "Yes, you can! That's the beauty of it!!" Even though this is just a comedy movie, there is a valuable Truth here. I believe God gave us free will so that we could ask questions. I do think there is a difference between honest questioning and the type of questioning that is dishonest and is just a stall tactic. The latter one is abusing free will, not using free will. If your will was truly free, then there would be the possibility of finding God. If you have decided ahead of time that no matter the evidence, no matter the reasoning, you WILL not believe...then your will is not free...it is imprisoned.

God wants children that freely choose him. It's the only real love in the universe. There is no other way. God can not make round squares. By insisting on the ability to find eternal happiness in some other thing besides God, you're asking Him to allow you to choose some Absolute besides Himself. He can't do that. God can only offer you Himself because all else is death in the long run.

Free will and imprisonment (mac):
First of all the free will part. I don't remember ever really being hung up on free will. It seemed obvious that I could freely choose from a variety of possible choices at any time. Besides if I was really as rebellious and resistant as I thought I was, then the thought of being controlled by anything made me choose not to. How could I choose to rebel, and against what, and to what end, if I was being controlled? I wasn't on autopilot. I wasn't stupid in an obscene way. I wasn't daring gravity to prove me wrong. Gravity had no problem proving her authority on me without me tempting her. I could however choose not to obey gravity, I

could choose to go against my animal instinct to stay afoot, to stay away from the edge. I knew what it was like to battle desires and instincts, and I knew what it was to give in to them. The free will to do either was self evident. I was able to look back at my life and see clearly in the wonderous view of hindsight, and see exactly where the choices I had made, my freely made choices by my own will, had led me. I was able to learn, change, and adjust. I was always able to hear my conscience and choose freely to obey it or not.

Here's the paradox. Like Sanchez said and I agreed, I was freely choosing to not even consider God. I was rebelling against that Ultimate Authority. I was obeying something though. I gave up what I thought was the Prison of God, for my very own homemade prison of a combination of my desires, my needs, my thoughts, my ideas, and my way. I wasn't choosing the objectively best method to do things. I was stubbornly choosing my own way. I imprisoned myself to myself. I was able to choose freely as long as it was my will I was choosing, nobody else's, no other little authority or Big Authority. I was my own authority, but not really. I was doing that obeying when it pleased me, and rebelling when it didn't. I freely chose honesty. So being honest, I chose to seek truth. I wanted to be right, but I wasn't going to take anybody's word for it. I chose not to have any guides or Sherpa's up the mountain, I chose to be stubborn on this journey. I chose to battle Sanchez not because he was an authority but precisely because he wasn't. The paradox is freely choosing to follow reason and therefore truth was leading me to see the flaws in my ways, in my thinking, in my approach. The truth was that I wasn't free, I had grudges, I was resistant, I was rebelling. Once I chose to submit to something besides myself, namely the Truth, only then was I able to see the walls that my own free will had built around my heart. Eventually by submitting my will to His I was able to free myself from myself. Thank God.


Hold on tight (mac):

Sanchez is about to lay some things down in order here that are important and necessary to this journey. It has a different feel than a lot of what we have been doing thus far. One reason is that to talk about this topic with the proper weight it needs to be done in a clear manner. Second is that though I did stumble over this a little it wasn't my major hang up. We definitely spoke about this multiple times and from many angles, but once some of my other more difficult objections to the Absolute were solved, I was able to move through some of these without as much difficulty. Third is that it's hard to do, these arguments are technical and difficult and they push our mental capacity to clearly lay them out. We say "it's heavy lifting" and can feel the mental fatigue of carrying logic out so far, while at the same time making it as clear as possible, all the while being as careful with each word as possible, while simultaneously continuing to 'stay connected' (more on this later, much more...) to the Source. I had the advantage of having Sanchez sit across from me explaining all of this to me in person, over time, and at a pace that I could grasp. I could and did stop him frequently to re explain. Sanchez is someone that doesn't mind re-explaining, it is a gift I have seen personally with myself, his own kids, colleagues, and students alike. He has a patience or maybe even a real joy in repeating what he has already said a thousand times over. I don't, and I haven't met anyone else who does, in every area of his life. All this is to say that I didn't mind stopping him, I didn't feel embarrassed, because he didn't make me feel that way. You won't have him to in front of you, so this might feel a bit like a fire hose of an argument coming at you. For that I would refer back to Sanchez's very own method of reading the greats. Read it through once without pause. Read it through again and take notes. Research anything you don't fully grasp and attempt to restate the arguments. Then finally reread it as if he were an old friend who is glad to re-state his words just for you, as he has done for me time and time again.

Why can't we just be "naturalist/materialist"? (sanchez): The first reason we can't just be naturalist is because the naturalist begins their belief system <u>assuming</u> there is nothing outside of nature. They have no proof or reason for this belief, it is simply accepted on faith.

Again, we have shown good reason for the existence of God, but here are the top four proofs against naturalism laid out as succinctly as I possibly could that we will explore in more detail later but that I will list now so we can show how naturalism fails as a source or explanation of the physical universe and our human condition. There are even more arguments in favor of God, but here I am just knocking down the most common naturalist arguments. Many of these arguments have been known for years, if not centuries. It's interesting that many believe they are the first to throw up an objection that was defeated hundreds of years ago. This shows that the person has not really studied their beliefs and instead started with the end in mind and then found arguments that fit their world view. This can be done in honest error; however, after you read this, it can no longer be honest error. Proceed with caution...count the costs...be willing to follow the logic to its final conclusion.

1. All physical things have a cause.

2. Objective moral values exist.

3. Reason exists.

4. If God can possibly exist in any possible mental concept, then he must exist in all possible concepts and, therefore; does exist in our actual experience.

One:

All physical things have a cause. Out of the gate, materialism/naturalism is defeated on its own premise of belief. The natural world can not be all there is and has ever been because science tells us that the physical universe had a very distinct beginning. This means there was a point where nothing existed. If this is so, then it would have remained in a state of nothingness and nothing would have happened and nothing would exist. But something does exist; therefore, naturalism can not be true.

Here, some try and throw out terms like "multiverse" and "quantum nothingness/pure nothingness".

The idea of 'multi universes' spawning more physical universes just moves the problem of nothing back one more step. We are still left with how the first physical universe came from no material. If there were an 'infinity' of physical universes spawning other physical universes, energy would have run out by now. Physical energy is not infinite, no matter how far back we take it. In fact, the further back you take it and the more you transfer it, the more unusable it gets, until it can no longer sustain life, nor create more universes. It exhausts itself.

The theory of "quantum nothingness/pure nothingness" is a mental and verbal trick that is dishonest. This is a description of the beginning of the universe that claims; at the beginning, there was this sort of 'space soup' of particles and energy that 'popped' in and out of existence until suddenly, BAM, everything. The verbal trick is that we know the word 'nothing' means absolutely nothing...no 'space soup'... no particles...no energy. It may very well be that there was a quantum state of energy and particles in the very first moments of the universe AFTER the state of nothingness, but energy and particles are 'something'...not 'nothing'. The mental trick here is pretending like we are talking about the moment before the 'space soup'. We are not. We are talking about a moment AFTER the nothingness when the 'space soup' existed. It's like you and I getting to New York and I ask you, "how did you get here?" And you say, "I've always been here." This is a good joke or even a reference to a particular block of time, but it is not an absolute statement and we are looking for the absolute beginning.

So, all physical things have a cause. The cause of our physical universe must be outside the physical universe itself. It must be outside of time, powerful; and even though not physically a human person, It is still personal (meaning It has characteristics, the ability to choose, and prefers some things over other thing). Its characteristics includes being a Creator. Its ability to choose is shown in deciding to create at all. It prefers at least one thing; creating versus not creating.

Here some try and argue that the physical universe could have decided to create itself. This is a self defeating premise from the get go because how could the physical universe choose to exist BEFORE it exists? How can a purely physical entity MENTALLY choose to exist (on the naturalist view, thoughts are by-products of a long string of physical causes, but there are no physical causes before the physical universe began to exist)?

Later, we will see that when some people say "the universe" chose to create itself, they are describing God without realizing it. Some descriptions are closer than others, but they all come down to the same thing in the end. You'll see.

And so, number one is defeated. Just this defeater is enough to abandon naturalism/materialism, but there are more reasons it can not be true.

Two:

Objective moral values exist. I am breaking these arguments down in isolation from Mac's journey because I want to help everyone to find the Truth. I will say that this is one he understood relatively quickly but we did have it come up again and again for 8 years.This is a tough pill to swallow for many especially because so many have come to believe the opposite almost from birth. When you are born and raised in a world that does not examine its beliefs because no one wants to admit the Truth, it is difficult to find the way out. During this portion of the book, you may find yourself floundering internally. You will find yourself picking up and putting down your core beliefs because you don't want to be caught red handed holding on to an inconsistency that will require you to reevaluate your life direction. It's like a bandage on a wound that has been there for too long. It will hurt to tear it off; it feels like more harm is being done than good; but in the end, it's the only way to clean the wound.

There are three major theories concerning objective morals. Actually, the fourth position is that there are no moral values. This person believes that anyone can do anything to anyone any time they want. Rape, murder, theft, and lying are only measured in if they will get caught and punished. For this animal, no reason can reach them. They are psychopaths better served by a mental health expert.

The first theory is that morals come from the culture/society of the individual and are; therefore, subjective. An example would be how in some cultures in the past and present, people have harmed children. Now, it is true that often a practice like child labor or child prostitution is practiced by a society almost unquestioningly and handed down from generation to generation; this does not make it objectively true or right. Even if everyone ever born believed it was "right or moral" and never in all of human history did someone object, it would still be objectively true that abusing children would be bad or wrong.

Society is not the standard of objective moral values. This is not necessarily a naturalist argument but is one for the objector that believes societies form 'naturally' and; therefore, moral values are formed 'naturally' and have no objective value. Even if our society today was to go back to the practice of child labor or prostitution, it would be objectively wrong. Societies, like individuals, can become worse than those that came before. It is not a necessarily upward trend.

The next major theory is that moral values are part of our evolution as a species and are not objective. This again would be like imagining a world where the humans there 'evolved' to believe lying was ok. They would be wrong. It would be like imagining a world where the humans there came up with a math system where 2+2 equalled 5. Their world would not function. The conscious mind added to free will makes it necessary that we need the truth to function. You see, a lie is not just one sided. By lying, you are inhibiting my ability to exercise correct free will and conscience. It would be like if I was trying to add up something and you kept taking away or adding to the number of things I was trying to count. Your actions are affecting my ability to come up with a true answer. Objective moral standards are not at the whim of DNA like hair color. They belong to the same category as primary colors or numbers. They are true across all possible and actual worlds. They are an object that is not subject to my understanding or acceptance.

Finally, we get to the possibility of morals being objective, outside of nature. Parts of the argument have been made above as refutation to other theories. Here are some other arguments. Objective moral values fall into two categories. Those that are values (good or bad) and those that are duties (right or wrong). Values deal with the worth of the action and duties deal with whether we ought to do the action or not. For example, it is objectively good to help others; however it is also objectively good to take care of yourself. Now our duty must come in to play and tell us which one we ought to do in a very particular moment. Even Mother Teresa had to eat some time in order to continue serving others. How would we decide which action is appropriate? Is it time for me to feed others or myself? What if I had to choose in a situation where I can not share? This is why objective moral values can not be part of evolution or a social construction. If we try and choose using those two, then the choice becomes arbitrary and could have been different. It becomes subjective, not objective. We would need guidance from a Source outside of space and time. It would, by Its very characteristic of objective values, be the ultimate Good. Objective moral values are expressions of God's character and He wants to direct us to our duties if we would freely choose to obey. This is the only Source of objective moral values that makes sense. Everything else is reading tea leaves in an attempt to make objective moral choices. It's impossible and contradictory in its very definition.

Three:

Another proof that God exists is the fact that reason exists. Without a power outside of nature, then reason is just the result of a long string of accidents or chance. Let's imagine that every time someone gave me a math problem, I answered 7. I would be right once in awhile, but it would not be reasonable. This is what we are claiming about ourselves, the universe, and reason when we remove God as the source. We are claiming that we just lucked into the right answer and; therefore, we are good at reasoning. Remember that if you believe all of the universe came from nothing; and you are part of the universe with no outside explanation or source, then your reason came from nothing. It is random and has no source or basis for reliability.

I was standing on reason, but what was reason standing on? (mac):

The truth here put a stop to me thinking that everything came from randomness, it stopped it dead in its tracks. How could such a powerful tool for figuring anything and everything out have 'evolved' out of a universe that lacked any reason to begin with? How could order come from chaos? How could reason come from randomness? Without God I was putting a tremendous weight on reason, it was one of my primary weapons against God and religion. I had never thought of the source for reason. Sanchez pointed out that I had put a lot faith in reason, so much so that I was basing all of my thoughts upon it. This observation actually did two things, it pointed out that I did in fact have faith in something and that I was putting a large portion of my faith in the reality of reason. I had faith in reality and I had faith in reason. I had no reason or source for either, I had nothing. I was faced with, either I had to pretend reason was based on chance, randomness, or evolved somehow out of nothingness, or come up with a better reason to reason. This powerful tool could not have been random, it worked too well, it was more foundational than mathematics, mathematics was based upon it. Science was based upon reason. Science also had no explanation for reason, they did what I had done, just take it for granted, as a given. But given from what or really from who? There had to be a giver of this gift. There had to be a source that gave us this beautiful and primary tool. Here was this extremely objective tool that I was basing my life on, and I had been using it to pervert objectivity. I had been using, no abusing reason to distort reality. I had just accepted reason as a weapon, and I chose to wield it for my own selfish ends. Not once had I looked up at who handed me the weapon. I just knew it was there and that it worked, it worked extremely well. I had no idea the real power of reason. It was as if I had been grabbing a sword by it's blade, and swinging the handle at the world. Sanchez was helping me to turn the sword around properly, so that I could stop be such a danger to myself. I was cutting my hands, I was doing nothing to the world besides showing others the same useless sword play I was into. The magical beauty of turning the sword around properly, is that the giver of my sword, used the sword to lead me back to Him. It didn't happen overnight, but with this revelation on reason I at once moved infinitely farther away from pretending reasoning came from randomness. I moved infinitely closer to the truth, that reasoning must've come from something, and that something must've been magnificent. If I was going to use reasoning and trust reasoning I had better figure out and trust its source. Otherwise I was left not trusting reasoning, and this would prove impossible. How could I reason my way to not trusting reasoning? I would have dismantled the bridge that got me there, undone the work that lead me to it. It would have left me with nothing, it would have been the death of everything, of the words I spoke, of me, and I knew it. What I didn't know was that trusting reasoning would lead me to its source, and in a very different and surprising way, my death.

(sanchez):

Four:

If God may possibly exist, then He must exist. Here it's a difficult concept because people think of God as a unicorn or leprechaun. They think, "I wouldn't say, IF a unicorn could possibly exist, then IT must exist." You are correct; however, this is because a unicorn is a mythical creature supposed to exist inside the universe. The unicorn is finite and not omnipotent, omnipresent, or omniscient. God would have to be all three of these things. This means God would be source of all things and would exist across all possible universes. We inhabit a possible universe. Therefore; God exists. I think this is the hardest line of reasoning for most people. I offer it for those few that want to stretch their understanding of logic and the universe.

I'm flawed (mac):

This last argument I have never understood. It seems like a trick or rather incomplete. However I'm flawed, I don't understand everything. I don't need to understand everything. I can't understand everything. I'm confident that I probably could understand this argument if I worked harder on it and studied more, but just because I don't get it doesn't mean the argument is flawed. More than likely it means that I am flawed. This simple idea is powerful. I knew theoretically that I was flawed before Sanchez, but I never really 'knew' it. I operated from a viewpoint that the world was flawed more than I was, so that if there was a problem it was out there, not in here. I think this was caused by growing up and having a pretty good childhood. I was successful at school and sports and had plenty of friends. I was told over and over that I was a good kid, later it turned into that I was a good person. I took this all to heart, if everybody was telling me how good I was, they must be right. The few times somebody went against my innate goodness, I could easily dismiss the person as being bad or flawed. They just couldn't see how good I really was. It wasn't until I got older that this mentality began to crumble. The lie I had been operating under was beginning to be exposed. So when I met Sanchez and he was able to reasonably explain the objective value in opera music, and admit that he was the flawed one in the equation of music, it was a strange relief. Finally somebody was just flat out saying that they were flawed. I couldn't say it, not even to myself, but I could feel something deep inside, a bit of relief. The ring of truth was beginning to resonate. It proved to be a small step in distance, but a huge step in direction. What I mean is that looking at my flaw in music was looking at a small flaw, I have much bigger, but looking at myself as flawed was a complete flip. It was huge in that I was actually looking in the right way at myself, seeing my flaws. I began really seeing myself and my flaws rather than trying desperately to ignore them. In explaining the objectivity in opera music, Sanchez was not only showing the objective goodness in opera music, he was subtly and truly showing me the objectively flawed me. He was doing this by understanding his own flaws and limitations first. For me, I had never really looked at my flaws, not really, not the ones that came from within. Little did I know that that was the beginning of a long and painful process of discovering the truth of my condition. Discovering the truth of my depravity might seem like strange thing to celebrate, but knowing my innate badness has paid huge dividends. Now when I don't get something I can't help but wonder is the thing off or is it me? So knowing how good Sanchez is at reasoning and especially these arguments, I can pretty well be certain that the flaw lies not in the argument, but in me.

Theism (mac):

After years of conversation and adventure with Sanchez. After reading and researching, and watching debates online. My position on God had shifted. I honestly set out to dismantle any further nonsense and notion that there was some Being 'up' there. But at every turn I was confronted with evidence and reason that pointed elsewhere. Every real thing that I had discovered couldn't have existed on it's own. Nothing was self sustaining. Reason, the wonderful and beautiful and powerful tool that she is could not have created herself. Pure Reason was the ultimate order maker, the ultimate arbiter of reality, everything I knew went through her at some point. All inferences of how reality worked was touched by her, yet Reason alone couldn't produce reason. Order could not have come from chaos or randomness. If everything has a reason, which it seems as it does, what reason did Reason herself have for existing? Only one answer fit. A Being that was the Source of Reason. The Perfect Reason for Reason is God. I couldn't stand on Reason alone for what was she standing on? Where did Math come from? What was the source of Pure Math? The same problem and answer dressed in a different color. Speaking of color, where did the colors come from? What about Goodness? How did we know what was good? There was this Objective Good out there and in here inside of me, my heart and soul knew it. Where though did it come from? How could such a clearly defined Good come from nothing, or come from randomness or chaos. This Good wasn't new, it wasn't invented, it was discovered and every human had access to it across the history of mankind. In the exact same line of thought, where did Rightness come from? Again same I found myself in the same theatre watching the same play, with only different character reading the lines. This Objective Morality did in fact exist, just as Reason did, but the explanations that were out there were cheap, besides one. Randomness and chaos and nothingness cannot produce anything that was so purely opposite, darkness cannot produce light. Where did Reality and Nature find their Origin? Where did EVERYTHING come from? There must be a Source. The profound yet simple idea of absolutes had dug itself into my conscious so deeply over these years that it had left the same question to be answered; where was this Absolute? Why couldn't it be possible for absolutely no absolutes? Why did so many who swore God didn't exist, hold such absurd statements of 'nothing matters'? 'It's all relative', 'Trust no one', 'Everything is meaningless', or 'truely there is no truth', all of these were clear contradictions and versions of the same illogical nonsensical idea that something came from nothing or objectively there is no objectivity or in reality there is no reality. It goes on and on. None of the ground that I was standing on was solid, logically, or otherwise, if I was to observe reality. The reality that made sense, the reality that I existed in and actually lived in contained Order, Reason, and Truth. If there was an Objective Morality that screamed for Truth and Goodness and Love and Honor, there must be a Source. A Source that preferred these Things. This Absolute must be the Source of Justice, if justice had a chance any chance at meaning. The Source of Everything must in fact prefer Truth to falsity, must prefer Existence to nothing, must prefer Good to evil, must prefer Order to chaos, must prefer Reason to randomness, must prefer Love to hate. My entire existence pointed this way, whether I liked it or not. All of my practical hard fought reasoning pointed this way. This Being must be Good, because He preferred Good. This Being must be Reasonable, because He preferred Reason. This Being must be Absolute, because He was the source of all Absolutes. This Source must be beyond Mother Nature because he was the Father of her. He must also be beyond space and time because He had created them both. He must be all places at all times because He was outside of space and time. He was the Author of the book of everything, he had access to every character for eternity, infinitely. He was infinite and limitless for the same reason, He existed outside of the limits of reality, He had to, He created Reality. He obviously must be powerful because he Created everything. He must be Creative, because He is the Source of Creativity. The definition of God had taken shape by looking at the evidence. There must be an all powerful, all knowing, personal, always present, infinite, good, just, creator of everything. The things that God preferred must be in His very Nature otherwise we would have to refer to the Source of them as God. The ground underneath me had changed, it had revealed itself to be faulty and crumbling. At first I thought I was standing on solid ground, but at every turn, with every conversation, my original position got weaker. I had to continue to move forward to dodge the trap that I kept finding myself in. The ground that Sanchez had been standing on all along seemed solid, stable, and true. The distance in the gap between where I had been, and had at one point seemed insurmountably far, now seemed narrow. Looking back from where I was now, the distance I had travelled was far. I had no idea that taking small but secure steps along this path would lead me so far from my original position. I could never again honestly take those same steps back to my original position. For at each and every previous step, the one that I had moved from was dismantled, crushed, disintegrated under the weight of reason, experience, and truth. To switch analogies, the small unexamined poorly crafted boat that I had been for years floating comfortably in within my own mud puddle had changed dramatically. My small rickety boat was no longer a heaping pile of rubbish, but a solid ship, that I had built purposely over years, with hard work. Not only hard work, but I had sought help from master craftsmen. I had done the work myself, but as an apprentice. I now knew where all the parts and pieces were, I could build another on my own, I could easily see the flaws in the other less seaworthy vessels. My old boat had been blown to pieces, ripped apart, I had salvaged only those pieces and planks that ended up being of good quality and true, and burned the rest. I also noticed while building my new sea vessel, that I had drifted into new waters, leaving my mud puddle, for at first a slow moving river, and then entering a harbor, and I finally was at the mouth of the sea. There was now all around real deep water and real dangers, the comforts of my mud were long gone, my old childhood boat was all but gone, only a few pieces remained woven into my new adult vessel of beliefs. The winds in the sea were picking up, the depths of the sea were frightfully real and full of unknown terrors. Was my ship as good as I thought? It was time to find out, it was time to leave the harbor, lift anchor, and raise the sails. It was time to leave my crumbling old absent and hollow land and take a leap onto new solid Earth. The leap had shrunk, it was still a leap, it was still dangerous, I was still hesitant, but now it was no longer a battle of reason. Now it was a battle with pride with emotion, with my old self and my old ways. Reason had brought me to the edge, there was still an abyss to leap over, but reason stepped aside, it was now faiths turn. Faith was what I needed to get me to jump, to get my feet to leave the ground, to ultimately get me across. I don't know that I could go back, I knew forward was unknown. Just like it's time now to stop these analogies, it was time stop stalling. Just like that, I held my breath and jumped... I opened my eyes, I had landed. I was now on God's side. Now what?

Theism, pantheism, and dualism (sanchez):
I'll start with pantheism. It is odd that this is the most common "enlightened" belief. The idea that the universe is god. This seems right because we want God to be understandable. We are committing the error of the Native American or other religions that believed god was a mountain or the ocean. We are simply making the physical object we want to call good bigger; however, whether it's a mountain or the universe, if we want to imagine it as God, it would have to be outside of nature to create all nature (the universe). It would also have to think and have a free will.

Dualism would not work because two equally powerful but opposite powers would not agree to inhabit the same space, so whatever created the space they share would actually be the Absolute power.

This leads us to theism. There must be one absolute source of all. This is the only explanation for why objective values exist, why physical space exists, and why reason exists. I explain this concept more on my side of the book.

One more serious debate (mac):
Somewhere around the time I found God, or He found me, Sanchez and I had a fairly heated and serious debate that lasted not as long as some of our earlier conversations, but was still proved very significant to my journey. Where it lacked in length it made up for in intensity. I was hanging on to an old idea, one that is somewhat at the heart of all of this. I was under the illusion or impression or spell or delusion, that with enough knowledge of good and evil, that this, in itself, was sufficient enough at being able to control whether or not I could actually choose good over evil. My argument was basically that the more

I realized the real harm of my actions, the real consequences of my choices, the more I would be able to choose to not do harm, to do good. Sanchez would listen like he always had, but would then fire back with something like this. "When I truly examine myself, and really watch what I do, even though I know 100% that the thing is wrong and harmful and even disgusting, there are times I still do them, even though I don't want to." My counterclaim was that then that means you just don't really want to or that you really don't 'get' how bad it is. I was trying to place on him alone the brokenness of all humanity, that he must be more lost and broken than me, because I didn't suffer his same fate. I was able to improve and control my goodness. We went back and forth around this for awhile. He was even willing to grant me ground in that I could grow and improve; we all could, to a point. He held strong and steady in the fact that we could not come in this lifetime or the next, within any distance resembling closeness to Perfection. This debate was interesting in my memory because at least part of it happened at work in front of others. Other colleagues and students were around. I think this helped to increase the intensity. There was an audience. I thought it was exhilarating in a way, and had the effect an audience always does in a fight, that is to increase the stakes. Around this time too, I was reading more of CS Lewis, and he too gave me an illustration of what Sanchez was trying to tell me. CS Lewis argued that you never realize how hard it is to be 'good' until you actually try it for a whole day. He explained that if you just watch yourself for a full day you will see the flashes of anger, the trappings of lust, the seeds of greed, the force of pride all pushing their way to the front of the line. He used this scarily powerful example, that if you announce yourself to the basement, and loudly stomp down the stairs, and wait, while slowly turning on the lights, the basement will appear quiet and clean just as you had left it. Here is where his genius makes me smile at his brilliance. He says, if you however are in a hurry and rush down to the basement flicking on the lights in a flash, then you will see all the rats scurrying away from the light. The truth of this hit me hard and sunk in deep. I could easily see that in my own life when surprises happened, when things didn't go just right, all the 'rats' of my soul and being would be caught in the light. And depending on the surprise, might even come out and show their ugly sharp teeth, and gross leathery tail to the world. This helped me to realize that even if I had known about the harm of my 'rats' it in no way helped me to eradicate them. My will was no match for them, and at best I could simply hide them. What I was mistaking for knowledge became more evidently just a more mature and sophisticated way of not showing the world my rats. It was a socializing or civilizing effect, a growing up, a maturing. I was getting better at being phony, along with getting better at recognizing my inherently flawed nature, and pausing longer before acting it. I wasn't however getting rid of my demons, just a bit better at recognizing them. Sanchez was saying the same thing, that he had also found that when he really, honestly looked at himself, he could very well see his rats, but in no way could control them on his own. His evil was a part of him, just as his arms were a part of his body, he couldn't very well cut off his own arms, he was left with them as part of reality. Evil was part of him, just as all his flaws were part him, part of his very own nature. I don't know what exactly did it, when precisely, or who was responsible for my finally admitting defeat. But I could no longer pretend that I was right. I could see exactly my grossness on a regular basis. Real talk, had exposed the truth of me, but had provided no answers. There were no solutions period, that I had found in the world in nature, in the natural. This went back to the heart of the story. I could not perfect myself. I was broken. Not just me, we all were. Being broken and flawed in such a violent way wasn't acceptable. There had to be a solution. There had to be a solution outside of us, not inside. We couldn't actually lift ourselves to Nirvana or heaven or the Light. All we could do was admit defeat. This was the last piece, this was my last ditch effort to resolve my issues with existence, with myself. This was my last realization that I alone could not win at life. I was doomed to fail from the gate. It was heavy. I did not want this to be true. I had fought long and hard for it not to be true. I had turned over every possible stone. I was left with the emptiness I had started with, only the naivety was gone. It was time to admit defeat and turn the one answer I had been avoiding all along. The debate had ended the conversation that had taken so many years and so many battles and so much searching was drawing to an end. Sanchez proved to be right once again, he never had pointed to himself as an answer, he was always pointing in one direction, he was always moving in the same direction that he was pointing. I was finally at the summit. I was finally to the place he had been pointing. He had successfully used reason to destroy all of my irrational objections. It was time to man up. It was time to put up or shut up. I was ready to look to the Supernatural. The Supernatural was pointing to one Man. He pinned the entire problem on one this one point in history, to this one Man. It was time see for myself what all the hype was about. It was time to actually read what He Himself had said and He Himself had done. It was time to look directly and honestly at Jesus.

CS Lewis's plain and simple argument (mac):
Around this time I went back to CS Lewis, I had been reading a lot of his books. Sanchez had been letting me have and borrow as many as I wanted. I went back to "Mere Christianity" it was safer, than the Bible. He lays out this argument for Jesus that is just so dang good and trapping. It goes like this. Either Jesus is who he says He is, or He is a Demon who is Evil beyond belief, or he is a lunatic, the crazy type that think they are a legit alien. Jesus doesn't leave room for us to believe that He was simply a

'good teacher' like Gandhi. That's it. Once you accept that He was a real person, then you're trapped. He did this on purpose. So before I even read what Jesus Himself said and did, CS Lewis made sure I knew what I was getting into. Either He was the Lord, the Truth, the Light and the Way, or he wasn't. Either this was God embodied here on Earth and that was it, or it simply wasn't. It was so clear and so simple, yet so profound. If or when I were to read about Jesus, the stakes were extremely high, the implications were clear. The costs were high. I really had no idea of how high, but at least I knew they were real costs. To face this, to really look at it, it just blows my mind, it's staggering. It has that cold and clear immovable property that arithmetic possesses. It's just such a vastly bigger deal than the sum of integers.

Jesus was a real guy (sanchez):

This step was also hard for Mac. Like most people, he thought Jesus was as real as the Easter Bunny or unicorns. Once again, I directed back to outside sources to show the historical fact that Jesus of Nazareth was born, lived, preached, and was crucified by the Romans. You can look for yourself in the encyclopedia

Britannica or on Wikipedia or any other unbiased source. We may disagree that he was the Son of God or that he was raised from the dead three days later, but there is no reasonable doubt He lived and died. Mac was sure I was wrong. He investigated on his own and found some biased sources that made claims that Jesus was a very common name or that made the weak argument that there aren't more independent sources than the ones we have to corroborate His life. I will point out here that for the person that does not want to know, no amount of evidence would convince. Jesus Himself could appear in all His glory and that unreasonable person would say to themselves, "look at that...I've gone crazy and am delusional." Seeing would not be believing. The person that refuses to accept that Jesus lived as a real man are on the level of the people that believe the Earth is flat or that the Queen of England is out to get them. No amount of proof would convince them. In fact, the more proof you provided, the more you would convince that person that you are lost or naive; and therefore, dismissible. The overwhelming majority of humans believe that Aristotle lived even though we have no direct evidence of his writing or life. They believe

Alexander the Great fought his wars and achieved glory on the battlefield with sources way more suspect than the sources we have for Jesus. Only now, something is at stake and so the proof is not enough. I agree that whether or not Socrates lived has very little felt impact on our daily lives, but if Jesus really did live...if He did what they accused him of...if He said what they heard him say...then the ramifications are severe. I will tell you this now...it's interesting that the world has been telling you Jesus is as real as leprechauns...what else are they wrong about?

This was difficult (mac):

It's interesting seeing this laid out so succinctly and so clearly. It seems rather short and quaint. Reading it here and now it seems rather pathetic that this was such a mountain to climb for me. Again this conversation took place over years. Coming to realize Jesus was a historical figure that walked the Earth meant something. I didn't know exactly what it meant then but I knew its weight was heavy. He was the number one villain out of all religions for me. It took me a long time to even say His name. Even now, I can feel the twinge of my past self's disgust with His name. It was clearly through ignorance of who He really is and was, and through the way He had been presented to me through the world, that my stomach was turned whenever I had thought of Him. I just didn't know Him, and the people who claimed they did the loudest might not have either. The branding and marketing of Jesus to me was distasteful, arrogant, and rude. It was flamboyant and strange. It was popular to 'love' Jesus. Like football and the flag, the military, and monster trucks, there was Jesus. He even had a bobble head doll. The amount of bumper stickers of, "real men love Jesus" of these hideous fish shapes, of the cross was ridiculous. People had put Jesus stuff, very cheap distasteful stuff, everywhere. Right along with Nascar and their favorite team's logo was some Jesus something or other. There were jeans with crosses sewn into their rear pockets, like look at my butt and while you're there, JESUS! There were mega churches just like stadiums to watch WWE wrestlemania. It was mania, a collective mania. Billboards, bumper stickers, and sandwich boards were the stuff of falsity and advertising. Their sole purpose is to spread propaganda and to trick me into buying something. So Jesus, especially this brand of Jesus, I wasn't buying. Guess what? I still don't, it still seems weird and off. So there was that, the over popularized noise of the American version of contemporary Christianity that poisoned my view of Jesus. There was also my personal interaction with those who proclaimed Christianity as their religion. Seriously everybody I had met up until Sanchez who believed in Jesus or proclaimed Him to be theirs were some of the most closed and lost people I had ever met. I'm not going to get too specific here, just because I don't want to do harm to prove a point. The amount of unexamined nonsense that came out of these people's mouths was absurd. It was like all they had was Jesus, but nothing else, no other bone of goodness. Whereas other people that didn't believe, they seemed more thoughtful, more genuine, more real. They seemed like they were at least trying to live a good life trying to figure things out. They were at least using their brain and their heart. There were some people that claimed Jesus, but when it came down to it they didn't use Him as any kind of excuse or reason for anything. Those people seemed alright, they almost seemed embarrassed by their belief, so they kept it quiet. They were 'good' but not because of Jesus. The third reason I had such a problem with Jesus is because of me. I can't stand most of authority. It almost all seems corrupt. Jesus was obviously some sort of authority figure. I also am not a 'joiner'. Large groups of people joining things to fit in or belong isn't me. It turns me off, it makes me feel suspect. I won't go any further here other than to say this wasn't always the case, I think I grew into it. So I was NOT about to join this gigantic tribe of Christians and start putting bumper stickers on my ride and wearing trendy clothes and attending a mega church. There was just no way.

So before I could even consider Jesus, just consider Him, I had the hurdles that 1) He wasn't even a real person. 2) The vast majority of people I knew to 'follow' Him were lost as could be. 3) The loudness of their irrational and strange marketing campaign seemed disingenuine and gross at the very least. And 4) I was an anarchist, thinker, and a non committing loner of sorts, and therefore there was zero chance of me joining this large silly club called Christianity.

Here is how Sanchez helped me to realize my 'reasons' for not even considering Jesus were really excuses. For 1) Sanchez already laid out the arguments, what really got me was

I was willing to accept all sorts of history based off less evidence but I was going to deny Jesus who had more evidence. I found myself in a situation that I was either going to have to concede He did in fact live and was part of human history just as I did with Julius Caesar or Napoleon, or I would have to deny all of human history, at least a huge part of it. So it took me a long time and many conversations, but if I was going to remain sane and consistent in my reasoning, I couldn't go around denying history, denying science, denying truth, denying that the Earth was spherical etc. OK fine Jesus was actually real, so what? I still was not even going to consider Him for anything but a good teacher. Who existed, but who people just over exaggerated His impact or meaning over time and made Him into something He never was. He at this point was like Elvis, just a bunch of overly obsessed followers who wanted to believe Elvis meant more than he actually did. For 2) it was actually pretty easy for Sanchez, he himself was a living breathing counterexample to every other Christian. He had no bumper stickers, he dressed normal, and he wasn't fancy. He was the most thoughtful person I had met, and still is to this day. His thoughtfulness wasn't limited to one area, it ran the gamut. He put thought into all sorts of areas of his life, and was in the simplest and most genuine sense, thoughtful of others. It took a long time for me to really believe and understand because he was such a unicorn in the Christian world, and a black swan in the world in general. Just the fact that Sanchez existed and was himself was enough for me to throw out my second 'reason' or excuse for avoiding Jesus. I could no longer say ALL Christians were brain dead sheep who drank the kool aid. Here was one Christian who had examined his beliefs and was willing to lay out all that he had found. He was still examining, tweaking, learning and open to being wrong. There was none of the prideful arrogance of every other 'believer' I had encountered. Sanchez was humble, yet sharp, extremely intelligent, extremely patient, and very real. He was battling through life like I was, well not exactly like I was, but in the same spirit. He was willing to admit when things were tough. Life is hard, it is a struggle, he never denied this. So many Christians seemed like they were forcing smiles and acting as if they were the happiest people around, it all seemed so phony. Sanchez didn't. Now that 1) and 2) were dismantled Sanchez used the math analogy to help me with 3). That is just because there were a ton of people that were bad at math, that in no way speaks to the validity of Math itself. A bad mathematician, doesn't mean that we ought to abandon Mathematics. That really was it. Again it didn't happen overnight, but I could not deny the truth in that statement. Sanchez didn't argue that Christians were right and I just couldn't see it because I didn't have faith or that I was flawed. He just told the truth, he AGREED with me! He too saw the weirdness in the commercialization of Jesus. He validated and confirmed my analysis. He was like yeah there are lots of whack ass Christians or people that claim Jesus (paraphrasing). He was also like yeah there are a bunch of whack ass people period. So what? You can't use the fact that people suck, as a reason to deny the validity of everything people do or believe, all you can do is say people are strange and weird and FLAWED. Mind blown, again, slowly but still exploded. An explosion in slow motion or in real time has the same effect, you sift through the rubble, dust yourself off, and rebuild.

Once 1) thru 3) were handled 4) was much quicker or was an easy result. It turns out there wasn't one 'type' of Christian. Obviously Sanchez was completely different than anything I had ever seen or even heard of, so there was a different version. I also eventually read a book called, "The Irresistible Revolution: Living as an Ordinary Radical" by Shane Claiborne, and that gave me a version of Christianity that seemed more along the line with what I thought was a type of Christianity that I could actually see myself being a part of. The book was written by a Christian who got fed up with the same modern American mega church weekend only Christianity that I had. The book was his story and analysis of what it meant to actually follow Jesus. The author sold everything set up a 'church' in the ghetto or slums of an inner city where he was from. He clothed and fed the homeless and was homeless himself. He had few possessions and lived a life of service. The books profits were even going to be used to give back to the poor communities of where he actually was living. He wasn't going overseas to be a missionary, he was staying local in his own community, helping out his actual neighbors. It was the first time I had read or seen anybody use

Christianity in a way that seemed genuinely good and selfless, besides Sanchez of course. So between the the book and Sanchez I could see that I could remain true to myself and still honestly explore Jesus. That is, I could remain be an anarchist (just so we're clear, what I mean by anarchist is simply to question authority and dismantle or at least disobey any illegitimate authority), be a thinker, be a doer, and not join anything that I didn't actually want to be a part of. And in doing so I could remain safe and intact, in at least considering Jesus. Or so I thought.

One or the other (sanchez):

I am not going to tackle all of the reasons for the Bible being a historically reliable source just yet. There are good reasons and you might want to go check them out ahead of time so as to save yourself time later on. Here, I just want to point out three major schools of thought.

One goes like this:

Well of course the Bible is filled with mystery and miracles. It was written by uneducated, delusional fishermen. However, when you point out that it's filled with platitudes that have shaped history and that it has a message that is unheard of throughout human existence..that's when the doubter switches to version two...

Well of course the Bible has platitudes that have shaped history and a message that is unheard of throughout human existence...it is a scam put together by some devious and intelligent people.

Well, which is it? Are they ignorant, delusion fishermen or devious, intelligent people? They can't be both. You can't hold both true. You see? You find yourself switching theories whenever the evidence makes you uncomfortable. The third major theory is that the Bible, specifically the New Testament (since we are focusing on the life and times of Jesus), is the real account of what happened at this time. Think about it. If they are ignorant and delusional, how could these plain men suddenly deliver pearls of wisdom that, when examined, reveal the deepest realities of the human condition? If they are devious and intelligent, why would they write down the most embarrassing moments of betrayal, doubt, and sin? The only theory that makes sense is that they wrote these things down and said what they said because they had experienced Jesus. They passed on words far above their human understanding and wrote down their darkest personal moments because that's what happened. They had no choice but to tell the Truth. No sugar coating, no saving themselves...just honesty.

Jesus (mac):

My wife had this pink leather bound NIV, life application Bible that her dad had bought her. Sanchez had recommended the NIV Bible, because it was written in the most current english and it had done the most accurate job in translating, out of all the versions he had researched. Sanchez also told me a few parts to read specifically. I don't remember exactly what they were, but it was the New Testament gospels and maybe two others after the Resurrection. After 8 years of in person conversations and deep philosophical debates, adventures, and a meaningful friendship, Sanchez sent me a text message. It was short and cold. It wasn't in the same vein that the previous 8 years had been. The energy and tone were different. The text said, "You should read these specific 4 books in the new testament" then "That should be enough to choose." Gulp... wait, what? I was going to have to choose?! That was weird, and heavy, and strange. To see it so clearly laid out in front of me, on a text for that matter, the gravity, and the gull of it was so biting. I can still feel the strange sting to this day. There was this, "Well, it's on you now. I can't help you anymore. I got you this far, you're on your own. Good luck." craziness, wrapped up in that little cold text. I remember reading it and just rereading it a few times and then waiting to see if he was going to send anymore. Then I remember going back later to it, and realizing that, that was it. That's all he was going to say. Dang... I guess I had better start reading.

I sat in my favorite spot, the same spot that I had read and watched debates, and learned about truth and reality. The spot where I had searched for meaning everywhere else, but here, in the Bible. Everything had led me to this moment. My wife was a little freaked out too, she was taking pictures of me reading this pink Bible. She knew not to interrupt me, but she also knew how momentous this was. When we had first met, I was adamant about the absence of religion, God, and especially Jesus in our house, in our relationship, and around our kids. We had many fights about her putting me, and us, and our kids, in the right spot in relation to her parents and their old religion. She would go to church and leave me at home. It was a begrudging acceptance on both our parts. Her parents didn't approve of my non belief and I definitely didn't approve of their 'belief' or their version of Christianity. Her parents and I didn't speak about it, we didn't speak much about anything.

When I actually read the new Testament Gospels I was stunned. I really was. It was nothing, as I expected. I don't really know what I had expected, I had never actually read it, but it wasn't this. I had pieces of it read to me as a child, in the old King James Version where the 'thy' and 'thou' and 'tis' shakespearean language proved an obvious hurdle to understanding. I was now an adult who had been studying truth for years. I had Jesus's words in front of me in red and in a language that was clear. All that was left was for me to read it with an open mind and heart. Read I did, and astonished I became. This guy Jesus spoke with crazy Authority. He performed Miracles left and right. He said that He came to divide. There was none of this hippy, peace, love, and good teacher bullshit I had been fed. He was fierce. He was clear headed. And He was deadly serious. He spoke about Truth, like I had come to know it. It was razor sharp and extremely focused. He was straight punking all these so called 'authority'. Nobody was safe, especially the religious people. The only Authority he accepted was His own, and God's, His Father. He showed zero signs of weakness. He was brave and bold. He was loving but firm in the good fierce way. He spoke of hot and cold, not lukewarm. He spit lukewarm out. He demanded passion, and strange extreme Faith. He was walking around going like, fig tree wither, and sinner you're forgiven and demon get out. He was future telling and smart as hell. Excuse the weird pun. He was super intelligent but cared about my heart about everyone's heart. I knew heart mattered, I had learned that, and here He was saying it. I was floored. He was bringing Truth and realness with reckless abandon. He went out and faced the devil himself for 40 days and it didn't even phase Him. This guy was a Truth rock star. It amazed me. I don't know where I got this holy calm monk impression, but the Jesus I was reading was radical. He drew clear lines. Clear distinctions. And did I mention, His dismantling of all earthly 'authority.' There were people trying to trick Him and He saw right through them. Those with power who had everything to lose, were desperately trying to trip Him up. He was having none of it. He in the same way would at times have me submit, to certain authority, not because they were right but because it was right to submit at times. He went to the extreme in every case, I was honestly in Awe. This Jesus was so unexpected. I don't remember how long I it took me to get through those 4 or so books Sanchez had recommended, but they had left their mark. This Lord left no room for me to waffle. I really couldn't honestly go anywhere else. He left me no choice. Logically before reading Him, I had three choices, but after reading Him there was only one. He was it, just as He had said, the Way, the Light, and the Truth. He emphasized what I had already learned, that Truth was a narrow path that many of us just didn't want to walk. If He wasn't the Way, then there couldn't be one, and we were all doomed. He gripped me. I could feel myself scared, I could feel myself being reluctant, I could feel myself trying to distract myself and find other things to do. But Jesus isn't one to be ignored. He either freaked people out and they made some excuse to not follow, or they fell to their knees and worshipped. Nobody was left untouched. It was one or the other. I was no different. I reacted. I had to.

I'm pretty sure, I put the book down and just let it all sink in. He was clear with count the costs. So I needed to do that. This wasn't going to be easy or costless, there was a price to pay. Just my entire life.  He talked about losing your family, separating father from son etc. Was I really willing to give everything up to be with Him? I remember sitting on it for a day or so, it was churning my insides up. I went to school that Monday morning and I remember laying it down. I was by myself and I began to pray, to talk aloud to God and Jesus. I was telling them that I was here, that I was ready. I was saying sorry for being gone so long for being so reluctant. What happened next, what's happened since then is stranger than I would like to admit. For now, I had walked down that long corridor, I had taken the most important leap of faith I had ever taken. I was going all in on Jesus. I was done carrying my own yoke. I had failed. It was His turn. I was grateful and I had counted the costs and I had made my decision. I closed the door to my past self, laid down my pride, asked for help, and I leapt and fell. I remember the fear of Him not being there when I jumped. What if I jumped into the abyss and I just kept falling? For that split second after jumping I could feel the freak out deep within the instinct to save myself, flared up. It was too late I had leapt, and He was there right where He had promised to be. Right where He had always been. I had no idea what was in store, but I was eager and ready to conquer this world and to conquer death, as long as it didn't kill me in the process, or rather.... precisely because it would.

Truth over comfort (sanchez):

Honestly, I didn't want to send that text to Mac. For me, I risked losing another 'friend'. It's a phenomenon Mac *knows well, now*; but at the time, the fear was one sided. There was a danger here. We could have argued and debated for eternity, but there comes a point where a person is no longer 'searching' and instead stalling. One is allowed and encouraged by God...the other is not. I was in danger of allowing Mac to raise 'arguments' to the Absolute. Some of you may even be thinking, "Why couldn't you continue going round and round?" Well because I had done that when I was younger and it almost lead to my spiritual death. I had raised arguments and reason to such a high level that I began to mistake it (or purposefully built and idol) for God. I did much harm for a couple of years as a young man. I was like a Levite of the Bible more concerned with my fancy arguments than what God wanted...what He wants from all of us...my heart.

The moment came with startling clarity. Mac brought me a book about 'mysticism' that was so badly written and so poorly argued that I looked at him stunned. At the time, I had no idea he was actually trying to help a mutual friend who had given him this book. Mac knew there was something off about the premise the author was proposing, but he couldn't put his finger on it. I don't know if he remembers this. It was very close to this incident that it became clear Mac had all the evidence and arguments he would need to make the decision to hear God directly or not. I prayed and received every word I typed to him in that text. I wanted to meet in person, but God probably knew I would fold under emotion. I wanted to give Mac an 'out' and think he just needed more time, but these were lies. I knew it. He knew it. It was with a trembling finger that I hit 'send'.

Car overheating (sanchez):

If you've ever owned a car that overheated, then you might know the trick of turning on your heater to release the heat building up in the engine. This is what trying to live without God is like. You can figure out all kinds of temporary tricks to keep the car moving down the road, but it is neither comfortable nor a good strategy in the long run. You will break down and ruin more than if you had just fixed the problem. I know some think, "but I don't know how to fix it and I can't afford to pay someone." Have you ever wondered why so many poor people are great cooks or mechanics? It's because necessity forced them to become good at it. You will be surprised what you can accomplish when you are desperate. Here's the problem...you have to want the answer. This whole God thing is impossible if you believe you have anything figured out away from Him. You are driving the vehicle of your life with the heater on and convincing yourself that "it's not that bad" or "I like the heat anyway". The problem with this analogy is that you are not the driver in this analogy...you're the engine (a freewill car like KITT from Knight Rider!) You're headed for disaster.

Not my first rodeo (sanchez):

The good news is that Truth has been studied long before you were alive. Great humans have thought long and hard about the idea of Truth and have left you their work to discover. It may seem daunting at first, but if you start and keep seeking for ultimate Truth, you will become a more efficient connoisseur. You will see the same arguments made from different angles and more refined the more you search and study. You will discover the amazing fact that humans from before Christianity and outside of Christianity and inside Christianity are all saying the same thing. The universe began. Objective moral values exist. There is an ultimate source outside of nature. It is absolutely stunning how in tune the great minds of humanity have been with these three Truths. Some got it more right than others, but a majority agree on the basic premises. You have been given a mind that can reason. Aristotle, Socrates, C.S. Lewis, and others can be your equals. You can stand on their shoulders and see new heights. They invite you to. Do not be afraid of discovering that you are more than randomness and nothing. You are an infinite being imbued with the spark of the Creator and you are being called to be a son or daughter of the Absolute. Claim your inheritance.

Malcolm X (sanchez):

I had not read Malcolm X's biography until Mac recommended it. I was very impressed. Here was a story (warts and all) that showed me a man on the path to Truth. Especially the end, he comes to realize how broken we all our; including his mentor and religious leader. After his discovery, he becomes much more tolerant and peace loving. It is a great book and I recommend everyone read it. The other reason the book touched me was because I found my own story echoed in the pages. When Malcolm begins to educate himself, he does so with the most fundamental tools and efforts. He reads the dictionary, encyclopedias, and other reference materials to become a better speaker, writer, and thinker. I have done this. I did not know others had done it and I really didn't care. I wanted to understand this life. I read the great Greek philosophers, the great saints, the best atheist, naturalists, and Christian works. I found common themes throughout all of them. A hunger to understand where we came from and what our purpose is. Some are closer than others, but all are trying to answer the big questions. I want to mention that as a Christian I was much more harsh on those that shared my religious beliefs because I didn't want to give them a pass if there was bad reasoning. This has lead me to recommend very few "Christian" authors. If their story wasn't honest (warts and all), if it didn't attempt to tackle the big issues, then I didn't recommend them. I also focused on the non christian writers because this is where my opponents would be coming from. Knowing Bertrand Russell, Walden, Benjamin Franklin (a deist at the end of his life), and others helped me to minister to those who had looked for answers anywhere else but in Christianity. I will also say that it is dangerous to believe only Christian authors have discovered truths. This is not true and leaves you unprepared to handle the common objections a true seeker may bring up. Just as a heart doctor must study all of medicine first, THEN choose to focus his medical practice on the heart...we must study all of truth, THEN choose to focus our ministry on Truth.

Doubts (sanchez):

Doubts are natural. The sane person wonders if they are crazy. The crazy person does not doubt that the Queen of England is trying to kill them. Of course, in my life, there have been times when I have thought, "what if I'm wrong?" No argument seems more flimsy and weak than the one you just got done defending. It is only as we live life day to day that the truth of our beliefs manifests itself. I have studied the claims of apocrypha and alternate theories of the life, ministry, and death of Jesus. Some of them, on the surface, cast a shadow on what I have believed true most of my life. However; when examined, they are found to be lacking in substance and reason and are simply thrown up in an attempt to provide conjecture as proof. Christian and non Christian historians alike have studied the apocrypha and agree they are not authentic documents. In fact, it becomes evident very quickly of the intellectual dishonesty by those that propose it and those that believe it. The attempts to not see Jesus as a historical figure flies in the face of knowledge as we know it and tells more about the person's desire to not know the truth about even the most simple of facts. We should reasonably doubt our positions to keep ourselves intellectually honest. However; we should not allow our preconceived position to have such a tight hold on us that we begin dismissing good evidence because it goes against our position. If there was another Absolute Truth, God would want you to follow it. The problem is that He is the only Absolute Truth, so He has nowhere else to direct you but to Himself.

Rungs on the ladder (mac):

There are four things I would like to add here, or at least dig at a bit more. One is that when I look at when my doubts are at their highest it's when my emotions are flaring not my reason. Two, the approach that Sanchez and I took to Him is one of reason. We started at the very bottom of the bottom. If we can believe that reality is in fact real then we can move up the ladder of reason all the way to Jesus, and through the narrow gate. Three, is that I'm actually open to being wrong or to there being another way, but every time I honestly look there is no where else to go. Honestly where else do we go? Four, it's a lonely road, it often seems that Sanchez and I are the only two on it.

The doubts that I have stem from an emotional place not a reasonable place. Doubts are actually the irrational fear side of me that get loud when I am weak. If I'm tired, hungry, worn out, or grumpy my doubts grow louder. For that matter all of my natural negative emotions grow louder. It's not a coincidence that when I'm suffering in some way that I begin to doubt the position that I have found myself in. It's when I am uncomfortable that I begin to wonder if there is a more comfortable position. I don't ask myself if there is a better more reasonable position. I ask myself is there a more comfortable less painful position. I ask if there is an easier way, not a better way. It's when pain begins to build that I begin to attempt an escape. It's the same reason that I don't want to exercise or eat healthy. I begin with a reasoned position that I ought to do both, but when the pain of actually exercising, and the pain of not eating junk food when it's presented, that's when I 'doubt' the reasons I began to exercise and eat healthy in the first place. It isn't even really doubt, it's a lack of resolve or strength or conviction. It's an emotional plea to escape that leads me to 'doubt' why I got trapped in the first place. It's the pressure of reality that squeezes me to abandon my beliefs, no matter how well reasoned they are. When I am rested and clear minded, when my emotional self is at bay, and I can focus on reason without the interference of emotion, that's when I can clearly see the position I have arrived at. When my natural self is taken care of or when I seek the help from the Supernatural, then the clarity my position is revealed and the deeper inner comfort outweighs the outer more shallow discomfort.

The reasoning that Sanchez and I followed to get to the position we hold is not only solid it's also meticulous as well as broad. Because we started so low, the leaps of faith for each step are not nearly as big as taking the leap without reasoning. I'm not hear claiming it's the better way, in fact maybe it's the weaker way. Maybe because my doubt muscle is so strong and my faith muscle so weak that I need the crutch of reasoning to prop up my underdeveloped faith muscle. Nonetheless this is the path I took. When I find myself in the emotional position of doubt, I can look at the ladder of reasoning that got me here, and grab on at any point. I can see clearly how I climbed each and every rung to the top. I can see the much smaller leap of faith it takes to admit that reality is real. It's not even really a leap when I look at it, it's actually a comfortable simple step. A common sense type of step. The leap, the extreme and dishonest, wild leap of faith, to assure myself that nothing is real, is the impossible nonsense taken to ensure I get the base life I deserve. I can see the absurd logic of that statement and exactly the nonsensical position it leads to if I choose to pretend that none of this is real. If none of this is real then it's a very short path to nihilism, chaos, and death. It's short and yet full of giant leaps of faith, and dishonest reasoning, or irrational rationality. Each step off of the ladder of Truth leads in this way to some illogical mess, some dishonest position onto a heaping pile of despair. Each rung on the ladder of Truth that I have honestly taken is clear and solid from the bottom to the top. Every position on this ladder is a short more reasoned true solid position, that I thoroughly doubted and fought against, before I made the leap, or rather the step. Another way to put it, is that I made sure that it was a short solid step before I got anywhere near taking it.

What's maddening is that while I was being so reluctant and patient and doubtful, even skeptical and cynical, I hadn't done that to the position I was currently occupying. I was taking wild leaps to unsecure false mud, and getting dirty, scraped, bloodied, and injured along the way. I somehow was completely willing to emotionally and irrationally leap anywhere, except the correct true most reasonable position. What this approach did was two fold; it made me realize in real time and space all that was wrong with the alternative positions, that in the end couldn't hold my weight, and ultimately made me live a life of despair; while simultaneously it forced me to realize just how solid and well reasoned the next rung on the ladder was that I needed to take it. It made me realize how close the next rung really was. It was like having a ladder directly to the Truth in front of me, as well as guide, Sanchez, helping me. While he sat patiently at each rung with his hand out, I was stubbornly attempting to run up, climb, dig, swing, scurry and tumble my way up, in the dark, during the rainy season. After every failed attempt I would reluctantly get back on the ladder, with his help, and take the next step. Then jump off again, and stubbornly try a different way, multiple different ways, before dragging my bruised and broken self back onto the ladder, and taking the very next short step. Though I don't recommend this method, for me what it's done rather well, is that no matter how uncomfortable and doubtful I become, I can always look down at every rung of the ladder, and on my own now see exactly how I got here. I can equally see just how dangerous and treacherous everywhere else but the ladder is. I personally tried and failed all along the way. I have the scars to prove it.

I'm still open to being wrong, I'm actually still looking for a better way. There are none, at least none so far. I can't honestly go back down the ladder to a lower worse position. I could maybe do it dishonestly but not honestly. I could walk away from Him, from the Truth at any moment, but now I would be purposely seeking something lower, my own death. I would be saying, "fuck it", "fuck life", and really "fuck Him." I can't think of a more eloquent way to say it. I'm sorry for the vulgarity of the phrase, but that is the real. It would be an emotional excuse or escape and it wouldn't last. I would be right back to Him. Even in my darkest, most doubtful hours, He is the best, by far, that I have ever found, heard of, or witnessed; by far. I'm not talking about for some far off eternity, but for right now. All of my eggs or in one basket, but it is the only true basket I have ever found, and my eggs, though aren't perfect, they're all I got. I've bet my life on it. Reluctantly yes, but also in profound awe and extreme love. I have nowhere else to go. It's like in every way possible, every road, every bit of reason, every road, path, and way; they all lead directly to Him. Everything else leads to somewhere else, somewhere destitute and false. It's strange. It's like I took a ladder up, but the minute I got here the ladder was kicked out from underneath me. Reasoning, logic, and truth work that way. I can see clearly the previous position, but I can no longer settle on it. It would be the equivalent to trying to make two plus two is five work. I can say it all day long till I grow weary, but I cant convince myself of its worth or value. It just isn't so. It's simple. Even if I want it to be true, I can't make it, I can't force it, I can't pretend it to be. I can't convince myself that Jesus isn't the way, just as much as I cant convince myself that I don't love my wife and kids. I can't pretend God isn't the Truth, any more than I can pretend reality isn't real. I've tried, I've looked, the position I'm in is honest, there is really nothing even close. Every step away from this position is an infinitely far leap that I cannot make. The gap is infinitely far away and the abyss between goes infinitely far down. So no matter how desperate I become, no matter what obstacles are in my way, I can't deny Him. Now faced with certain death or torture or the harm of my family I might crumble, I might like the Apostle Peter, deny Jesus. I can't say for sure what I will do. If anything remotely close to that tests my faith, I can't honestly claim any result. But so far, even when everything seems off, untrue, and emotionally crazy, or extremely foolish, I still have nowhere else to go, nothing else to turn to, I return back to Him. With my head down, and my spirit low, I ask again, "How can I serve you?" "What can I do for you?" Then I listen and I obey.

It's a lonely road. Every single person I have ever talked to has a weaker position. They are stuck somewhere on the ladder or really they are stuck somewhere off the ladder. They are always at a position I have already examined as weaker than the one I'm on. Sometimes they seem to grasp a rung, and even seem to begin to climb, but then they fall off, and never return. Sometimes they seem to remain comfortable on a lower rung and never honestly look to the next. They stay on their less solid position for good. When I point out their flaw, or their weak position, they can't defend it, and they can't dismantle mine. They just quit the discussion. It's actually strange. It's lonely. I had no idea how narrow the path would be. I'm not here coming from an arrogant, look at me, I found the answer kind of way. Though I easily can get there, when my heart hardens and my emotional frustration gets the best of me, then my pride gets all self righteous. That is not the sentiment here, it's not the sentiment that breeds honest inquiry. The position I'm trying to convey is more of wanting to be proved wrong or shown a better way. I'm actually open in this way to being shown the proper path if I am in fact on the wrong path. Just as I climbed the ladder to get here, I'm willing to admit an error in any position and take a different step in any stronger direction. The position I currently find myself is lonely. If you have an honest, less lonely position, then by all means, please help. Show me. I've looked, I've listened, and this is the most correct, best, most true way that I have found. Everyone else has weaker position, so far, I could be wrong. We've tried to lay our position out here in this book. It seems though there is simply a reluctance, the freewill of the masses to choose anything but Him. It's not an intelligence thing, or an educated or learned thing, it's a heart thing, a particular choice, a willful ignorance. I understand the person that is actually ignorant, but the willfully ignorance is extremely puzzling. The purposeful blindness, seems silly. The childish covering of ears, and closing of eyes, along with the sticking out of the proverbial tongue, is honestly confusing. There's a paradox here; even though there is a deep connected cure for the existential loneliness I once felt, there is now an external more shallow loneliness in the world. There is an external lack of others that are willing to seek His kingdom, but a deep internal togetherness with Him.  The deeper thirst is now quenched with living water, but there is now and external thirst to share with others. These words are our attempt at keeping the former, and quenching the latter.

Heaven and gnashing of teeth (mac):
One of the ideas that Sanchez repeated throughout this journey, is that nobody knows who is actually going to Heaven. Somehow this simple idea, that most 'Christians' were wrong when they

assumed that they were definitely, no matter what, going to Heaven, made me able to realize the arrogance of the typical believer was misplaced, and more importantly unfounded. One of the things that was so troubling for me about 'religious' people in general, was their overconfidence. The hypocrisy of going to church on Sunday, and 'sinning' the rest of the week just seemed ridiculous to me. It still does. Sanchez would say that even according to Scripture, Jesus Himself, was clear that nobody would know who would get into His Kingdom. Another mind blowing seed had been planted. Sanchez would say, "I think in the end, we'll all be surprised at who gets into Heaven and who doesn't." Here was a Christian that wasn't at all confident that he himself would get in, let alone anybody else. This admission proved important for me. It seemed ridiculous to give yourself a 'pass' in this life for a guaranteed golden ticket in the next. This idea had the ring of Truth that I had become used to finding in my search for Truth. How could every moment matter so much, and at the same time not at all? These believers that threw in the towel in all their minute to minute daily moments were claiming that in their reality, only one moment actually mattered, the moment that they gave their life to Christ. It just didn't hold true, it didn't hold up to the test of reality. What I had learned was how important my intention and heart were, that every moment was important, that life itself was made up of these seemingly insignificant moments. The 'big' moments had proven to be far and few between. When placed side by side with 'small' moments in comparison, these 'big' moments didn't stand a chance. The weight and significance sided with the mundane, the regular, the normal parts of life. It's not that the 'big' moments didn't matter at all, it's that everything mattered. The death of my friend mattered, but it didn't matter more than my rage following his death. How I dealt with his death on a daily basis over the days and years that followed, proved significant to myself and those around me. This observation happened over and over in my life. There were many moments, that at the time, when they were actually happening, didn't seem 'big' or significant at all, and that it wasn't until much later, upon reflection, that those moments turned out to be incredibly significant. This is in fact exactly what I'm claiming about the many conversations Sanchez and I had. I didn't realize until years later how important Sanchez and his words and actions throughout the journey proved to be. It's not that all along I thought they were insignificant, it's just that I had no idea exactly how huge and extremely significant they actually were. The cumulative effect, the taking them all together in one bunch, the collection of all of those moments with Sanchez have proven to be the largest and most significant 'moment' in my life to date. This is exactly and technically what I'm saying in regards to this particular idea; the claim that anyone could make with certainty in entering Heaven was null and void. It didn't negate the reality of Heaven, in fact for me, it enhanced the likelihood of its existence, because what Sanchez was saying seemed so much more in line with how the world actually worked, and because in general the ignorant and arrogant people making their claim were wrong, by definition. It all seemed to make the possibility of an after life more plausible.

Once I finally was able to read the New Testament, I was able to see that Sanchez had been correct. Jesus left no room for misguidance. Jesus said throughout the Gospels that there were going to be many that would claim Him and that He would

would ultimately say get away from me you evil doer. He would tell them He would spit the lukewarm out of his mouth. He explicitly said only the Father in Heaven knows who will enter His Kingdom. It was everywhere and it was clear. These 'Christians' just weren't reading or listening or seeing. They were doing what everyone who is living in falsity does, they were cherry picking their truth. They were making truth subjective. I knew all too well the pitfalls of this approach, by this point it made me sick. Sick with regret, and sick with the danger and dishonor it did to the actual truth. It was another indicator that what I was reading and the path I was on was indeed correct. Far from being overly comforted or confident, it made me more careful and focused. The path had narrowed. Moments mattered even more than before. There were and are ample warnings from Jesus Himself about the many ways to miss the gate, and I wasn't trying to get close yet miss the mark.

This leads me to another important part of this journey for me. I was never looking to escape death. I have always been looking to escape life. I don't mean to be extra grim here, but it was living that had proven to be difficult dying seemed easy in relation. Especially if there were no God, death was just nothingness. What fascinated me about the Scripture, and especially the words of Jesus, was that the words and message and Truth all seemed to apply directly to life itself. Directly to the present moment. He repeats the gnashing of teeth several times throughout as a description of Hell. I was drawn to this because I had witnessed this gnashing of teeth in my own soul. Whenever my wife and I fought my insides would gnash their teeth. It was Hell right in the middle of me in my own life. Whenever I had resentment, deep anger, strife; gnashing of teeth. Whenever I felt wronged or slighted, whenever contempt would creep into my heart, my insides, my soul, and spirit would gnash uncontrollably. Here was Jesus describing exactly how this would happen and exactly why it would happen. He was throwing it down, in a very clear and direct way. He wasn't being vague about anything really, it was the opposite of vague, it was all deadly accurate. He was also describing how to reach God's Kingdom. Here Jesus was describing Heaven, it was the opposite of teeth gnashing. It was deep and endless joy, lightness of spirit, deep calmness and ultimate goodness. This too had the similar effect that the description of Hell had. I had experienced deep joy and moments of deep meaning. I had seen glimpses of this Kingdom, in love, in family, in conversation, in music, in art, in creativity, and in friendship. I had been in places in my heart and mind that had soared to poetic heights. The profound idea that we were all moving each other closer to either heaven or hell in each and every moment seemed as true and real as anything I had learned up until this point. I still to this day am more concerned with the present moment here in life, than I am with my immortal soul. It's not what appealed or does appeal to me. I think it true, but I think it the wrong focus. I only have today, right now, this very moment, a real yet admittedly slight chance at attempting to get anyone including myself a little bit closer to Him and His Kingdom. At least I can aim at avoiding Hell and gnashing of teeth. This is what this book has been about. I hope you the reader is closer to Him and His Glorious Kingdom than you were before you turned these pages.

Beware (sanchez):

If accepting Jesus once was all it took, then Judas will be in heaven. If rejecting Jesus once was all it took, then Peter will be in hell. What's the difference between these two men? Well, one of them turned back to Jesus and asked for forgiveness. He then gave his life moment by moment to Him because the reality of his offense was all too real. He had denied Jesus...like the rich man that walked away...like the other prisoner that mocked Jesus on the cross and did not repent. If Peter had died in that moment of betrayal or killed himself, he would have been as cursed as Judas...perhaps even the devil himself. He had seen the face of God in Jesus and he still turned away. It's the unforgivable sin. It's my sin. Daily, I turn away from Jesus in thought and deed. I have turned people away from the kingdom with my actions. I have harmed the very people He sent me to protect and help save. I do not deserve to go to Heaven. Here's the good news... Jesus died for my sin. It is great news! However, we cannot be like the servant that was forgiven his great debt and then turned around and threw his neighbor in jail for owing him pennies. Remember, that the master came back and said, "since you made this choice to live like you weren't forgiven...now you're not. Off to jail with you." We cannot simply claim Jesus in the 'big' moments and then sin to our heart's content in the small moments. I am a hypocrite even as I write these words. I am a sinner. I am the chief of sinners. And yet, He calls me. He waits for me at the end of the road to return broken and covered in pig shit. This is the point...I can barely talk about my ability to come back to Jesus... with what assurance can I speak on others? On liars, murderers, adulterers, betrayers, and cowards (I just described every 'great' man in the Bible). Faith and works is a tough debate. It's one for the person on the other side of the decision to follow Jesus, but I will say that when I honestly examine my own life...I see only the faith that Jesus is interested in the work of my heart. We as Christians would better serve the world by laying bare our fears of our own salvation rather than talking with so much confidence about the fate of other's salvation. I think we will be surprised who we will see in Heaven. I may not even be there. I pray I will be. I pray I can serve faithfully as long as I can. He doesn't care what place you take in the race...He cares that you keep getting back up and finish the race. This is good news.

# Volume 2: After Jesus

Now what? (mac):

So I am now officially a new believer. I went and joined the masses, the gigantic cult of Christianity. I was and am reluctant to even call myself that. I fought so hard against it for so long that it was embarrassing to admit defeat. I came to believe because it was true, not because I wanted it to be true. What I wanted is that the answer to be anything but Christianity, and here I was a converted Christian. Don't get me wrong here, Jesus and God were new and exciting. I was excited that I had an answer, one that seemed to make the most sense, by far, than any other answer I had ever heard of, period. I just want to be clear I was and am down for Jesus, God, and the Holy Spirit. I wasn't and am not down for everyone who claims them. I'm down for the cause but not necessarily down for the community around the cause. Something like that. It's not that I'm against them either. It's more that group identity is too crude of an identifier, Christianity is such a large and diverse group that it says almost nothing to claim to be a part of it. In fact, almost always in my experience, claiming Christianity leads to assumptions, preconceived notions, prejudices, and judgements that are entirely false. It's a lot like saying that I am a white American male, once I say that a whole bunch of false assumptions begin to bombard your senses. I then have to spend more time dismantling those false assumptions than I do actually describing who I am. The only way to identify anyone is on an individual basis, regardless of what group they belong to. It's way harder to do, and probably impossible on some level, but I know all too well what linking myself to any category causes. Discrimination, confusion, and then offense. So calling myself a Christian causes people to stumble and miss the mark shooting too high or too low, depending on what kind of baggage they carry regarding Christianity.

But I digress. I'm a new believer in Christ. He is exactly who He says He is. So what do I do? I in all my amateur and naive excitement, immediately get on my bike and go out into the world looking for someone to serve. I find the first dirty homeless man, who looks in bad shape and who could use a hand in life. I roll up on him, all excited and overly eager, and I ask if he would like any help. The response I got was not what I expected. He just looked at me like, "who the hell are you?" He looked at me like I was the weirdo, like I was the one who needed help. I quickly pedaled on. I left deflated and went back home, tail between my legs, emotional excitement turned to emotional embarrassment and confusion. I had been so caught up in my new belief, so excited in finally finding 'the answer', so in love with Jesus, that I hadn't really thought of how to be a follower? How exactly was I to behave like a Christian? It obviously wasn't a gun ho, save the world on my bike, missionary, craziness, I had just tried to pull off. It wasn't what I had been doing before hand either. So I was stuck, I had went from disbelief or unbelief to belief, but I hadn't figured out exactly what that meant. I hadn't read the whole Bible, just the parts Sanchez had recommended. So confused, and a bit disheartened, I hit Sanchez up, and was like, "We need to talk."

Under the fig tree (mac):

Shortly after my first feeble attempt at embodying Christ, Sanchez came over to my place. We went out back and sat at the picnic table under my fig tree. We had been talking for at least 8 years by this point. We had been meeting up and talking just like this for years, but this conversation, this was entirely different. I was now a believer. I was grateful. Sanchez was happy, we were both excited. He was weary and maybe a bit exhausted as well. He had certainly went to great lengths to show me the Truth. It had taken so many different and varied conversations to get me to this point. He had joined my band, playing harmonica. He had left his young family to travel to Boston with me for 10 days, and again to Utah, on a road trip for a week. He had frequently went out and stayed out late with me. I was single and lost. He would come hang out with me while I stumbled through alcohol, drugs, and women. He had scrambled with me often. He had went to the mountains and explored with me. He went 4 wheeling all the time with me. He went to chop down trees and harvest wood with me. He stayed and hung out when I tattooed myself and others. He helped me move several times. It wasn't like I wasn't being his friend as well, but I was never carrying the burden of truth, having to constantly help to save his soul. He lead the way on needing help with building and repairing his fences, and I helped him move too. He showed up to work one day on a motorcycle, and I of course had to go out and buy one like that weekend. We rode motorcycles for a summer, finding all kinds of excuses to get out and ride. Until on one of our best trips, he goes and decides (it was a complete accident) to lay his bike down, crash into a cliff, and scare the daylights out of all of us. Motorcycle riding was short lived, yet very fun. On the whole though he was much more adaptable toward my whims than I toward his. I also in fairness was and am just more 'whimmy' than he, especially back then. Anyway under the fig tree this conversation though one of many, was entirely distinct. It began by me describing to him my embarrassing attempt at being a Christian. The fresh attempt that day on my bicycle, and the awkwardness of the homeless man. Somewhere in there, after my story, he lays this on me; He goes, "Well this whole time I've known you, I've been listening to God." Wait what?! He goes on to explain in his very thorough, straight forward, and patient way this stunning revelation. He obviously must explain in more detail, I mean he did just admit to hearing God! More detail, please. Sanchez went on to explain about listening to the quiet voice deep inside. The one that isn't his own louder stream of consciousness. The voice that he could only hear after he had laid himself down, not before. I was like wait, wait, wait, "You mean this whole time, these last 8 years, you have been obeying God, and following what He told you?" "You mean the God of the entire Universe wanted you to help me?!" And equally as stunning and marvelous was that, "You didn't tell me?" And Sanchez was like, "Yeah, it was the call."

'The call' would become the central theme to our relationship and to my life from that point on. Sanchez went on to explain that once Jesus died and was resurrected God sent the Holy Spirit in order to act as an intermediary to God. It was a wild and strange way, but it actually made complete sense. How could we figure out in every moment, what it was that God wanted? How could we choose what He would have wanted? How could we follow Him, without Him being there for us to follow? If God had in fact wanted me to be in a personal relationship with Him, then I must be able to relate to Him. God didn't want me to be in a relationship with the Bible or with a church, like many Christians had fallen in the common trap of worshipping. He wanted me to be in a relation to Him. So I needed to get to know Him and be able to hear Him and talk to

Him, just like any real relationship. Obviously with some major differences, being that this is the Absolute we're talking about. Sanchez went on to explain that the Bible itself was made up of men who had in fact been in contact with God. That these men were flawed men, who had walked with God or ran from Him. Sanchez explained that Jesus had asked us to pray incessantly, that is to pray without ceasing. This is what Jesus Himself was doing while He was on earth. He was in constant and continuous contact with His Father. He was doing His Father's Will, leading us all by example. Jesus was demonstrating to all who will listen and see, what we all were meant to do. The reasoning of it that Sanchez laid out was extremely powerful, and the practice at least in theory was extremely simple. I couldn't rely, like I had been, on reason alone, all that meant was some form or another of rationalizing my actions to my own will. I couldn't now after becoming a Christian, carry a Bible around with me and randomly flip pages to see what exactly I was supposed to do. Neither could I memorize the entire Bible and somehow call forward the exact line for the perfect moment. In the end, that would have been a sneakier version of my will, cherry picking verses to suit my own ends. I couldn't read signs and use my flawed interpretations to maneuver through life, how could I protect against reading the sign in order to do what I wanted. No none of these methods would do, I needed to know God's Will. I needed the Supernatural to interact with me, and I to Him. Ok simple. Not quite. How exactly was I to actually hear His voice?

Under the fig tree Sanchez first described how 'the calls' weren't what he necessarily expected or most of the time wanted. Sometimes they were what he wanted but in the end that didn't matter. What mattered was whether on not he obeyed. He told me that lots of the calls he received were mundane, and sometimes they were downright strange. This became the first of many more conversations to come on this very topic, and we will almost definitely be going into more detail later. The trap I had fallen into right when I accepted the Truth of Jesus, when I went out into the world to 'save' it and 'serve' it on my own, was that what I thought it meant to serve and save the world, was most definitely not what God wanted. Sanchez explained that we had to be open to big life changing calls like moving to Africa to open up a church and serve the people there, or feed the hungry in

South America or build an ark like Noah, or even that we might be called to leave each other.(That one stung, but it also showed how deadly serious this all was.) He told me about the disciples in the Bible after Jesus had died and resurrected. They all were dispersed throughout the world following Jesus and the Holy Spirit. Many of them ultimately faced death, the Holy Spirit had lead them right to it, at least on this side of Eternity. This was the first of many times that I heard Sanchez say, "I hope I don't get those calls, I really don't. Even Jesus asked for the cup to be passed. If I do get a tough call, I have no real choice. If He is God, then I have to obey." It was all extremely eye opening. I didn't get to pick the version of Christian I was to become. I had to shut up, open my heart and mind, then listen and obey. This was very strange and obviously extremely new. However I was excited to get started, I had come this far, what else did I have to lose. A lot it turned out, I was a bit scared at the beginning, time would tell that I wasn't scared enough.

This conversation with Sanchez, under the fig tree was remarkable. It has stood out as a pivotal moment in my life. This part of the book is all about the results of all of our conversations, but especially that one on. I needed to get with Jesus directly. I needed to figure out what He wanted, what God wanted, I needed the Holy Spirit to guide me. How exactly was I to do that? Here again Sanchez helped out. He explained that it was a combination of knowing just how bankrupt I was on my own, and then submitting my broken self to Him; while at the same time knowing how truly Great and Awesome God was. Not Awesome like 'cool dude', more like the Awe He inspired in His Greatness kind of way. I needed to get more real with myself in an even deeper way than before, and put my pride down. I needed the old me to die. Then, and only then, could He lift me up to do His work. Sanchez explained that God uses everyone to do His work, to do His Glory. One way or the other God would win. It was up to us how He used us. We could be slaves, servants, or sons. It was all in our approach to Him. If we flat out denied God, He would use us an an example of filth to show others the wrong way, we would be slaves to sin, to evil, to our own nature. We would be working for Him in chains, not the way He intended. We could be servants which is good, ideal. He can use us as servants, and we can even be good and faithful servants, but a servant isn't family. He couldn't fully trust us to fulfill his Will, a servant doesn't love their master. The servant is obeying out of duty not love. They would rather not obey, but they know they should. They aren't going to receive the inheritance from their master, they aren't His sons and daughters. Servants aren't fully invested, servants come in fear. On the other hand, we could be God's children, His sons or daughters. We could come to Him in love, with a joyous heart and have a real, full relationship with Him, just as a son or daughter has with their earthly parents in the proper way. One where they love each other, and are honest with each other. A relationship where there is pride in the right sense of each other in the relationship. A relationship that is based in love, respect, and truth. The Ultimate Power of the Universe and his family all together in His Kingdom, enjoying His inheritance. Ok, so if I wanted to be His son, I needed to approach him with honor, love, gratefulness, and trusting Him more than I trusted me. I needed to bow down in my heart, mind, and spirit. I needed to honestly seek His Will, and I needed to wait for Him to give it.

Now that I knew that Sanchez had been listening and following God's will all along, it made perfect sense. How in the heck was he able to so patiently say all the right things, at the right times, for 8 long years? How was he able to go on adventure after adventure with me and remain in tact and faithful? He had been listening, that's how. I think it's a real and honest miracle, that I am now a Christian, a real Supernatural feat. I was the most reluctant and rebellious sheep in the heard. I was the most lost, I had been lost for a long time. God used this unlikely shepard, Sanchez, to come get me, and bring me back from death. I am grateful and amazed. It was my turn now. I had walked through the narrow gate, but this wasn't a one time thing. This was an infinite thing. I needed to walk through the narrow gate day to day, and moment to moment. Oh, I thought, in that revelatory kind of way, getting to Jesus wasn't the end, it was truly, just the beginning.

Sanchez also told me that day under the fig tree about the deep comfort and peace in walking with God, that he had experienced. Up until that point truth had always been uncomfortable on the inside for me, and rather comfortable on the outside in my actual experience. It was always hard and uncomfortable to learn how bad and wrong I actually was. It hurt psychologically, mentally, and emotionally. It was always tearing off the planks of my old boat and rebuilding the new one that felt painful. I was always laying down some form of my pride to keep the pride of being right in tact. Now I was learning for the first time that deep inside I would finally have the peace and comfort I had always sought, but never in the right places. I was ready to experience this deep peace inwardly, but was I ready for the external discomfort that came along with it? I'm still trying to figure that out. Here is the story of our attempt at following God. It's real and imperfect. It's full of foolish steps and mistakes. There is plenty of adventure and conflict. I am actually scared to tell this story, it doesn't paint me or even this way, in the best light, or at least the light I would have picked to paint it in. Out of the two volumes to this story, this one by far is definitely scarier. The costs seem to be higher, but that is probably, most definitely, exactly, and precisely why, we should tell it. Good luck.

Hearing the voice (sanchez):

In my past, when I have ministered to others and we get to the point of talking about the voice of God...I get different reactions. The seeker thinks you're crazy. Their line of thought is usually something like, "there's no way God is talking to you. That's what crazy people say." Believers usually are uncomfortable with the conversation. There is a strange belief in "Christianity" that God only speaks through the Bible or only in vague 'feelings' or random prompting. I would say that the Bible is very clear that His sheep will know His voice. That we are to listen if we have ears. At the same time, "Christians" will also let slip here and there that they have "felt the prompting of the Holy Spirit" in some moment in their life. I believe this is what God wants with us all the time. The call to pray without ceasing is really an invitation to hear God's voice and listen to His prompting as much and as often as possible. I know the concerns are: how do we know we're hearing the voice of God; and, evil and crazy people claim to hear God's voice and use it to do evil. For the first one, you will know it is the voice of God because it is usually not what you would personally pick and it is received after praying intensely. God also allows us to find confirmation in His word (though not always as specific as we would like) and through other believers. Here, "Christians" do this all the time. I do believe you get better at recognizing the Holy Spirit's tone of voice and style. It's like a child that gets used to hearing, responding, and obeying their earthly father's voice. Now, on Earth, we don't always have access to our earthly fathers or they are flawed as humans and so we can not always turn to them for comfort, advice, or direction; however, this is not the case with God. He directs us to pray to Him and seek His will at all times. It's both the easiest commandment and the hardest. I find that most "Christians" are so afraid of being led astray that they refuse to try and hear God's voice. It's like someone that has been cheated on in a relationship. They develop trust issues not just with the other person, but even with themselves. They do not want to risk betrayal. Again, this may actually be necessary on Earth with earthly relationships, but this is not what God tells us. He commands us to listen to His voice. By the way, it should be obvious that I am not referencing an audible voice. I mean more like a stream of consciousness that is not mine and directs me (although I have the free will choice to not obey) and is confirmed by scripture and can be checked with fellow believers that have also practiced hearing God. There are times where I do not have the opportunity to do these checks because the call is urgent and immediate; however, the times I have got it wrong, when I look back, I can see how my selfish, prideful, or stubborn self got in the way. There are other times where I have made assumptions on what God wants only to find out later I was using God as an excuse to do what I wanted. No matter how 'good' that decision turned out, I was in the wrong. I ask for forgiveness, repent as much as I can, and then get back to God's will for my life. I am not perfect. I do not know why God would choose to die for me. I often feel unworthy and get angry with myself for betraying my Lord and Savior with each sin. I sometimes want to 'give up' because I am unworthy. I don't deserve to be His servant. Yet, God says to me, "Get up. You're my son. Let's get back to work." He rarely allows me a pity party. When I bring up my brokenness (if I have truly repented), I usually get, "That's forgiven, don't bring it up again. Get back to work." It's not harsh. It's loving and reassuring.

'The call' (mac):

After the fig tree conversation. Probably the very same day. I went to pray in a totally new and different way. I hadn't really been praying at all up until then. I was newly converted, and newly lost, in a different way than I had been. This new way I prayed wasn't a physical position or location, it was very much an internal practice. I sat at my kitchen table when nobody was around and closed my eyes. I internally began to 'talk' to God. I first in my mind bowed way down. I literally pictured myself kneeling, but not just kneeling. I was completely laying my chest on the ground with my hands sprawled out in front of me. I was so close to the ground that I had to turn my head to the side. I was submitting. It was kind of like what you would do to a cop that was going to arrest you but also had their gun pointed at you. Only it wasn't exactly like that. I was doing this out of love not fear. I was coming to Him with open arms willingly submitting. It was like the cop or Judge, in that I had done something wrong, but it was also my Father who loved me deeply. I was coming to the God of the Universe, down very low with all of my heart, but with nothing. I was admitting how inadequate and completely empty I was. I was completely bankrupt. I was coming to the King with nothing to offer besides my pathetic self. I asked Him to forgive me. I really meant it. I thanked Him for bringing me back to Him. I asked Him to help me hear Him. I asked Him to help me kill the old me. I asked Him to replace me with the Holy Spirit. I asked to follow Jesus. Please help me, I said in my heart. Right then and right there sitting at my kitchen table with my soul bent way down in humility, in humble approach, submitting my will to His... I felt it. I heard Him. I felt his presence. The Holy Spirit had arrived. Then it was gone. So I refocused and reprayed. There it was again. That feeling, that voice, that deep mental and spiritual feeling in my mind. It was like, "Hi I forgive you", and I felt forgiven. It was too much. My eyes swelled. What in the heck was happening. Oops lost it, refocus re-pray, re-lay myself down. There It was again. It was like I had to purposely tune into it, in the right way. It was definitely there though. He was definitely there. He told me to get up. I literally felt Him pick me up from my internal kneeling, submitting, and worshiping position. I was filled with joy deep and un altered joy. Deep love that I had never felt before, filled my entire being. I can still feel it and here

Him as I am writing this. I just wanted to sit in that feeling, and He wanted me to sit in it too. That hole that I had tried so desperately to fill and never really managed was filled immediately and fully, in an instant. I was home. Not externally,(though I was actually in my house), internally, in spirit I had arrived home. Or more likely, the Spirit had made a Home in me. Whatever was the case, my heart swelled and my mind was in tune. Then it was gone again. It was as if I had to purposefully turn me off inside, and bow way down to hear Him. It was strange. It still is strange. The second I lost focus on Him and allowed my normal internal voice, the one I had been used to, the loud one, to take over, He was gone. It was like my normal consciousness, the one that is me, the one that wants things, the one that's always talking, my ego, my self, was a constant faucet that was turned 'on' always. When I prayed and laid that person down, put myself to death, then and only then, could I hear and feel the Holy Spirit. In the days, months, and years to follow it's gotten easier to tune into that voice. I no longer have to have my eyes closed in the bowing submitting position. My heart and soul still do that but it's faster now. It's easier to get to Him in a way. I know His voice and His feeling way better now. Back then it took a real effort to focus and clearly remove myself from the equation.

At the picnic table earlier that day Sanchez described the voice in this way; He said, "Remember following the 'vibe' and sometimes feeling the 'on-ness' of a certain decision or choice or place we were at?" I did remember of course. I had learned to feel the 'vibe' of the universe. Through travelling and music, I had learned to tune in, on a macro level to something vague, and seemingly random. I could only tell when it was 'right' or when it was 'wrong'. A lot of the time, it seemed far off, or like it wasn't 'on' or 'off'. It was more like grey, fuzzy, and vague. It was nothing like this new thing, none of the deepness, and specific voice and actual 'in tune' feeling in my heart and mind. Sanchez went on to explain that the 'vibe' I had felt before was like a far off echo of Him. It was like I could hear the drum beat of the band or concert from a far away distance. The 'voice' or 'the call' was like hearing the voice of the lead singer of the band up close and personal. The analogy would prove correct. Along my journey to Truth, the 'vibe' had gotten easier to feel. Now finally hearing God, feeling the Holy Spirit, and getting to know exactly what Jesus was saying was up close and very personal. Instead of the distant randomness of the 'vibe', I was now in a very personal relationship with this Trinity of the Supernatural. I pictured an outdoor stadium sized concert. I had been stumbling around lost in the wilderness far far away. I could only hear the faintest sound in the distance. The deep but quiet thump of the bass drum. As I approached, I could hear more of the instruments and could tell that it was music that I was hearing, not just a rythmic noise. It became easier to track the direction it was coming from. The path narrowed and my focus became consumed by the sound. That music guided me in a directly to the concert. When I got to the gate, I could get a clearer but still vague sense that there was actually a whole band in the venue. I could hear that there was a singer singing. There was a powerful vocalist inside, but being outside the venue, I couldn't quite catch the words, just a little of the melody of His voice. The entry fee was my soul. I had to pay with my will. It cost me my heart, and it was paid in faith. Once I stepped through that narrow gate into the venue, I could now hear the whole band and the lead singer's voice playing right along. It was all so amazing, His voice was powerful yet calm. He was in rhythm, and sync with the whole band, but He could've performed without them. As I walked closer to the stage, it got more crowded, it was harder to move, but the singers voice got clearer and clearer, and the music got lower and lower. Once I finally worked my way directly to the front, the music had faded away completely. I could hear only the singer, the band was no longer playing. The singer was off the mic, and had stopped singing. He was now talking directly to me, holding out His hand for me. Pulling me up to Him. All the people had disappeared, Jesus pulled me close, smiled, and whispered in my ear, while embracing me, "welcome home son".

For the first few days the call was to "be with Me." God wanted me to get to know Him. Feel Him. He wanted me to be able to hear His voice and feel His presence. I would ask, "What can I do for you?" or "How can I serve you?" The call was just to 'love and be with Me'. On my way to work shortly after I broke down in tears of Joy. I had never done that before. I was overwhelmed with awe and gratitude. God wanted me to be with

Him. I could hear Him, the Creator of everything. I could feel Him. The void was gone. A deep peace and comfort soaked me to the bones of my soul. I had felt falling in love with my wife. That was and is a deeply personal and beautiful thing. This was different, yet similar. That feeling with my wife of close intimate goodness had become more inconsistent and more volatile. This new feeling with God had a less fierce and dramatic emotion. It was a more still and deep comfort and belonging, that I had only caught glimpses of while staring deeply into my wife's eyes. I had not felt a sense of belonging to the world for my entire adult life besides sprinklings of seemingly random occurrences. When I look even further back I can trace its roots to elementary school and beyond. The deep loneliness that had always gnawed on me was suddenly gone. Just like that. The existential boredom was gone just like that. The lost wandering, was gone just like that. I was extremely grateful to Sanchez, and still am for his part. He followed and listened to God. He stuck with Him, and together they brought me out of the darkness. What if he hadn't? Who would He have been able to send? What if it would've been another 30 years of lostness? I was and am deeply grateful. I was floored. Driving to work I was just bawling like a baby, it was all so incredible. I got to my classroom and finally stopped crying, but I was still in awe. I got one of my first 'calls', besides to be with Him. To this day it is one of my favorite 'calls'. It was to tell Sanchez ,"well done"and "good job." Coming from the God of the Universe that was as good as it got. For God to be proud of you, man that was amazing, and I got to honor my friend with it. I think I text him and told him to come by my classroom before school. When he walked in, I could tell he thought something was wrong. He gave that concerned look like, "Is everything ok?" I smiled through my post crying emotionally drained face and said, "thank you." Not thank you like polite excuse me and thank you. No this was like thank you for helping me find Him and saving my soul. I was like, "I'm getting to tell you, well done and good job, and of course thank you". It was hard in a way. I hadn't ever really been that vulnerable as an adult, in front of another man before or specifically in front of my friend. I mean we were close, but I'm not a crier. Either is he. I still haven't seen him cry. Anyway he accepted gracefully and tried to deflect a little bit of the compliment, but I know he heard me. Then we just sat at my desk and talked like we always had, it was of a lighter in tone and we laughed, while we reminisced. There was one major difference sitting there and talking in those moments following. This difference would end up lingering and lasting from then on. We were now talking as true brothers... Brothers in Christ.

How do we know? (mac):

I'm going to talk about the heart of the matter at hand. That is, how do we actually know that we are hearing God. Fair enough. Good question, if you are really seeking the truth. If you are just trying to dismantle or dissuade or poke holes, then the question is not a question at all, it's an accusation. An accusation of this type is not only damaging to the accused, but also to you the accuser. I can easily ask it back. How do you know I'm not hearing Him? How do you know He isn't trying to talk to you right now? There is no middle ground here, either I am hearing Him and everybody can and should hear and obey, or I'm not hearing Him, and in that case I am crazy or demonic. Just as Jesus left us this choice I myself leave it to you.

Back to the honest question; How do I know that I am hearing God? This goes back to how did I know anything before God. How did I know what was good or bad, or right or wrong? How did I know what to do next or not to do next, what to say, or not to say? How did I live, function, and make decisions before God? Before God, I would use a combination of: reason, my conscience, my gut or intuition, my feelings, my wants and desires, my experience, my impulses and instincts, some person of authority, or others council to make all of my decisions. Simply put, I would rely on me, myself. I would judge for myself what I ought to do. This method got me by, it still could. This method, relying on self, would inevitably fail at some point. Why would it fail? Because I'm a man, a human. I am flawed so all of my faculties are flawed. I could however feel when something was wrong, or at least way wrong, like lying, stealing, cheating, or taking advantage of someone. I knew that hurting someone on purpose, taking out my anger on someone, scaring someone for real, etc. these all 'felt' wrong. From early on in childhood, I could feel the burden of sin. That feeling never left, I still have that, the guilt of transgression. As I got older I learned to use other faculties such as reason, and council of others etc., along with my original conscience. Into adulthood I began to rely more heavily on reason, trying to subdue my own conscience, but that often lead to rationalization. I explain rationalization in volume 1, but basically perverting reasoning to my own ends, to establish my own gains, to excuse my own reckless behavior, and badness. My conscience was still there but I tried my best to will it to go away, or at the very least to persuade it to break away from its old primitive ways. There was a lot of doing things in the heat of the moment, and not feeling the wrongness till later when my heart and mind were calmer and therefore clearer. In effect, I wouldn't know it was wrong until it was too late. Before God this was an all together, all too common phenomenon; Me thinking things were good and right, and then later, inevitably feeling the pain of guilt. Something or someone would put me on notice that in fact, I had messed up. That probably most definitely, 'should've known better' or that if I would have been more considerate things would've been better.

Before God, I could also feel and know when things were good. I could use all of the faculties, emotion, reason, council, authority, and observation to tell when I had done good or that something was good to do. It was right, good, and true to help others, love others, be kind, to forgive others, correct others, and keep goodness on my heart and mind. Instead of the pains of guilt there was the deep joy and proudness that went along with doing good. Part of the whole point of all my searching and seeking was to maximize the good and minimize the bad. How could I do more good while at the same time do less bad? I would still end up getting it wrong time and time again. I would be trying to help, but sometimes would make a situation worse. Hindsight was always showing what would have been better, what I could have done better.

   With God, all of my old ability to 'know' right from wrong, and good from evil is still available to me, plus I have God. So I still use all of the same faculties, reason, conscience, counsel of others, gut and intuition etc, but I now have this peculiar addition. I have this other voice to commune with. I have an entirely different Will to go to. It isn't mine, my own inner voice doesn't leave, my own conscience is still present, my own emotions, memories of past experiences, me all of me, still here. The 'call' the voice, the other will, God, the Holy Spirit, Jesus, is clearly not me. I didn't have access to it before I found God and laid it all down at His feet. I do now. It often is not what I want, or what I would do. The results of following this other Will, this voice, by in large have been good. Way better than I would have thought, before acting upon the call. In other words, the call often goes directly against all of me, it goes against my reason, past experience, wy own wants and desires, it goes against my gut or intuition, it flies right in the face of what I think I ought to do. The thing is once I follow this voice, things work out better than expected. They work out in ways I wouldn't have imagined. Hindsight almost always leaves me going that was perfect, couldn't have done anything better. I'm not constantly missing the mark. I'm not constantly second guessing as I did before. Often the 'call' seems crazy and not all that clear that it's good or right, it's also not clear, that it's bad before I implement the call before I choose to obey. Matter of fact, the further away from the 'calls' I get, in general, the better I feel about them. The evidence of hindsight grows with time in favor of, and showing that the 'calls' were in truth, the right calls. I'm way less guilty now than ever before. There is never a time when I go, "man I shouldn't have listened and followed the call" It's always the case that I should've been more 'prayed up' or I should've been more 'connected' to the Absolute. It's only the times that I get off of Him and go off on my own that hindsight tells me otherwise. The actual results in my life when I do follow the voice turn out so unexpectedly better, it's not even a fair comparison.

       The source of the evil I have commited and still commit is myself. I am the evil one who commits sins against others. I am the one who wants to force my will into the world. I am the one who screws things up. I am the flawed one. I am the bankrupt soul who needs redemption. I am the fallen one. I am the chief among sinners. I am the one who needs the filth washed from me. It is in me to be the murderer. I have wished plenty of people dead including myself. I have lusted for many women. My heart wants revenge. I want to cause harm to others. I want take what isn't mine. I want what I want, when I want it. I am impatient. I am gross. I am disgusting. It is me who holds grudges, and keeps tallies of those who owe me, those who did me wrong. So when you ask me, or when I ask myself as I often do; How do I know it isn't the devil or some evil spirit that I'm hearing and then obeying? That's easy, it isn't me. I am the source of the evil. I am the one that wants to know what God knows. I am the one that wants power. I am the corrupt agent. So I pray to kill my evil self, and I bow before Goodness Itself. I bow before Reason itself, I bow before the King, and ask for His way, for His Light, for the Truth. Then, and only then do I hear, then I listen. I always have a choice. I could choose not to listen. I could choose to walk away. I could choose to not obey. Thats easy. I can always leave Him. I still foolishly look for a better way. I fought against my sick self, my mentally ill self, my pathetic self important self to find Him. Once I did I fell to my knees, but then in my depravity I run away. I continue to battle myself to lay myself down, to find Him. My pride of wanting to know the Truth led me to the Source of all Truth. The Source asks me to lay down my reason, my pride, my will. I feel myself fighting still. I have all the Reason in the Universe to tell me to listen and obey, yet I still find 'reasons' to doubt.

For the believer, but not the follower (mac):

We know that our reasoning alone is flawed. So how do we know when we're reasoning correctly and when we aren't? Besides the method of the non believer I named above, its when our reasoning lines up with Scripture and what we already know to be true from it. The problem with relying on Scripture alone is; how do we prevent ourselves from using Scripture as a means to our own ends? Even if we are using our own faculties of truth, like, it rings true, feels right, real honest talk, and shining light on our real intention; How do we know what He wants from us? Either you're in His will or you're not. Either you are following Him or you're not. Reading a piece of scripture to justify an action, is the definition of rationalizing. In fact it's the worse kind. What better way to hide evil intention than being close to but not in His Will. Evil is the separation from God, and what better way to separate from God, but to lift up a 'good' like Scripture in His place. The self-righteous, the self-proclaimed authority, the self-pious, the self-Christian doesn't work. There is only one Will that matters, God's Will, everyone else's and everything else, is off the mark. Because reason got me to Him, I often try to raise reason up above God, I still struggle with His will when I can't see the reason for it. When it doesn't make sense to me, I think it doesn't make Sense, or that there is no Reason for it. I have to continually lay down, my own reason, my own understanding and trust His. You might be raising church or the Bible up in His place. A false idol is anything but Him that we worship instead of Him. The closer we get to Him, the easier it is to fall into the trap of worshipping a piece of His essence. It's easy to miss the narrow gate and create an absolute out of something 'good', but that isn't God. It's easy to pervert and manipulate the gifts He has given us into something they were never meant to be; a substitute for Him.

Father in law (mac):

One of the first 'calls' I got surprised me. I was so ready to start a church or go to Africa to minister and help the poor children. I was ready to house a homeless man. I was pretty gung ho about the whole thing. I was naively confident about hearing the voice of God and following Him. I was like let's do this, I was all in. I was like whatever You want, I'm in. I want to serve You and only You. Ok so that's what I prayed, and what I got was, "You need to go talk with your father in law. You need to tell him how he's hurt you. You need to tell him how he was a stumbling block to Me, to Truth." Just to be sure I've been clear and to exercise caution while being completely transparent, let me try to explain this voice again. It's not a voice in the sense of audibly hearing something external. It's not even a voice as in an audible internal voice like, "Luke this is your father!" from the Star Wars movies. It's actually difficult to explain. It's more like a meeting of consciousness and not consciousness, something else, the unknown. It's not my conscience. It's my conscious self and then this different other thing, feeling, sensation, or voice. Almost like being on drugs or high in some way, but not, it's more specific than that. Maybe more like or a heightened connection to something greater. It's hard to explain without using religious words like, Spirit or Ghost or God. That's what I'm convinced it is obviously, but the call is to try and explain it as clearly as possible. I'm stuck feeling like I'm trying to explain the color blue to you. There is nothing really like it, we all know it but it's actually really difficult to explain. Anyway I hear it or it happens only when I focus and turn myself off, only then this other voice comes in. Sometimes it's me asking, "Is this God, is this Jesus? Is this what you want?" And the feeling of affirmation or yes is overwhelming, and when it's not God, it's quiet, it's nothing, it's gone. There are all kinds of thoughts that pop into my head, but when it's from Him, it's different. It comes from a different place. There is a nudging, an ought to, or an ought not to. There's a, "pay attention to this!", and there is quite often, "don't worry about it." I can check in with it as many times as I like, and it's always the same. When I'm tired it's harder to hear. When I'm sick, or extra emotional it's' harder to sense and to feel it. When I'm laying down its harder to get to. I have to be awake. I have to be focused and I have to lay it down. I can really hear Him when I'm bathing or meditating. When I am alone and it's quiet and I really focus. In the morning when my family is still asleep and I can hear more clearly. I have access though anywhere and anytime. He is everywhere always. When I get too caught up in the results of the 'call' or the Reasons for it, I lose it. When I care too much about whatever the thing is, I get in the way, and it's hard to get back to Him. When I ask directly, "Is this Jesus?", I get, "yes."

When I ask, "Is this just something inside of me that's tricking me?" I get nothing silence. "Jesus?", "Yes!" "Demon?", nothing. "Alien?", nothing. "God?", "Yes!". "Holy Spirit?", "Yes!" and "Jesus?" again, I get the loudest deepest, "Yes!" back. So I check all the time, all day, everyday. "Is this you? Is this what you want?" Or sometimes I ask for things like health, and financial stability, or to go to the beach with my family, or direction. I ask for a more meaningful career or a more specific aim, but mostly it's "What can I do for you?", and then I get whatever the 'call' is, and then I try to obey. Sometimes it's easy like go to work, or relax, and sometimes difficult and I'm like, "Wait, what?!" That's how this father in law 'call' was, "Wait, What?!" My enthusiasm quickly turned to fear and anxiety. Apprehension. I was in no way prepared to hear that. How in the world did that make any sense? It was so far out of my realm of possibilities, that I was literally stunned. I had to (unknowingly at the time, but would end up doing over and over again from then on), double, triple, and quadruple check. Then I had to check again. Then I had to sleep on it, and check again. Then I had to talk to Sanchez and tell him what the 'call' was and have him check with Him. Then I had to check with my wife, and see what she thought. (eventually she was able to hear God too, but I don't think should could at this point). It was my first experience with wrestling with God. The 'call' was clear it didn't waver, but I sure did, it just seemed like too much. It seemed like it would just cause more harm than good. It seemed like it would make an already strenuous and tense relationship and situation worse.

We had been married for only a year or so at this point. We had been dating for several years. Her father, my father in law, had been a thorn in our relationship A thorn in me. She dearly loved him and was very close, but he didn't like me and I definitely didn't like him. He had done several things to me, and to others, that made me not respect him, and not want to be around him. At that point the way I dealt with him was to just avoid him as much as possible. I hated him, he had given me good reason to hate him, and I obliged. I took his tempting, negative, and nasty shots at me, and I went, "OK, that's easy, you want to hate? So can I!" He definitely started the hate dance, but once he was on the floor, I jumped in head first. I willingly and almost gladly accepted his invitation. And so began the gnashing of teeth, to the music of resentment.

What exactly had he done to make me hate him so much? A little bit of everything. He had backed his younger daughters actions, my wife's sister, when she had claimed, "The whole family doesn't think you two should get married." When I tried to calmly talk to her about it, and asked her where she had gotten that from. She had nothing to say, nothing to backup her claim. She literally ran away crying. She was 19 at the time, an adult, and her dad acted like I was the one that had said and did horrible things. He had basically cosigned her claim that nobody in her family did in fact want me to marry their daughter or sister. That hurt. His actions hurt worse than his daughter's, because he backed her play and blamed me for her crying.

Another time, I had made my wife a desk. Beforehand I had told her that I would gladly do the labor for free, but that I couldn't afford the material. (I was broke, I still am broke) She went to her dad for the money, and he told her to just have me give him the receipt when I was was done with the desk. He would then pay me back. Deal! So I built her a desk, it cost around $100 in materials. When I gave her the receipt along with her new desk she loved it. She gave her dad the receipt. He then dragged his feet in paying me back. I was confused. He was a well to do, federal employee life insurance and retirement benefits salesman. He had a nice house, a boat, he travelled often, he went shopping all the time, spent money on dinners, watches, clothes, shoes, and all kinds of frivolous treats. He had nice truck, on fancy rims. He was proud of his money. He flaunted it. When he didn't pay me back, I told wife (then girlfriend), that I needed the money. It wasn't a luxury to me. My money situation was tight. I didn't need it exactly, but I definitely was in a different financial position than he was, and it was messing my finances up. More importantly to me was that we had made an agreement, and now he was playing games. Anyway after she went to talk to him about the money for her desk again, she came back to me crying. She said her dad had thrown the money at her in anger. He had said to her, "After all the dinners I took him to and paid for he is going to press me for $100?! Here take it!!" Um?! No!! I was pissed. She asked me not to make it worse. So I kept my mouth shut, but I was ready to blow him up. First he had treated his daughter poorly, and made her upset. He hurt her feelings, and caused real pain, in trying to harm me. Second is that he had been claiming that the dinners were gifts up until that point. He always insisted that he paid. He proudly spent his money to take everyone out to eat, and I had been grateful. I brought this story to Sanchez at the time and we used our normal analysis and real talk to quickly dismantle what in fact was so wrong with his line of reasoning and behavior. We realized, that now all of a sudden, the real came out. The truth was that those dinners hadn't been gifts at all. They weren't free to me. There was a catch a hidden cost, those dinners had been IOU's, that he was writing on my behalf, without me knowing. He was going to hang every dime he ever spent on me, over my head. Any 'gift' he gave me was turned into, something that I owed him in return. Not only that but that he was going to spring the IOU on me whenever it was convenient for him without warning. That was gross and low. It was clear. What I did in response, was to explain to my future wife how wrong that was, and how I wasn't going to be going to anymore dinners, ever again. I wanted to have nothing to do with him. She was in the middle of us and neither of us were talking to each other. I used the excuse that he was a piece of crap, and that talking to him would just make things worse. I had learned that fighting with someone who was demonizing me only made things worse. At that time, not being 'connected' it probably would have.

After we got married, my father in law left my mother in law for another woman. It was a mess. Here was a man who claimed to be a Christian, and just like his money, he was proud of it. He flaunted it. He was the typical, cross wearing, republican, rush limbaugh listening, loud, obnoxious, fish bumper sticker, American loving, Fox news watching, so called Christian. He went to a megachurch, wore Christian clothes, and carried a Bible. Yet here he was committing adultery and leaving his wife and family to deal with his mess. During this time, he needed a favor. He asked my newly married wife and I, if we could take his dog for him. I did not want to, but she was excited, and so were our two boys. So I obliged, but there were some conditions. I called him and said that we would take the dog as long as he paid for the food for a year (we were still broke, we still are), and that he didn't get the dog back if his new "life" didn't work out. In other words, he wasn't going to let my family get attached to the dog, and then come rip her away when things didn't work out with this new woman. He agreed. Later my wife tells me that when she talked to her dad, that he said, "The adoption hadn't been friendly." Really?! The gull, the audacity of this guy. First of all, it wasn't unfriendly it just was what it was. It wasn't like we were in this fairy tale situation, that he was pretending to be in. He was leaving his wife. He was acting as if that wasn't wrong. He was acting like he was doing us a favor. Neither of these were true. We had to go pick up the dog at his old house, and watch the pain he was causing to my wife's mother. She was obviously a mess, it was crushing her. Taking the dog was symbolic. Her husband was really leaving her, after 20 or so years, he was abandoning her. It was terrible. Yet he was acting like, "Why aren't you happy for me?" He was acting like he was the victim. It was bizarre, even for him, the level of mental gymnastics he was pulling off to do this. He was worried about the "friendliness" of the adoption, rather than the souls of all those people around him that he was moving closer to Hell. Besides, he had over the years done many things to make our relationship 'unfriendly.' We didn't talk, we weren't close. It was always strained and awkward around him. He didn't ask me about me. He didn't know me in the slightest. He didn't care. I was married to his daughter, and there was a feeble, thin, almost non existent relationship between us. What was he doing worrying about this twisted dog adoption and its relative friendliness?

He eventually did come back from his drunken adulterous escapade to his wife and home. We kept the dog. He was always asking for me to go to church with them, or really asking my wife to ask me. My wife was going with them regularly, and for some reason (I think I was getting closer to finding Him, and this was a perfect excuse to hate Christianity) I said ok. I was anxious, nervous, and reluctant. This was a giant megachurch, in the wealthiest part of our area, it was everything I hated about modern religion. When we finally go I want to sit in the back next to the exit, in case I get too uncomfortable. Of course they choose to sit me right up front and center, so that I was staring directly at the pastors crotch. Needless to say, I didn't enjoy my time, I was extremely uncomfortable. I could feel everyone looking at us, (they weren't) I could feel the judgement they were placing on me the only non believer out of the thousands of people there. (they weren't) It was all just too much. I wasn't a Christian, and this rock star, loud, really loud flamboyant place was just too much for me. Especially right up front. Thanks, but no thanks. I think he (maybe my wife and the rest of her family too) was under the impression that going to church would make me come to Jesus. It did the opposite. The type of church and the aggressive, up front, right in the middle, seating was the opposite of what I needed. He was just inconsiderate of me, who I was, and what I needed. This was about my father in law and what he wanted. This had nothing to do with me, a potential believer coming to God. My wife got it. She knew me and could tell I wasn't having any of it. She understood the mistake immediately. I only got through that because of her touches and comfort. The whole experience, just pushed me farther away from Christ, and by that point I was so incredibly close.

When I called him on the phone to meet up, he was surprised, but without hesitation, obliged. We met at a local restaurant at lunch. After all my checking and rechecking, the 'call' was clear. I was to go meet up with my father in law and lay out all the issues I had had with him. I was to lay out all the harm he caused. I had actually written a list, it was the 'call'. With the amount of nerves and hesitation I had, I most definitely would have forgotten something. We sat down across from each other in a booth. We ordered our food, and I got right to it. I was way too nervous, and excited, and anxious to really make any small talk. Here was this man that didn't know me, that I was about to reveal my heart to him. I was feeling very uncomfortably vulnerable. What if he argued with me or got mad or started blaming me for all of it? If he was the piece of crap that I had come to know, then that is exactly what he was going to do. This was where faith in Him was being tested against my own human reasoning. My reasoning was pretty sound, my evidence had mounted, my experience was in line, but the 'call' flew directly against all that. It was time to trust and obey or run away. So I just stayed 'connected' to Him. I bowed to God, instead of my instinct to run and hide. I looked at my father in law took a deep breath, chugged some beer, and began to explain. I explained from the beginning of meeting him, all of the different instances, in specific detail, that had bothered me, and that had harmed me. He sat patiently across from me watching me and listening. He was still and quiet. I got through all of the things I have already laid out, and added more. Like the time he asked me to get married in the church, when I wasn't a Christian. The audacity to ask such a thing, when we had zero relationship seemed off and bizarre. That was like asking me to get married on the moon. I told him about the harm his response was when we announced our engagement, he hadn't been excited. He wasn't happy. It had been awkward. I explained how he had been a major stumbling block in my search for God. He sat there quietly and listened and watched me. I struggled through the list, it was hard and emotional. It was scary. When I was finally finished, he asked if there was anything else. I kind of awkwardly laughed, I said, "No, I think that's it." I thought isn't that enough? I prayed and got that I was done. It felt really good to actually confess and say all of the things that I had been carrying around for all these years. My father in law without pause said, "I'm sorry, please forgive me." He teared up with real emotion. He said, "I'm guilty of all those things you said." He cried, and he made me tear up. He said, "I didn't care about you, I have no real excuse." He told me how much he loved his daughter, and that he had a certain image of who she would marry and it wasn't me. Fair enough. I was the opposite of everything he was. I wasn't flamboyant, but I was definitely proud of who I was, and I was proud that I was nothing like him. Anyway, my father in law did great. He did amazingly well. I had never seen a man be so incredibly humble, especially under criticism, I was stunned. I asked him if there was anything I had done to harm him. He said, "No, you've been great. This was all me." He owned everything, every bit of it. I was and am still am so impressed by him. I was and am so impressed by God. I had no idea that he was able to own his crap like that. It was as if in one conversation, this heavy huge weight was lifted, and he and I were extremely close, at least way closer than we had been. In one conversation the previous five or so years were wiped clean. I was able to easily forgive him for it all right then and there. This was a miracle. This was some extremely powerful supernatural craziness. I went home that day from our lunch straight to my wife, and I told her everything. She was crying. He had texted her something nice about me, before I had even gotten home. Something like that I did well at lunch and that he was impressed. I was like no, he did! He had honestly and in a real way apologized. He owned it all, everything he had said and done to cause harm. And he humbly with real humility, asked for forgiveness. I was so proud of him. I was so impressed by him and by God. I still am.

God blockers (sanchez):

One of the biggest obstacles to God can be his followers. When Mac would tell me about what was happening with his soon to be father in-law, I would be stunned. Passive aggressive jokes and pride in their 'christianity' as though it was an exclusive country club were the kind of behaviors that Mac and others used as an excuse to never know God. It would be like if members of a certain gym were all out of shape but acted prideful about their memberships. Looking at the results, no one outside would want to commit to the membership dues. Our lack of flavor in this world hurts the lost. If there is any judging to be done, leave it to God. He calls us to love our neighbors. I do agree that, in the end, each person is responsible for their response to God's revelation to them in their lives. Whether it is through nature, reasoning, miracles, etc., each person must answer to the Creator one day. However, it is very clear that we "Christians" are his ambassadors. We all (Christian and non Christian alike) affect each other's eternity. There are no neutral interactions. God forgive me for the wrongs I have done. Thank you for the good you have allowed me to do.

It's the end of the world as we know it...(sanchez):
I want to take a moment to talk about how odd it is that the "Christian" culture is fascinated with the 'end of the world'. Having been apart of church culture my whole life, I have seen this come up again and again. Revelations is very clear that no one...not even the Son of Man will know the hour. It seems prideful to believe some guy with a sandwich board figured it out before Jesus. It is blasphemy. It doesn't seem like Jesus wants us to spend a lot of time worrying about the unknown time of the Apocalypse, but would rather we keep that same train of thought while reaching out to others to tell them the

Truth. We should be desperate to save others while there is time, but not so consumed by the unpredictable event that we take our focus off serving His children. I think this is what will happen if we approach the problem from the wrong side. We should be giving swimming lessons rather than standing on the beach screaming our heads off about the dangers of the ocean. Plus, the end of the world might be tonight for you or me or anyone. Rather than worrying about the global Revelation, we can be helping lost people with their personal revelation into Truth and Love. The other side effect of focusing on the end is that some use this as an excuse to give up on the lost. Why paint a sinking boat? This gets into our thinking and service and the next thing you know...you find yourself in a dark place. You start saying to yourself, "these sinners have had more than enough time and more than enough chances to know God. If they haven't got it by now, they don't want to and they never will." You'll begin seeing your ministry as pointless and futile. You will find yourself painted into a corner where you know all the answers but you forget who He sent in this time and place. He sent you. He sent me. We are responsible for our fellow humans. Yes, the boat is sinking. It's time to start calmly giving reasoned instructions that are easy to understand and will help the most people survive the impending disaster.

You think YOU'RE upset? (sanchez):
One of the worst things anyone could say to someone who is suffering is "everything happens for a reason". I don't think most people understand how wrong and hurtful those words are. They are usually said because we want to say something, but we're not sure what to say (next time just offer them a bottle of water and ask them to share their story). The point is that this phrase is wrong on the big and little "T" truth level. I do believe God can take any situation and turn it to His glory, but I do not believe he wants sin and the broad reaching effects of sin any more than we do. There are three sources of evil. One is the devil (I am not an expert here so I will leave this one alone for now). Two is 'natural' causes. These come from the laws of the universe acting in accordance with the fallen universe. Car accidents are just that...accidents. God grieves over them just as much as us. (Can he perform miracles? Of course, but that is another topic.) I do believe there was a time when the laws of

nature obeyed man's will because our will was in alignment with God. After the Fall (we'll get to Bible stories in the next part), nature remained the same but we lost control over it because we were no longer in His will. Finally, the largest and most common source of evil is abuse of our freewill. Even evil we would attribute to the devil or nature, can sometimes be traced back to a human abusing their free will. A drunk driver, a mugger, or any number of free will agents are usually the source of evil. God would rather those people had been in His will and not committed evil. However; when we ask for all evil to be removed from this world, what we are really asking for is a world that can not exist. We are asking for a world where freewill agents have no choice but to do good. We are asking for square circles and married bachelors. I, too, have suffered in this life and prayed with so much passion for God to fix the evil being done to me or someone I love. It's easy when the pain belongs to someone else, but when it's ME...I want an exception. Especially, when I see non-believers seeming to prosper, I think, "what's the point of being your son if everyone else looks to be doing better?" Once the emotional tantrum is done, I see. This world is not my home.

I'm asking God for comfort over Truth. I'm asking him to love me less...and He won't. Not everything happens for a reason...not in the way we mean it when we say it. Everything can be turned to His glory, but we must start with our hearts turning to Him.

Sticker shock (sanchez):

I personally have never put a bumper sticker on any car I've ever owned. I don't think bumper stickers are inherently wrong, but they symbolize the idea that I can be reduced to one or two simple statements. Even the person that puts dozens of stickers on would be annoyed to find out that all we other drivers do is look at maybe one or two of the bumper stickers and then mentally say to ourselves, "yeah... whatever weirdo...". They don't even do what they are intended to do. They don't really sum up your beliefs into a simple and succinct message. I find most bumper sticker Christians are actually showing their desperate desire to convince others that they have convictions. "Real Men Pray"...did you pray about putting that sticker on your car? "My Boss is a Jewish Carpenter"...did He direct you to display that? I'm not talking about hiding your light under a bush...oh no! I mean usually the person with those stickers is so obsessed with convincing others they are with Christ that they forget or don't want to check with Christ if that's what He's called them to do. I think it's a bit of over compensation. I may lie, cheat, and steal...but hey...I have the fish on my car...that's all that matters. Let me be clear. I do believe we must fly our flags for God when directed. We must be ready to answer when called to duty. We must not be ashamed of service; however, we should be sure we are not trying to push it in people's faces just for the bragging rights. We must guard against name dropping, with some kind of weird personal pride, the name of our Savior. Putting a bumper sticker on your car and thinking that makes you a Christian is like standing in your garage and thinking that makes you a car. He is more concerned with you displaying your commitment to Him in your relationship with God and others than on your bumper.

Minister (mac):

All of a sudden everything was about getting people to Him. Every moment of every day we are either getting one another closer to Heaven or closer to Hell. The idea that everything mattered became intensified after getting to together with God.

It was as if in my truth seeking days prior to Him my actions were of an artist painting with a big messy bucket of one primary color, let's say blue. I was only really painting in broad strokes. I could only give what I had. Since I wasn't connected but was only seeking I could only 'paint' the world with this truth seeking color blue. It wasn't very accurate, it was pretty clumsy, it was messy, it wasn't very precise. It was broad stroke trying to 'help' people. Once I got 'connected' everything changed. Now I had access to all the colors and the brush I was using got a lot finer. The picture I was painting was specific and different for each individual. I was amazed at the depth and accuracy that listening and obeying the Absolute got me. It became all about walking with Him, and simultaneously ministering to others. Sanchez had been ministering to me for years while all I could do was try to help him. I didn't have the Absolute, I was lost, so all I could do was give it a random one dimensional shot at doing good or helping others. Sanchez was being called by God Himself, in very specific ways, in very specific detail to minister to me. It was all about getting me to Him. Now it was my turn. Now that I was connected to the

'Source' my job in the world became getting others to Him. That's it. I never even heard the word minister until after I found Jesus, then and only then did Sanchez share. I've used the word for years, and picked the definition up out of context. I always used it and meant it as being connected to God while trying to help others get closer to Him. It didn't always mean talking by any stretch, it just meant doing for others. Loving others. Staying connected and focused on Him while at the same time focused on someone else. When I finally looked up the definition, there are 2 that stand out. The noun that means 'a person used to deliver something, as in Angels that deliver the Divine Will' or the verb that means 'to attend to the needs of someone, as in a doctor ministers to patients by giving them the medicine they need'. Both of these are it. Sanchez had been delivering the Divine Will to me, he was attending to my needs as a non believer, trying to get me to Him. The minute I was able to get connected to the Divine Will, it was my turn. It was hard at first to minister to Sanchez himself, because, it had been so long the other way around. I was hesitant. Sanchez assured me that, no that is exactly how it works. Once we're "in", we are equals, we are true brothers. Following the Divine Will is the only thing that matters. If God wanted me to minister to him then that's what I needed to do. It's funny that Sanchez needed to minister to me about ministering to him, but that's what happened. Little did I know then, but definitely do I know now, ministering to others that are not 'connected' is heavy lifting. It's only by the Grace of God that we are able to minister to anybody else. It's only with the help of the Supernatural that we can even come close to actually ministering to anyone. Again we can only give what we ourselves possess, if we are not tied to the Holy Spirit, it is impossible for us to get anyone else to Him. Another lesson I had to learn was that everyone's journey is different. Not everyone was going to take 8 years to find him through the logical reasoned arguments that Sanchez helped through. In fact it was Sanchez who explained to me that I was the rare, weird case, there were many paths to our Creator. So we needed to be open to everything, anytime, anywhere, and to everyone. The God of the Universe wanted us all to be with Him, and that meant, we as ministers needed to meet people where they were at. The only way we could know what they needed and where they were at, was to ask the Divine Will, listen and obey. I became a doctor, a spiritual doctor with the medicine of the Divine Will. I would spend everyday since then, trying my best to lay down my will for His, and minister to any and everyone around me, however He had me do it.

After our incredible first conversation, the 'call' was to minister to my father in law. He already believed in God, but wasn't connected to Him. I spent many sessions with him in person. We spent more time talking about truth and how to find it, then we did about the Bible. My father in law had been putting the Bible, church, tithing, and his pastor above God. Over the next couple of years I met with him and brought him intense Truth. He would take what I would say back to His pastor and he would come back unconvinced. He would be with me in the moment and he would claim to understand everything clearly. He would listen make a few arguments and then agree. Then he would go to his pastor and he would come back, back in square one. He began to think that I was just a good arguer and that I should meet up with his pastor directly. He began to back out of our sessions. He came back to me with, "How do you know it's not the devil you are hearing?", or simply, "I've never heard it explained that way." These two weak objections were his way or his code for, "You go ahead with your strange opinion or interpretation of God, but I'm going to stay over here and do what I've always done." Over the couple of years I spent with him in deep ministry, I brought him CS Lewis to read, I brought him Oswald Chambers to read. I wrote up arguments using the very Scripture he worshipped to show him that I was in fact in line with Scripture and that it was he who was cherry picking. I stayed connected and gave him all the 'medicine' I was required. I even picked up golf to minister to him out on the course, but in the end he backed away. His heart hardened back to his old ways and the 'call' was to stop the intense ministry. We grew close during those years of meeting up smoking cigars and speaking about Truth and being real and following Him, but he made a choice. I learned the powerful lesson that I have learned many times since. Free will is powerful, everyone has a choice. Everyone has the potential for a soft heart or a hard heart. Everyone has the ability to get to Him directly or to run away to something else, something lesser. Sanchez said it well when he said, "God is first, and everything else is 2nd, and 2nd is infinitely far away from Him." Sanchez reminded then as he does now, even Jesus Himself in the flesh couldn't convince people of the Truth. People literally saw Him perform miracle after miracle and heard Him speak with Ultimate Authority. They heard Him and saw Him and witnessed Him speak Truth like they never had heard before. And yet they still were like, "eh, nah, not for me, unimpressed. You go ahead with your Jesus, God, Savior of the world Holy Spirit gibberish. I'm going to go back to my false idols and play in my old puke." Like a doctor that's done everything in their power to help, and his long time patient just continues to be the old stubborn mule they've always been. After years of trying, the prognosis is death, and there is nothing left to do to save him. The doctor shifts his attention from his health, and begins to talk to him about the weather and sports, as a way to comfort, rather than repair. That's what it's like between my father in-law law and me.

The Rambler (mac):

Toward the end of the couple intense years of ministry with my father in law and after many attempts by him, the 'call' was finally to go meet up with His pastor. I went with an open mind and heart, and I was prayed up and connected. I had met the pastor before he in fact was the one who married my wife and I the second time.(A story for another time). When I wrote my own vows that I received directly from God, he was very impressed. He had said that the more he read them the more he was impressed. He said they were very, very good. He was an older pastor who had pastored a small local church for many, many years. He was my wife's pastor as a kid growing up, and he was still my father in law's pastor. The 'call' for me was to try and get the pastor to see that if he was trying to convince my father in law that I was wrong then he was trying to get him further away from God. The conversation quickly turned into an interrogation. He asked me to explain just exactly what I meant by 'hearing' God. So I began to explain, but I was uncomfortable, I could feel the accusation in the question. I did the best I could staying connected and explaining what it was I was hearing. He interrupted me and said, "Everyone who heard

God in the Bible heard Him audibly" I said, "What about Jesus? He was connected always, He told us to pray incessantly. And what about the Holy Spirit, He says when He leaves He will send the Holy Spirit in His place?" His response was that, "You sound like a cult leader. Cult leaders claim to hear the voice of God." I was stunned, he went there. Wow. I said, "I am not trying to lead a cult, I am trying to follow God, and my only hope is to get other to follow Him, not me. Cult leaders want followers for themselves or claim they are the only ones that can hear Him. I want no followers, and I'm claiming anyone can hear Him." He asked, "How do you know you're hearing Him?" I said, "Reason, logic, experience, results of hearing of obeying, and faith." I asked, "how do you know you when you're in God's Will?" He seemed a bit offended, like he was the one asking questions. He said, "I have Scripture, tradition, and years of experience." I said, "You really liked, and thought it good and true, our wedding vows. Those came from the same voice as the one who has brought me here." He didn't answer, instead he shrugged and said, "Just be careful, if you're wrong you could end up in Hell." Now it was my turn to look at him crazy, I responded, "You too should be careful, because one of us is right and one of us is wrong. If I'm right, then you are the one that should be worried." That was it. I haven't seen him since. My father in law said whatever you said got him fired up, he did a whole sermon on God's Will, and wrote a blog about it. My father in law had made his choice, and I had made mine.

If looks could kill (sanchez):

I met the Rambler at the rehearsal dinner for Mac's wedding. We were lined up and about to practice walking out. This dude was dressed in jeans with a jean jacket, huge belt buckle, boots, and a cowboy hat. As a joke compliment (because I can admire someone that commits wholeheartedly to a look), I said, "look, it's the Rambler." He turned around and looked at me like he wanted to kill me. I attempted a half hearted apology because I really meant no harm, but he was having none of it. Of course, I have been instructed to forgive him and I ask for his forgiveness too. The point of the story is that this man is the type of "Christian" I have come to expect and know. If it's not directly in the Bible, they don't believe it; at least, that's what they say. Where in the Bible does it say to dress as a cowboy? So not

EVERYTHING is in the Bible. How do we navigate the nuts and bolts of life? Take for example that the Bible is about believers that had no Bible. Peter did not have the New Testament to which to refer. Paul did not have the Bible as we know it to direct him. Both Peter and Paul spend a majority of their time referring to the prompting of the Holy Spirit, being in relationship with fellow believers, and obeying God's will. Jesus tells us He will send a counselor to be with us. Even the most dedicated fundamentalist agrees that without the Holy Spirit's discernment, the Bible is a mystery. Mac's conversations with the Rambler are typical of the church today. It is like we have returned to the days of the religious leaders being more concerned with your 'bona fides' than your heart. We will listen to a man with a theology degree more than the Holy Spirit. There is a modern attempt to re-establish a priesthood that claim to be the only ones that can correctly handle the Bible. I agree that the Bible is inspired by God and is useful for instruction and edification, but in the end, God has always wanted our hearts over our knowledge. He tells us to be like children when it comes to knowing Him and obeying Him. To do so out of love and faith, rather than memorization. Heaven will be the removal of all barriers between the Trinity and our souls. May it be on Earth as it will be in heaven.

The Bible (mac):

Toward the beginning of finding God, one of the 'calls' was to read the Bible. Not skim it, not just read the New Testament, but the entire Scripture, Old and New Testament from cover to cover. So I did. I would mostly get up early, stay prayed up and connected and read. It was fascinating, strange, weird, and not what I had expected. I don't know what I had expected, but it wasn't this. This was just story after story of flawed people, stumbling through the world, and how God would interact with them. There was a lot of people doing a lot of bad things. There were kings with concubines, incest, drinking, and general craziness. There were Angels and Demons, weird miracles, amazing wonders, and entire peoples conquering and enslaving each other. There were long lists of detailed and specific rules and then pages and pages of detailed descriptions of temples and tabernacles. There were prophets running around naked proclaiming God's word, and nobody listening for years. There were poems and strange and ancient names. It was all a complete big mess of craziness. It was long, so long. Some of those books and chapters were excruciatingly boring. There were some that had beautiful wisdom and poetry written in them too. It was dense and not everything stood out as extremely meaningful. Reading it connected was like, "pay attention to this!", or "this is on!" or "remember this!", but other parts were like, "don't worry about this", or "read all of this part, but read fast." The New Testament was the same, though more dense with important parts, especially what Jesus said and did Himself. That was really 'on' as far as the connection and Truth. After the Gospels and into the early Church, it began to become more hit and miss again, where some parts were really on and others not so much. The Bible ends with the book of Revelation. That book is the craziest book of all. I could see after reading the Entire Bible how some people would gravitate toward some section, or cherry pick some verse to their liking. I could see how you could read it and find whatever you were looking for. It also became clear that the whole thing had only one point, to point us to God, that Scripture was there to get us to Him. The Bible wasn't the only way God spoke to us or used to get us to Him. The Bible itself was story after story of God using dreams, storms, prophets, Jesus, bread falling from the sky, miracles, and plenty of words, and signs to get everyone to Him. It was all about how to get to Him. It was all about how good, just and loving He was, and about how bad, awful, and scary it was to be away from Him. Some of it seemed literal and some seemed metaphorical. Things of this world are not perfect, and the Bible had the same ring of truth that all the rest of reality had. It was good and full of truth, but it wasn't Absolutely perfect. The Bible wasn't worth worshipping. If I was going to worship it, what parts would I worship? There were plenty of contradictions throughout, plenty of paradoxes. If I were to hold anyone thing higher than the rest, besides God Himself, it would be off. I had already fallen prey to that way of thinking and living before God, I wasn't about to do it again here at the Bible. Reading the Bible from front to back, only convinced me more that Sanchez had it right. That we had it right. That it was impossible to use the Bible without God first. Without being connected, who's will would be in control? It was an easy answer, my own.


Friends and family (mac):

There were people in my life that were watching me, they were interested in my journey, and ultimately in my conversion to Christianity. I had a handful of friends, fellow teachers, former students, fellow classmates, some old friends, and some new, that were interested. My immediate and extended family were watching as well, albeit from a distance. Everyone had different reactions to me finding Truth. Some, like my parents and parent in laws, were extremely happy about me becoming a believer, that is until they quickly realized I wasn't approaching this new 'way', like they were, or had. More on them later. The ones that were friends, were part of the journey and conversations, as I approached Jesus. They all became part of my ministry immediately following my accepting of Christ. Each one of their stories could and would take a long time to tell, and they have their own version of the events, I'm sure. The 'call' here is that I'm going to talk about all of them, all together, as one collection.

Even though each story is different, and each relationship is different, unique, and special, there are enough commonalities and overlaps that I can do this story justice without stepping on any one of their toes. I was called at different times, and at different levels to minister to each of them like I had my father in law. These were all grown men. They all knew me before my conversion and after. They could all observe the change in me. I didn't hide it. In fact the 'call' was often to share more than I wanted. I was 'called' to confess my lust for some of their wives for example. That was uncomfortable to say the least. I was 'called' to express my insecurities and be vulnerable. I was 'called' to use my own flaws as an example of everything I was talking about. Sanchez was part of many, but not all of the ministering that I was doing, that we were being 'called' to do. He too was 'called' to minister to some of our friends and colleagues. We would meet in my classroom and talk throughout the day. Sometimes we would meet out at my house or a restaurant or someone else's house. The only mission was to stay 'connected' to Him, and bring them closer to Him. It's a powerful and beautiful thing that happens when ministering to others, it simultaneously brings myself and them closer to Him all in the exact same moment. These were intense and amazing times. There was so much Goodness and Truth that was being discussed, that looking back I am fond and nostalgic for those times. I had imagined that we were going to be a tight group of believers. I thought we were going to have a deep long lasting bond as friends and brothers. I thought that together we would make a huge impact in the world bringing many collectively to 'the Way', to Christ. We were about to conquer the world with the help of the Almighty. I was hopeful and naive. All of things that Sanchez had done for me, we were doing for them. We were helping them with real life stuff, real talk, truth seeking, and the nitty gritty nuts and bolts of real adult life. We were ministering to them about their relationships with their wives, their kids, their other friends, and colleagues. We were helping them move homes, with home repairs, financial advice, whatever it took to be good friends. We were prayed up and moving them all to more solid ground. One of them in particular became a believer in my wake, we went up to the mountains and I was able to baptize Him. It was so special, and he too began to hear God. He too was able to minister to me. It was all going so well… until it wasn't. Each and everyone of the men that I or Sanchez and I were ministering to, almost in sync… turned and walked away. Each of them had their own rationalization, reason, or excuse. Literally, within a few months, they were all gone. Everyone had left, except my wife and kids, and Sanchez. My brother and sisters were more distant, my parents, and all of my friends. Anybody that either I, or Sanchez and I, had been 'called' to minister to, were now gone. Each one walked away, some blamed their wives, some blamed the harshness of Truth, some blamed God, some blamed their own weakness, some blamed predestination, and some blamed us or me. In all we're talking about 10 men. We aren't talking about hundreds or thousands of men. The problem is that these 10 men were all I had. They were the only people I would call friends. All at once, just like that, they all walked away. I remember asking them each individually towards the end, what I had done. Nobody had a sufficient answer. Nobody could claim that I hadn't been there for them or I hadn't spoken the truth or hadn't helped them in anyway they needed. They just left. That hurt deeply. It still hurts. It's strange. Both Sanchez and my wife stuck around. They both saw what I saw, everyone walked away, they chose to, not I. I didn't push them away, they ran away.

Sanchez and I would talk and analyze and discuss this very topic for years to come. We still do. Immediately after the words of Jesus came to mind. That He had come to divide, not unite became all too real. The separating of brothers and mother and son, hit close to home. The prophet is only without honor in their own hometown. Sanchez and I decided that they all didn't walk away from us necessarily, we saw that they in fact, had walked away from God. We also saw in each one a lie by omission. They all had been deceitful and left something out on purpose. The lie went something like, "I just want to be friends, so I will allow you to 'minister' to me, while the whole time crossing my fingers behind my back. I will pretend I understand and agree with you, but I will secretly keep my heart hard to what you are saying and doing." Literally each one had some version of this that eventually came out in the end. They all walked away. None of them wanted to look out how lost, bankrupt, and broken they were. And by default, how lost, bankrupt, and broken all of their relationships were. They didn't want to see that they were passing this their own evil ways onto their kids, wives, and other friends and families. They didn't want to bear the responsibility of life, and of the simple, yet devastating truth; that we are all leading people to Heaven or Hell every moment throughout our entire life. Sanchez and I could see the results in each of their lives, just like in our own, where not being in His Will had proven disastrous. It all came down to not wanting to see, not wanting to hear, not wanting face Him. In some way or another they decided this was all a bit too much. One indicator was that we had had to implement a 'safe' word. Sanchez and I never used, nor needed to use a 'safe' word, before them, and since them. For them though, they all needed a 'safe' word, a word they could say when the heat of truth was getting too hot. They would say 'Nantucket' to indicate for us to back off. 'Nantucket' meant that they were done, that they were mentally and emotionally at their limit. It was strange to us during the ministry, but looking back it makes a lot more sense. They were all, on some level, keeping something from us. We had learned from 'real talk', that the people who would give up, were always hiding something, or were not used to feeling the burden of their broken selves. The weight of reality was too much. We would say that it was too real for them, 'Nantucket'. Sanchez and I had been searching for the Real all along. We wanted the Real. We were desperate to know the Truth. If we were off, then we wanted to know immediately. When we found we were off, we honestly looked at it and felt it. We sat in our filth and prayed for clarity and direction. We knew the process of going through Hell to get to Him. We knew all about the burning off of the dead wood of deception and delusion. That's what we were forced to do when the 10 of them walked away. We had to face the reality of their lies and deception. We had to look long and hard at our role, if any, we had played. Burning off the impurities is painful, and this was no exception, it was hard, it still is. It's been a long hard road to realize my friends and family weren't willing to face the Truth, but were willing to sacrifice our relationship to avoid it. The more lost and living in falsity they were, the more they claimed that I had pushed them away. The closer to the Truth they were, the better they were able to admit their own fault in turning and walking away, leaving our relationship to fizzle out.

Another one bites the dust (sanchez):

I had explained to Mac that my road had been a particularly lonely one. Most people do not want to commit to God wholeheartedly. We like God as a hobby or even as a general philosophy, but not as a master or Father. I was immensely thankful that Mac had come to believe and even more astounded he was willing to live wholeheartedly for God. I had never had someone make it to step two...ever...in my life! Usually, the strain and intensity of trying to give every moment to God consciously is too much for people. Again, even I don't do it. I fail a lot. However, most people mentally try to serve God in moderation. It's the one thing He says not to do. Be cold or hot...but don't be room temperature. At first, through Mac's ministry, there were suddenly more people meeting and praying and listening for God's voice than I had ever seen. I'm sad it slowly ended. In each case, either Mac or I or both would talk with the individual and ask why. The reasons boiled down to not believing you can know God on that level and they just wanted to be friends around superficial stuff. We still know them and say "hi" and talk about work (they even slyly try insinuating that every once in awhile they 'hear the voice' before smiling and walking away). It is tough. We are not special...we don't want to be the only ones... we're writing this as an S.O.S. to find others or find out we're wrong. Hot or cold...not lukewarm.

(mac):

During this season of ministry and since, Sanchez and I looked closely at each of our own bedside manners when ministering. We looked generally at the phenomenon of bedside manner as well. We came to the conclusion, after many conversations, that bedside manner mattered, it was important, but not absolutely or more important than everything else. It was important for a doctor to understand when a patient needed more comfort or when they needed a harder reality check. The medicine or procedure might be identical from one doctor to another, but the approach or mode of the delivery of that medicine or procedure could make it easier or more difficult to take. It's the difference in ripping the band aid off quickly or slowly pulling it away. Both methods have a proper time and place, one isn't necessarily better than the other. In the end, we decided that the truth or medicine was what is most important, this was the thing that would ultimately save a life, but that it was better to go to a doctor that understood when it was time to be gentle and when it was time to be quick and to the point. As far as how Sanchez and I's individual bedside manners are, we are very different. Just like we look different, talk different, think different, dress different, have different backgrounds, and have different tastes and preferences, we also have different temperments when ministering. We could say the exact same thing (we often actually did this) in our own unique style, and the person receiving the message would hear it from me and not him or vice versa hear it from him and not me. More commonly though, they wouldn't hear it from either of us. This last option, where neither of us were successful, we realized, was the truth in almost every one that didn't take their medicine. They would blame the doctor for being too gentile or too abrasive and either way wouldn't take their medicine. This is how delivering the Divine Will turned out to be. It mattered very little that I was more passionate and abrasive or that Sanchez was more calm and gentle, the message was not heard either way. We both would pray and get that we weren't off in our approach, that we were in fact connected to Him, that indeed the Holy Spirit was working through us to bring His lost sheep to Him. Sometimes my method worked better than his or his better than mine, but more often than not, neither method worked. It didn't matter what we threw at them or how we threw it, if they had their hearts hard, and their fingers covering their own ears, and their eyes closed, they weren't going to see or hear a thing. In the end, bedside manner mattered, both Sanchez and I have different modes of ministering, the Truth mattered more than the mode, and neither can penetrate the unwillingly. Freewill is a powerful thing.

**Mary Poppins was wrong (sanchez):**
A spoonful of sugar is supposed to help the medicine go down. Mac and I discovered this is not true. My bedside manner is definitely less direct and blunt as Mac's, but it's the same message. Hear God, know God, obey God. Time after Time, someone we were ministering to would LITERALLY say, "you (Mac) are being too harsh. Sanchez says it better" or "you (Mac)

are right" and they would cry and go away and not come back. The point is that no matter how the medicine tasted, in the end, they didn't believe they were that sick...if at all! Except for hypochondriacs, no one would take medicine for a disease they didn't have. Imagine someone going through the difficulty of radiation treatment and they didn't have cancer...that's insane! So really, in the end, we have to come to realize how sick we really are in order to accept that we need medicine. Then we can work on the flavor. But, blaming the physician's assistant for not having bubble gum flavored penicillin and refusing to take the medicine when you are deathly ill, is even more insane.

Church (mac):

Another 'call' I received early on was to attend church. Not just any church, not the church that I would've picked. No the 'call' was to attend the exact same church that my wife had already attended. The megachurch in the wealthiest part of our area. The one I had hated on for years. The very same church that my wife's family had taken me and had plopped me right in front for me to suffer at the highest level possible. Each weekend my wife and I would pray and get the 'call' to go to a service, either on Saturday evening or Sunday morning. This church had lots of services throughout the weekend, it was and still is, extremely popular. It was interesting because the 'call' more often than not was to attend the service without my wife's family. Sometimes we brought our two older boys and they went to the children's play area, but mostly it was just my wife and I. It was like a little date night. There were obvious differences on my returning to this same church that had proven to be such a disaster the first time around. Obviously one major change, was that I was 'connected' and it was the 'call'. Being 'called' to do something is way different than choosing to do that very same thing on my own. Completely and utterly different. There is generally a deep surreal peace and comfort when following the 'call'. The external world often gets more uncomfortable when following Him, while internally my world gets more peaceful. It's almost as if the more uncomfortable it gets on the outside, the more uncertain I am of myself, the more I have to lean on Him. It's a strange and interesting paradox in my journey. Before Christianity I spent a lot of my life avoiding uncomfortable, external situations, my insides were always full of emotion and turmoil. I was constantly over thinking things and worrying about too many details. I was always on guard in public spaces. I was on heightened awareness and defense in crowds. Even in restaurants I always had to sit with my back away from any potential threats. Places with large crowds, like the megachurch, concerts, fairs, and shopping malls, gave me anxiety. (Unless I was drinking or on drugs, then I would be the one making others nervous.) So I spent my days avoiding crowds as much as possible. Instead I would spend my time engaged in a highly focused activity like scrambling, playing music, tattooing, building, creating etc. Anything that was not too focused on lots of people. I still have that in me, it is part part of me, it's part of who I am. There are reasons for my crowd avoidance that I won't go into here, but I will say that some fairly dangerous and traumatic things have happened to me in crowded areas. Anyway once I started listening and following the voice, there was an immediately calming presence inside of me. A deep trust and bond with the Absolute. I trusted that He would lead me down the right path, and as long as I got out of the way, obeyed the 'call', stayed 'prayed up,' and 'connected,' everything would be fine. Everything would be better than fine, everything would be the very best it could possibly be. Even if I died, I thought, at least I would die holding the Hand of the Creator. Now that I was armed with this new shield of faith, belief, and deep comfort, now that I was in the Divine Will, my anxiety associated with crowds dissipated to a vague and distant memory. Going to malls when it was the 'call' actually became enjoyable. I can't say that attending church was always enjoyable but it was sometimes, and at least it wasn't like that first time, unbearingly uncomfortable.

The first thing that my wife and I did differently when we attended a service, is that we sat toward the back, just the two of us. It was nice, like a little date. One of the first things I noticed, was the wide variety of people at this megachurch. I had expected them all to be a certain type. You know, extremely well dressed and attractive, young and overly energetic, and outwardly proud of their Jesus. There was some of this for sure, but sitting in the back, being able to observe the people from a comfortable distance proved to be eye opening. My newly found connectedness to the Absolute, along with my wife being by my side, allowed my guard to be lowered and my attention to focus outward. When I had attended the same church before, not connected, lost, and sat with my back to the crowd, I was inwardly focused. My demons had been eating my insides alive, I was focused on the gnashing of teeth. This time around, I could actually see and hear, and it wasn't so bad. It also wasn't the best thing ever. I wasn't and still am not overly impressed by it, but at least I could see it for what it was, and more importantly in this case, what it wasn't. The pastors were good in general, the messages were a mixed bag. There was a lot of sales pitch type of services. It always seemed like they were overly excited about the next big thing 'God' was doing in their church. They used the same NIV Bible I was used to, which was nice. In fact they handed out brand new ones to you when you walked in. Actually they handed us all kinds of junk mail. Super nice glossy pamphlets and brochures, describing the lesson of the day, upcoming events, and of course a tithe envelope. We were 'called' to participate in tithing too. We would pray before each service and ask, what, if any we ought to tithe. We would get the 'call' and stop by the atm on the way to church. It was easy, we had no issue with tithing, I still don't. Every service, everybody got special glossy handouts. I always thought it to be such a waste, we just threw them out when we got home. Not the Bibles of course, just all the frilly papers. Every once in a while the church would have a guest speaker, doing the megachurch circuit tour. That was interesting, the variety of different approaches to Christianity was in one way unsettling, but in a surprising way more comforting. Everyone was attempting to figure this thing out. There is a pretty incredible depth in Christianity that I was unaware of before coming into it. The variety of speakers, and preachers, and stories of just how much Christ had worked miracles in people's lives was overwhelming. The music at this church was at a very high quality contemporary Christian pop level. Full stage, professional lighting, amazing band with singers, guitarists, bass players, drummers, and back up singers. You name it they had it. My wife loved the music. I was impressed by the quality of production, but not necessarily all the music. Some of it admittingly was really good in message and in sound, but nothing so much that I wanted to listen to it outside of church.

(Thankfully I haven't gotten that call.) It was also pretty powerful to hear the entire crowd sing, and 'worship' together. I personally could've done without it, but it was pretty obvious to see how effective it was for my wife and many others. I would pray and get up and go through the motions, but mostly I just felt a bit awkward, and would have preferred to stay seated, but what do I know. The 'call' was most of the time, but not always, to get up and participate, so I did. I guess what I'm getting at, is that church, tithing, the music, and the pastors, the whole thing wasn't as bad as I had thought, and there was definitely some good aspects of it, but it didn't necessarily get me any closer to Him. I mean anytime I listen and obey, I am attempting to seek His Will, so in that way I was getting closer to Him, but there are other ways for me that are easier or that I had a stronger connection to Him. For example, writing this book, or ministering to my friends and family, or during our time as law enforcement community chaplains, or simply mowing the lawn or taking a shower, all have proven to get me closer to Him. That's my goal most of the time, when I'm not being a coward, is to get closer to Him.

I was humbled in many ways by attending the mega church, but I also received during multiple services, when I prayed, that parts of the message were 'off'. It seemed like at times they were leading people to the Bible, or to the church, rather than to God Himself. I want to be clear here, that they often did great job. All of the pastors and speakers and worship leaders had amazing true things to say. More times than not the message was on point. Other times though, the message missed the mark. One time in particular stands out. This time it was the best most popular pastor who gave the sermon. This pastor was popular for a reason, he was funny, entertaining, spoke well, was passionate, was self effacing, and humble, and he loved Jesus. He loved what he did, and he was proud in the right way to do it. His sermon on this particular weekend was to have everyone in the church go home, bake cookies, and then deliver those cookies to their neighbor. While giving their neighbors the cookies, the whole church, everyone was to invite their neighbor to church the following weekend. It was a cute, cheeky, and funny way to get more people in the doors of the church. I prayed and got that it was 'off', and to not make any cookies, or invite anyone to church. At the time my friend and his wife were attending the same church and had heard the same sermon. This was one of the men that I had ministered to heavily. In fact, this was the one friend, that I had personally baptized. The following Monday after the cookie sermon, my friend told me about his prior evening. He said his wife was stressing out, trying to make cookies for their neighbors. He said that their dinner and evening were ruined, because of the craziness his wife was doing trying to obey the pastor. She ended up delivering the cookies and inviting her neighbors to church, but their home was in strife. My response was usual and simple. I asked if she had prayed about that? I asked if he had prayed about helping her? This one example had many truths in it. One is that the church were getting people to obey the pastors rather than obey God. Two is that my friend didn't pray about helping his wife. Three was that she didn't pray about whether she ought to bake cookies. And four, this was foreshadowing the lie and betrayal my friend would ultimately commit. He was to mine and Sanchez's face, saying 'yes' he understood and believed and was himself following Jesus as we were, but in reality he was going home to his wife and allowing her to rule the nest. However, It seemed like the church was at least partially to blame for the cookie fiasco at my friend's house. I heard first hand what following anything but Him would lead to. I saw the harm it caused. I prayed and got the 'call' to reach out to the most popular pastor at the megachurch. Crap.

I emailed the pastor, and waited for a reply. His secretary got back to me. It took many emails back and forth to finally get an appointment. He was trying to get me to see a lower level pastor. It wasn't the 'call', so I persisted. An unusually long and tiresome email chain, finally resulted in a meeting. The appointment I got was for between services for a few minutes out in the seats. It was all so bizarre. It seemed obvious that I was purposely squeezed in, so that he had a way out. I get it, I was just one of many that wanted his time. It still felt like I was a burden or a hassle to him and the church in general. Such a burden that I had to be scheduled in the most awkward sliver of time as humanly possible to meet but to not disrupt a thing. I had had better success emailing and reaching my favorite atheist public intellectual, MIT professor Noam Chomsky than I had reaching my own pastor. Anyway the day finally arrived, only a few months later than I had expected. I was nervous and excited. I had 3 things I was to tell him. (I had the longest time in the history of mankind to prepare for this meeting.) We met shook hands and sat. I got right to it. He was friendly and kind. I told him I was a bit nervous to be talking to the head honcho, and he tried calming me down by saying, "I'm just a man like you." So I said, "I've been praying and I got the "call" to tell you three things. First, thank you for seeing me and for all that you do. Second, well done,( this was the second well done I was able to give and I was proud to give it.)" I continued, "Well done bringing people to Him. From God He wants you to know well done. Finally that cookie sermon was off." I paused, his face began to change. I continued, "Maybe you ought to get people to Him, rather than get people to obey you or the church." His whole demeanor changed. He looked disgusted. The kind smile was gone. The offended pastor was now sitting in front of me. He said, "I think people are too inwardly focused, so I'm going to continue to get them to be outwardly focused." Then he asked, "What would you have me do? What solution do you have?" I said, "I don't know the 'call' is to say direct them to Him. Have them pray and find out if thats what they are to do. Like check to see if 'go make cookies' is the 'call'." I said, "Pray about what to say, or whether I'm on or off. I'm telling you that I got 'called' to come here and tell you, that's what I get." He shortly and defiantly said, "I will, I will pray about it." He then asked, "Is that it?" I said, "yes." He said, "Why couldn't you have just emailed me?" I said that, "It wasn't the 'call'." That was it, the conversation lasted maybe five minutes. Then his 'nice', 'kind' face came back on, as he shook my hand, and hurried away. Blink, blink, what just happened? Everyone that I was close to knew that I had to meet up with him, it had been a long drawn out ordeal, that I was nervous about. I came back and told them all the story. It was clear that the pastor wasn't connected to God all the time, like I was trying to be. He obviously prayed and was doing something right. His reasoning though was flawed. His claim that people were too inwardly focused, was generally true, but it couldn't be an absolute. Here was the pastor of the church, putting a platitude way up too high. He was doing what I had done before Christ, he was putting things out of place. The problem is that even if it was absolute, on our own we wouldn't be able to find the right outward focus. Surely though there are at least sometimes the 'call' might be inward. He might 'call' us to self reflection and/or self correction. I mean just in my friends example of the cookies, it might've been the 'call' to not bake cookies and to stay in for the night and focus on her own family. It seems so obvious that baking cookies and inviting people to church or getting everyone to think of others is not the absolute. This line of thinking seemed much more like the modern self help gurus. It was a perversion of ancient wisdom. It was the white knuckling our way through life. Christianity was admitting defeat, it was realizing that no matter what we pick, if it isn't God, then we were doomed to fail. If we weren't submitting our will and living through the Holy Spirit, we were doomed for death. If all we needed were a few platitudes, then what was the point of all this anyway. I could have easily stayed a non believer if this were the case. I was good at picking platitudes to live by. The problem was that I had tried my best, I was the best at picking a quote to live by and throwing myself head first into it. Every time there would be the taste of ash left in my mouth, from a platitude not being able to sustain me through any number of life's complexities. That is one of the many factors in me laying down my life and allowing Jesus to enter in my place, that crap just didn't work. Period.

Eventually the call was to stop attending church, we tried a smaller church once, and I was shocked at how much worse it was compared to the megachurch. The megachurch was better. Who woulda thought? Not me. Anyway like I said eventually the 'call' was to stop attending church all together and also to stop tithing. We got the 'call' that all our money was His money, so we needed to be praying about every penny we spent. We needed to direct our funds through His always. We needed to direct everything through Him, always. It made sense, rather than giving Him just 10%, we ought to give Him everything. Rather than giving Him an hour a week on Sunday, we ought to give Him every moment, everyday, all week. Some of the people watching our journey, pretty much every other Christian that we knew, besides Sanchez, had an issue with this. They would all say some variation of, but the Bible tells us we ought to tithe and go to church. My response was something like we're called to be a part of the Church, not a church. We are called to be a part of the body of Christ. What we call the Church, that is every Christian ever. We aren't called to attend a little church necessarily. Besides Jesus Himself said whenever two or more meet in my name I will be there. Anytime I was meeting with anyone it was in His name. I was 'called' to, so I was always at 'church' in that way. The tithing argument I already made, all of my money wasn't mine, it was all His. So anytime I was spending any of it, it was because of Him and for Him.  I'm not here claiming that all Christians leave church and stop tithing. I'm here claiming that those are not to be worshipped or held as absolutes. Jesus was clear about this. The story of the good samaritan was about doing 'good' regardless. Jesus spoke about taking care of any strife you have with a fellow believer even before approaching the altar. He was clear that He was the Way, not church, or tithing. Jesus spent many times in the temples battling the 'church' officials, with working and doing good works on the Sabbath. He wants our hearts and minds at all times. He was clear that the greatest commands were to love God and love others. Those two were the ones that every other law and command fell under. The only way that makes sense in how to uphold those commands is to stay connected to God. Every other method will lead to some human error to some lesser human will. Even with the best 'intentions, we will still miss the mark. He was clear that the gate was narrow. Either God is the Absolute or He isn't. Everything else is second. Infinitely second, including but not limited to: the Bible, church, and tithing.

A recipe for disaster (sanchez):

The call for me is to attend church. It's not always to attend church. Sometimes it's to attend a family function out of town or go on vacation with the family. Notice, that other "Christians" may do this, but if they didn't pray about it, then they are outside of God's will. I know many will judge Mac for not attending church. They will point to the Bible and to tradition and other evidence that he should be attending church. If church were an absolute, then no reason would be acceptable for 'missing'. You don't get to go on vacation or be sick or take care of your family. It would be like the parable of the Levite or the priest in the Good Samaritan. You would be so concerned with going to your religious ceremony that you are willing to ignore the person in need right in front of you. This person may be you or your wife or your kid or any number of people. Again, if God is calling you to go to church, then go in His will. You have to, but reserve your judgement on those that are called not to go. Again, this is assuming they are called to not go. This is different than being lazy or trying to disobey. In our cases, I must go...Mac does not...so far. Even if you have the prideful honor of saying, "I've never missed a day of church in my life".

Great...but if God was trying to call you somewhere else one of those Sundays...you sinned. Jesus was in the desert for 40 days and nights. No church. Paul on his island prison. No church. Christians throughout history that were persecuted and hunted. No church. Not the way we think of it. We know man was made for the Sabbath, not the Sabbath for man. Jesus tells us who wouldn't go out and save their farm animal even if it was the Sabbath. When He says "church" He is very explicitly referencing the body of believers. Never once is He referring to a particular branch or building. Once more, I do believe if God is calling you to attend church, you must and you should with a joyful heart. However; it must also be held in its proper place below God.

In fact, it is the blind devotion to church and the Bible that leads to cults. It's the Holy Spirit that protects us from being led astray. Cult leaders and the devil can use church and Bible to trick "Christians" because they place them both above the Trinity. Even if all a leader does is convince a congregation to make cookies for their neighbors, if this was not God's will then it is sinful. Anything outside of His will is death.

Too high or too low (mac):

This is a good place to talk about one of the major lessons and themes I have learned and realized after I found Him. (or He found me, there's a certain mystery how much of that was me and how much was Him). The lesson is that without Him, I was, and we are all putting things either too high or too low in our lives. We all are flawed. We all have baggage. We all fall victim to culture and the 'times' we're living in. We all have tastes and preferences. We're all trained to care about what we think, what our opinions are, what we feel, what our passions are, etc. We can all relate to growing up and realizing what we liked as a child has changed. We can see that as a child we had lower or different tastes and preferences than we do now. Now as an adult, some of the things we once hated, we now enjoy. Like maybe wine, or smelly cheese, or we once loved driving, now we can't stand it etc. Well once I got with God, He helped me realize that I had been doing this as an adult with everything. I was misplacing and mistaking 'things' true value or worth. I was relying way too much on my flawed self to place a figurative price tag of things. With people, places, objects, music, food health, etc., they all were either overpriced or underpriced in my life according to me. I was learning with that when I had ranked things in life as 'important' or 'unimportant' that I was almost always 'off' in some way. Usually, but not always in some major ways.

I already mentioned crowded places that I had placed too low, and because I placed them too low, I wasn't able to see the benefits or goodness that crowded places actually had. The same thing happened with music, I had placed it too high, the 'call', once I began listening to Him, was to sell all of my musical equipment. With tattooing the 'call', instead of giving it away or selling it, was to throw that equipment away in the garbage. Both were hard in their own way, but either God was right or I was. With His help I could see that I had been placing tattoos too high in my life. I had been getting tattooed, and then giving homemade tattoos, for over ten years of my life at that point. Upon reflection and praying tattooing had been a way to mark permanently, on a temporary body, some deep meaning, that wasn't Him. It was basically pictorial representations of my idols. I don't think God likes tattoos in general. I think the act of tattooing and the motivation and intention behind it misses the mark. I think when we are getting tattooed we are all on some level saying, "fuck it". Whenever we say this to ourselves or out loud, I'm pretty sure we are really saying, 'fuck God'... I think that we all are trying, in some way when we get tattooed, to put an idol on our skin, even if it's the cross or His name. It's the same phenomenon when somebody over emotionally proclaims their love and loyalty for you. Sanchez and I have discovered that this is often a 'tell' or an indicator of the exact opposite being true. The person displaying over confidence in an overly emotional way, is in reality showing their lack of confidence it that very thing. Tattoos are somehow this way, they are a combination of an exaggerated emotional claim to something, coupled with an implied, 'fuck it'. I think that, at the very least, they are a 'cultural' thing that people are not being 'called' to do. I can't say any of this for sure, but I know for me my tattoos are definitely a real lack of confidence in whatever they represent, an oversell of my own loves or loyalties, if you will. They are equally a 'fuck it' (albeit unknowingly) to God, and clear markings of my past lost self. No matter what the reason for your tattoo, if you weren't being 'called' to it, your reason is off.

Music was similar to tattoos for me, but not exactly. In general I think music is more of a neutral medium like painting, than tattooing is, I already explained why tattooing, in and of itself, is not a neutral medium. Music is different in that, the Source of Music is God, so making music can be made in a 'good' way. It depends what's in your heart and soul, and whether you're being 'called' to it, just like tattooing, but it differs from tattooing in that, you actually can glorify God through music. For me I had definitely worshipped music itself, as if it was an end in itself. Like tattooing I had been playing music for well over ten years by the time I found God. It held a higher place for me than did tattooing. Music was probably the biggest idol I had worshipped until then. I had sought answers through music and had placed it very high in my search. Like everything else before Him, I missed the mark. Music had helped me express my darkness and let out my lostness, in a 'healthy' way. In reality placing so much of my life on music was unhealthy, but at it wasn't physically unhealthy like drugs. Which made it easier to worship, because music was 'good' for me. Music had helped me to bare my brokenness, but it was a band aid over a wound, or weak substitute for the real thing. It wasn't sustainable. It wasn't holding me up like I had thought, it was holding me back. No matter what we use to prop up our soul or our life, if it isn't God it won't last. The props we pick only clutter up our life and end up acting as chains and stumbling blocks on our way to the Source. God is the only proper true piece we are missing deep within. We get the urge to seek the key to our lock and we settle on any key before we reach the only one that works. Once I found Jesus, He wanted all of me. He needed to help me first see the clutter in my soul, that I had created trying to find Him. After He showed me the clutter, He then asked me to hand them to Him one by one. Some of what I gave Him, He gave right back, but now in its proper place, like my family. Others like music, He had me walk away from for a time. And still others, like tattooing, He had me stay away permanently. God needed to make room for other things, so He asked me to sell my musical instruments and equipment. So I sold it all.

God was literally and spiritually cleaning House. Scrambling, I had placed too high, building too low. I had placed food and health too high, I had put exercise and healthy eating too high in my life. I cared too much about physical health and not nearly enough about spiritual health. It was time to let that go. It was time to hand all of me, all of my health to Him. He then showed me over the next few years, that I had put too much emphasis what fed me physically and not nearly enough on what fed me spiritually. He showed me it was better to be physically unhealthy, than to be spiritually unhealthy. God would provide both, He would provide the 'food' to sustain my life in every way. All I had to do is let Him. 'Man does not live on bread alone', I was unaware of how starved my spirit had actually been until He began to feed me.

Since then He has given some things back that He originally took away. Always with whatever He gives me I must keep a light grip. He might want it back. I find that I am like a child and I only have room for so many things at once. God wants to take something away so that He can give me something better, but I am reluctant. I hold on tight an defiantly say, "mine." He will persist in showing me the things that I try and hold onto too tightly. The only thing He wants us too hold tight is Him.  He is either the Absolute or He is not. Anything else I place too high or too low is off. It's my will, not His. I had been placing reason too high, gripping it too tightly. I have had to continually battle that one, letting my own reason go, so that He could hand me faith. A stronger faith in His Reason, a stronger faith in Him. I had been putting my intelligence too high, and had to be shown my arrogance. I wasn't as smart as I thought I was. I shouldn't be placing others intelligence that low nor mine that high.  We are all stupid when it comes to Him. I had been placing my mechanical and building skills too low, He had to show me I could do a lot more. I could not only repair small and large engines, appliances, tools and equipment, and build and repair houses, but I was good at it. I was good with my hands and mind working together. I in general had put manual labor too low, that was partly thanks to my dad who placed college and mental work too high because he struggled in the back breaking construction industry for 30 years. He had placed working with his hands too low and passed that on to me. He is really good with his hands and mind too, but never honored those skills because school had made him feel dumb. It turns out I'm good at working with my hands, and I enjoy it.

I had placed my use of language too low, and cursing too high, or not low enough. I knew that what came from our hearts and out our mouth would defile me, and I was speaking from my heart in truth. I was being too free with cursing. I had been so used to cursing that I didn't realize how loose my tongue had become. My heart was good but the language I used to express it was too vulgar. Sanchez had to minister to me about my cursing, he simply had to tell me to pray about it. Sanchez explained that it might become a stumbling block for some if my tongue was too loose. He was right, when I prayed, I got to reign it in. It was vulgar, but that wasn't the problem, the problem is that it had become a habit that I wasn't fully conscious of and therefore didn't have full control over. For a time, I gave it up. Eventually God gave it back. Just as too loose of a tongue can be a stumbling block for some, so too can too tight of a tongue. Only running my words through Him can I get it right. God doesn't put cursing as low as some people might think. In my journey with Him, He has shown me that what is in my heart when I curse is what matters not cursing itself. When He gave it back, again I ran too far ahead of Him with it. I was cursing too freely, not staying prayed up. I was cursing out of anger or using it too flippantly. It was easy to fall back into old habits. He had to remind me to bring it back, to speak more carefully, to stay prayed up with Him.

I had put myself and my feelings too high without Him, and those around me too low. How was I to help anyone if my starting point was their inferiority somehow? I thought, I was gross, but I wasn't the grossest. I was bad, but not the worst. I had to be shown my filth up close and personal. I had to realize I was in fact worse than those around me. I had potential to be great through Him, but only if I laid my gross ass down.

Without God, I had put platitudes and life lessons way too high, I needed to stop saying them and stop caring about them. I had even put small 't' truth too high, I needed to put big 'T' Truth where it belonged, at the top. With Him I realized, sometimes it was better to keep my mouth shut, than to speak. Sometimes it was better to not give an answer, even though I knew it. Sometimes it was better not to correct, even though they were in error. God only knew what those around me needed from me, more times than not it was less than I thought. Either way I was 'off' the mark, I needed to stay close to Him, if I was too have a chance at helping others.

I had been putting my job way too high, it turned out that I was causing more harm than good trying to 'help' these kids. By trying to help them without being connected, I was actually harming them. The 'call' was way different than I had expected. I needed to be doing way less with the students, not more. I needed to shut up and teach math. I needed to stop being so relatable, so cool, and so personal with them. I needed to stop getting close to them and acting like their friend. I needed to stop giving them advice and life lessons. I was putting teaching way too high, school in general way too high. We as teachers and administrator were causing harm than good. We were missing the mark. I want to be clear here that not every single adult is harming kids, but most of us, and especially me were. We are an authority and we have power and we're corrupt. Only being connected to the Absolute could I see how often I had let my authority and power blind me. I needed to remove myself from the front and center position, and just stay out of the kids way. Teaching was just a job, I had been making it for years more than that. I had been placing its importance way too high. I had been trying to save the world through teaching, trying to force my will upon them. God told me to 'chill out' in a major way. I needed to put school way lower, in almost every way. Formal education, the entire system from Kindergarten to higher education was being placed too high by me and everyone else. The entire system was doing more harm than good, and I was apart of it. I don't mean that education and learning are bad in and of themselves, I mean that the way our system does it is wrong. This could be the subject of an entirely different book, and maybe it will be, so I will have to cut it short here. I just want to say that in the institution of organized education there is a major perversion that is unavoidable. It takes what should be an end it itself, that is a way to discover God's greatness, and perverts it to a means to something less. It bastardized and separates the true purpose of learning to some other less important and filthy end. It's like sex without the commitment of marriage, it takes something that ought to be sacred and pure and changes it into something less and perverse. Just as the institution of slavery is wrong so is the institution of formalized public education. There is good to be done within the institution of slavery but the underlying harm it causes outweighs the small good that can and does happen at the local level. I'm sure this needs more explanation, and that leaving this at an end here will make some of you want to squirm in your skin, but I must.

My worst misplacing errors were in people, I had placed some people too high and others too low. I had automatically put sales people too low, when many didn't deserve it. Some sales people had a real gift for it, and they were more important and useful than I had realized. It pains me to admit, but once I found God I quickly realized I had been placing my wife and kids too low. But especially my wife. I didn't trust her enough. I didn't include her in enough of the decisions about our life. I didn't give her enough responsibility. I blamed her too much and too easily, for things that weren't to belaid at her feet. I didn't honor her enough. My kids too were misplaced in my life. I was too annoyed by them, too harsh on them, and too angry with them. I didn't play with them enough. I wasn't taking fatherhood as seriously enough in the right places, and I was taking it too seriously in the wrong places. I was all around misplacing everything regarding the family that I was leading. By putting God first, He helped me to clean up the mess I was making and to put everything in its proper place. In my small immediate family is where I have felt the biggest most consistent change and connection with Him over the years. How I interact with my wife and kids, and how we all interact with each other has proven to be so much better and right and good and amazing and unexpected with Him. His presence has blessed every relationship within my household by an incomprehensible magnitude. There were times that I had to confess gross things to my wife and it would hurt her, but God would bring us closer. Often I needed to just be quiet and wait until my wife was ready. My job was to get her to God. Her job was to first get to Him, then help our family get to Him. When she got 'connected' everything changed for the better. Our purpose changed. Our burden was lifted and lightened. We had the gift of the Supernatural Holy Spirit in our lives. She got more responsibility with the houses finances and shopping. I was able to let go of many of the household responsibilities and burdens I had been carrying and keeping from her, while at the same time was given more responsibility in raising our kids. He in no small way saved our marriage. He directly lowered the amount of strife and grossness in our home. My kids could tell too. I had to stop calling them nicknames and names in general, I had to start playing with them more, and honoring them more. I prayed with them, and I told them about God. They witnessed the change He had made in me, they still talk about how sudden and drastic it all was. They trusted me more because I in turn trusted God.

They felt safer and more able to talk to me. They were stoked when God led me to take them to ice cream, and in return they understood easier when God was like it's not. I placed my burden on Him and He took it, just like He said He would. It was way lighter in our home after Him. It was more important though how we treated each other, it got stricter in not allowing for evil to seep into our home and hearts. There was a new huge emphasis on owning our transgressions against each other, apologizing, and forgiving each other. Before God I rarely apologized, after Him we all apologize, all the time. It's not that we got worse, in fact we are all way better. We treat each other way better, it's just that we now are able to see the plank in our own eye. It's amazing how getting with Perfection allows you to see how imperfect we actually are. Our home and my family is a good, safe place. Its not complete chaos and it's not overly ordered either. It's not perfect by any means, but it's infinitely better than it was. My family, my home, and my relationship with my wife and kids have proven to be the biggest and clearest ministry and miraculous change since finding him, without comparison

Even Sanchez got put in his proper place in my life. In some ways I putting him too high, and in others too low. I turns out that I had to honor him more as a friend, and in fact recognize that he was my best friend, and really truly my only friend. I also had to lower him as my spiritual teacher, and at the same time give him more credit as a logician. I needed to rely on my own connection with God and not his. Sanchez had carried me long enough I needed to trust my connection more than I trusted Sanchez and his connection. It was the only way to remain on equal footing. I needed to be fully reliant upon God in order to help and minister to Him, and Sanchez needed to do the same for me. As a logician and clear thinker, I needed to put him even higher. I knew he was good, but with God He showed me that Sanchez had a real gift in the world of reason. Sanchez is paradoxically horrible at local earthly directions but amazing at the direction of Truth. He can reason and use logic quickly and efficiently like no other. I am good, but he is great. Part of what threw me off before God about Sanchez is that he is an english teacher, where as I am a math teacher. I was always under the misconception that mathematicians were better logicians by default. I have come to realize that this is wrong. In english, literature, and philosophy is where the best reasoning and reasoners need to exist. It is in these arenas, dealing with man and his complexities that the higher intelligence is needed. In math or mere symbolic logic, we are dealing with literally less moving parts and therefore less complex problems. In math the problems might be long and in that way complicated, but there are not dealing with the soul of man like Sanchez and CS Lewis were dealing with. Also it seems the stakes are much lower when solving problems in math in relation to solving the problems of being itself. Even in applied math if we were to miscalculate, say the building of a bridge. The worst that can happen is the death of a handful of people. In comparison, if we miscalculate the story of Man's existence in the universe, we could lead an endless number of souls to eternal death. The complexities, subtleties, nuances and problems of real life are a laughably great distance away from the puniness of math. Sanchez has honed his skills using the fields of english, religion, and philosophy. Through God I had to realize I had been fiddling around in mathematics not realizing I was in a field that gave me false security in my ability to reason. I had to play catch up to Sanchez in the field of reason, I still in many ways do. I needed to realize he was better than I was at reasoning, that he had a gift, and that I should feel lucky to be able to learn from him, not frustrated at myself for not being his equal in that way. I guess that means I was putting my own skills, gifts, and talents too low or too high. More than that, because I spent so long being lost, I just didn't know what they were. I still don't. Maybe this book will shed some light.

Antique roadshow (sanchez):

If you've ever watched a show where people bring in items to be appraised, it is a mixture of sad, funny, and astounding. One person comes in and believes they have a priceless piece of American history...only to discover it's worthless. Another comes in with something they found while cleaning out their parent's attic and find out it's worth an incredible amount of money. Notice, the person that brought it in had no idea (good or bad) what they had. It took an expert in the field to point out what makes it worth what it's REALLY worth. This is how it is when we put anything too high or too low without God telling us. We may think, "Really, you want me to just sit here and watch a movie with my family? I could be out making money or saving lives or winning souls to the kingdom!" But what would it matter if you saved the whole world...and lost your soul? This is what being outside of God's will does. You could move mountains or raise the dead or heal the sick and none of it would matter if that's not what He's calling you to do. We rarely have any idea how valuable or meaningless any action, word, or state of being is. How could we? It would take an entity capable of seeing all of infinity to judge each moment. This is why following God moment to moment is so important. We can't simply randomly choose actions based on culture, tradition, or whim and then hope He blesses them. Again, I think God can turn anything to His glory, but He would rather we trust and obey.

Prophecy (mac):

I've reached a point where it's time to talk about a subject I don't necessarily want to talk about, but it's the 'call', so I must. Prophecy. When I look it up, it simply means someone who communicates with God, someone who has a message from God. So in that way, what this entire book has been about, is that we are all called to be prophets. We all have access to the voice of

God. That through Jesus, the Holy Spirit can and does act as a mediator between us and the Divine Will. With this use of the word prophecy I have no issue. The type of prophecy that I'm going to talk about here is different. I am talking about the kind of prophecy where God tells us about the future, what will come. First, is it even possible to prophecy in this way? If you've made it this far and think it impossible, then you probably should stop. Maybe if you've made it this far you're still on the fence and unsure if this is at all possible. Or obviously you've made it this far and trust that it is entirely possible. Either way, here goes some more. If God is Supernatural, He is outside of nature. He therefore is outside of space and time, and can easily see the beginning of time as well as the end of time. In fact, He can see all of space and time, just as an author can see their entire book laid open in front of them. Since God is infinite, He has an infinite amount of time for each of us individually. He is also all powerful so he can perform any number of miracles. The Bible is full of prophets, angels, and miracles alike. So here goes my own story of prophecy.

Very shortly after finding God, I was out mowing the lawn, communing with Him as I was beginning to get used to. I was still very amazed at the whole thing, I was happy to be in tune with the Almighty. I was drawing nearer to Him as He was to me. I have found that there are actually levels of closeness to Him. There are obviously times when we are not near Him, the more in sin, the more we gnash our teeth, the more we are doing wrong, the more stubborn we are, and the harder our heart is, the further we get from Him. The same phenomenon happens in reverse. The more I lay my life down, the more I open my heart, the more I care only about Him, the tighter I hold onto Him, the more I seek His Will, and the more in love with Him, the closer we get to Him. This is in a big way how eternity will be. Without the physical limitations of our own reality, we will either be drawing nearer to Him, or further from Him... for eternity. Anyway, I'm mowing the lawn drawing nearer to Him and I get the 'call' that my wife's pregnant. I get the 'call' to stop mowing and walk into the house and tell her she is pregnant. I get the 'call' to tell her not to worry, and that we're having a girl.... Pause... blink, blink, um?! My wife wasn't showing any signs of being pregnant. My wife wasn't feeling in anyway pregnant. There was no evidence whatsoever to make her or I think this that we were having a baby. I double, triple, and quadruple checked the 'call', it was clear. I walk into our house and have my wife sit at our kitchen table. I hold her hands and tell her what God told me. She was stunned and shocked and began to tear up. It was heavy and strange. She quickly went out to get a pregnancy test. She took it, the results were negative. Confusion. It was January. She kept taking those tests every few days. Negative, negative,...negative. Until a month or so later, she got one that said positive. Excited. Relieved. Nervous. We schedule an appointment with her doctor, and her doctor confirms she is indeed pregnant. Now I'm anxiously waiting for the ultrasound date that tells us the sex of our baby. It's weeks away. My wife makes a special appointment for mothers day, for both our moms to come see what the sex is. It's one of those fancy ultrasound places that do a 3D, high definition, ultrasound, that are clearer and nicer than the usual black and white, 2D version. We were all nervous and excited, I was too, but most certainly to see if I was hearing God or just fooling myself. I really didn't care what the sex was personally, I just wanted a healthy baby. I only cared to prove if the 'call' was right or not. When the technician said, "It's a girl!" Phew, I could stop holding my breath like I had been for weeks leading up to this point. Amazing. Our daughter was born in October. God had let me know she was pregnant on, or very near, the exact day my daughter was conceived. I was amazed. I still am. My wife was amazed. The doctor was amazed. (The 'call' was to tell her the story and let her in on this whole God and voice thing). Sanchez was amazed. Everyone else was either out of the loop or skeptical, most of them were out of the loop. I'm still to this day overwhelmed by the intensity and craziness of that prophecy. It was such clear evidence that God was not only very real, but also that I was actually communicating with Him. At the time, I was like give me more, I'm ready. All I can say to that, is be careful what you wish for.

One of my friends that I was ministering to during the next couple of years had been a friend since junior high. I grew up going to his house and he to mine. His house was alway the house through high school and into college, that we would 'party' at. His mom would always be there keeping an eye on us, and allowing us to have a 'safe' place to drink, smoke, and fornicate as we please. I'm not here trying to place any judgement on her or him. She was always good to me and I love her, just as I love him. In fact, when I was in a band and had released an album, she was the only one that asked if I was 'Ok'. There were some dark songs on the album that I had written, and she was genuinely concerned about me. I think everyone else either was scared to bring it up, or realized, that since I was talking about it, that that was evidence enough that I was fine. At least fine enough. Ok so fast forward 15 years since the partying days of highschool and college, and 8 or so years since the album, to me finding God. I am taking a bath and I get the 'call' that my friends mom is going to die. I 'get' that she is going to die tomorrow. I also 'get' that I need to call my friend and tell him. Dang. This was hard. Why me? I knew immediately the craziness and the weight of this 'call'. If I was right it was horrible, she was going to die. Yet at the same time powerful, because God was using me as His prophet. If I was wrong, it was horrible. To put this false alarm on my friend would be awful, and it meant that I wasn't hearing God. I double, triple, quadruple checked, as usual. I got out of the bath and called my friend. I told him exactly what the 'call' had been. He was very gracious with me, he was grateful, and he was obviously concerned and scared about his mom. After I made that call, I immediately called Sanchez and told him what had happened. He was like me, dang!? He also understood the implications of the 'call'. There was no escaping reason now. Either, my friend's mom was going to die tomorrow or she wasn't. Either I was hearing God or I wasn't. Ugh. This was on a Saturday evening, the next day, Sunday, was a horribly long wait for the news. Monday morning rolls around and I get the text from my friend...his mom was still alive and well. Emotion flooded me. I got to work and was sobbing. I felt ashamed, embarrassed, relieved, lost, angry, confused, deeply sad, overwhelmingly glad, and extremely foolish. I felt all of this, all at once. I couldn't handle it. I was literally losing my mind and soul. I stopped praying and just sat raw and exposed. It was a teacher work day the next day, so no kids, thankfully. Sanchez came down to my room, so did my friend whose mom didn't die.

My friend told me that he ended up having a really good conversation with his mom that night I called. He told me that his mom had mocked God and defiantly said she wasn't going anywhere. I, through tears, said I was so sorry for putting him through that. He forgave me, but he wasn't happy. He even took a shot at me, and said why don't you tell my mom that. He was hurt, as was I. It stung, but I deserved it. I had put him through a weekend of terror. A couple of other friends that we had been ministering to came down and saw how distraught I was. It was a solemn day. Sanchez stayed with me through a lot of that day. I went home early. I cried at home, my wife was upset too. She understood how big this all was. One of the other guys I was ministering too who hadn't found God, who eventually walked away from me and God, but at the time, was extremely interested, called me. I told him what happened. He didn't think it was as cut and dry as I was making it, he actually was comforting me, ministering to me. It was nice, I was grateful. I was raw, and lost. He thought that somehow I could be hearing Him and that this would all work out. He had more faith in me and God, than I did at that point. Eventually in the evening that day, I went back to Him. I had no place else to go. I had found Him, and it had been amazing up until then. I needed answers.

Over the next few days and weeks I prayed heavily looking for answers. This is what I 'got'. I 'got' that she did die. I 'got' that she had mocked God, and so she died 'spiritually'. I 'got' that I was too caught up in reason, that I needed to have faith, not reason as my guide. I 'got' that God was beyond Reason. That was it, that's all I 'got'. That was years ago. I still to this day, and every time since that I've checked (its come up a lot), get those 'answers'. Those 'answers' all have their own problems. They all lead to many more questions, and don't feel or sound sufficient. First, if she had died 'spiritually', hadn't God forced her hand? Didn't He create a situation, that backed her into a corner? And why didn't He say that from the beginning, that she was going to die 'spiritually', not actually? Why didn't He just tell me that she was going to 'spiritually' die, instead of lead me to believe she was actually, physically going to die? It's as if He wanted me to stumble and lose faith in Him. This 'answer' seemed like a sneaky way out. It seemed, and still seems, like someone who got caught in a lie and they go, "Well actually what I meant was…" It just doesn't sit well, it doesn't have that ring of truth that got me to Him in the first place. The second 'answer' that I 'got', that God was outside Reason, seemed strange too. How could God be outside of His own nature. I understand how His Reason can be more accurate and pure, than my reason. This is obvious. It definitely helps me to understand this when God seemingly does crazy things, like Tsunamis earthquakes, and floods, and people die from them. Or when babies die or kids suffer from illness, it helps to go, well His Reason is supreme, and we just can't know it. His Reason is too complicated, but He is Good so He has His Reasons for the pain and suffering. I get that, but how can God be beyond His own Reason? Those are the 'answers' I get. They don't give me much solace or comfort. How do I even trust God after that call? This is something that I've been battling since then, up until this very moment, and will continue to battle, for God only knows how much longer. Irony intended.

After my daughter was born I got another 'call' that my wife was pregnant. This time there was a strange complication during the early stages of the pregnancy. I 'got' that it was another girl. Then there were signs of a miscarriage. Even pregnancy tests that showed she was pregnant, then that she wasn't, then that she was again. She was either still pregnant, or had had a miscarriage, then immediately got pregnant again. It was all together strange. Even my wife's doctor was confused. We all were. I still 'got' that she was pregnant, and that it was a girl. When the doctor said it was a boy, and that they could see it clearly on the ultrasound, I prayed again. I 'got' that it was a girl.  I was confused. One of my friends, the one I had baptized, said that he 'got' that my wife did have a miscarriage and that the baby that had passed, was a girl. He said this new baby was a boy. I still 'got' that it was a girl. I still believed what I was getting over what the doctor said. (albeit after the mom is dead 'call' I was definitely more skeptical and doubtful.) When my son was finally born, and I saw clearly that he was in fact a boy and not a girl, again I was confused. It was a weird feeling to be disappointed at the birth of my son. I still have guilt about that. I was disappointed in him my son I was disappointed in God or myself. This was the second, drastically wrong 'call' I had received. Or was it? I mean it is entirely possible that we had a miscarriage. The due dates had shifted. My wifes doctor was confused by it, it was a mystery to all of us. We had a healthy baby boy. When I prayed again, I got that it had been a girl, and that now, obviously, it was a boy. I didn't get my boy was a 'spiritual' girl, thankfully. I found myself lost and confused about this God, voice, 'call', thing, whatever it was.

On the one hand I had had amazing 'calls', all of my relationships were truer, and better.  I felt His presence, I asked constantly if this was actually Him. He said "yes" always, without fail. I had had thousands of 'calls' by then. They had by in large all (minus a few big ones) worked out unexpectedly, and perfectly. On the other hand, I had these two very strange 'false prophet' type of 'calls'. 'Calls' that when I went back to Him to see if I was 'off', I got a resounding, "no". 'Calls' that made no sense in reality, but that God assured me made sense to Him. That He had His Reasons. When I asked my wife, and Sanchez, if I was 'off', they both, independently, 'got' that I was, in fact, hearing Him. I still get, and they still get, that I am hearing Him. Since then, I have struggled. I honestly can't go back to non belief, there is just too much logical and experiential evidence for

His existence, and for His Divine intervention in my life. I can't honestly turn into a sign reading, Bible thumping Christian either, for the same reasons I hadn't done so up until this point. It kept coming back to, I either am, or I am not, hearing God. That's as basic and fundamental as I can make this conundrum. Sanchez tried to explain that the problem must be me. He uses the analogy of antennae, or walkie talkies, when he tries to explain what might have happened. Sanchez explains, that if there is an error, it must be on our end. He says that since God is perfect, and we, obviously, are not, the fault must lie on our side. Just like a bad connection with a faulty cheap radio equipment, small antenna, or cheap walkie talkies work in real life. The fuzz from bad connection, can and does lead to us to make wrong interpretations of what we 'hear'. In other words it was I, if there was a mistake made, making mistakes in what I 'heard' not in God communicating it incorrectly. This makes sense, and it helps for a moment, but I always get back to the same sticking points with this explanation. One is that, if our reception is that faulty, how do we know then, what 'calls' are right, and what 'calls' are wrong due to a bad connection? It makes the entire game rigged in a way, that makes me not want to play. We're back to a random roll the dice life, sometimes it's God, and sometimes it's God but I just can't get the message right. How do I know which it is if they both sound the same on my end? That just doesn't work. It's always God I hear, but sometimes I just can't hear clearly, even when I check multiple times. Even when I check with my wife and Sanchez, and they 'get' that it is God, and that I'm hearing correctly. Besides that issue, during the two major 'false calls', I was extremely close to Him, my connection was clear, I checked multiple times, I heard that as clearly, if not clearer, than many of the other 'true calls'. Plus, I have since checked, and I still 'get' that I wasn't 'off'. I still 'get' that it wasn't a bad connection. I still get that those were, in fact, the 'right calls'. So this leads me back to, either I'm 'on' and I do hear the voice of God. And those two aberrations or anomalies, are not aberrations or anomalies at all, but are somehow, outside of my ability to reason and understand that those calls were not only correct, but also necessary, justified, and ultimately good. Or the alternative is true, that none of what I'm hearing is Him, and it's just some deep psychological trick that I'm playing on myself. It's something I have made myself believe in, even though it's not true. I believe in something that my mind had made up. This other 'voice', that has improved my life beyond belief, and given me a deep sense of purpose, meaning, and peace, is all an elaborate illusion. That I, in the end, am delusional. I guess it could also be a demon, or some other less than perfect spirit that has possessed me, but that just seems like, a fancier version of a not God delusion. When I boil it down, it has to be the case that either, it is God, Jesus, and the Holy Spirit, or it isn't. The 'isn't' maybe leaves some other options, none of which are good, but that are relatively unimportant next to the big true dilemma. Is it God or not?

No news is good news (sanchez):
This is a tough subject to tackle and deal with. I have not received the gift of prophecy as Mac has. Here and there, in small ways, I have been guided by God about future events but nothing on the scale that Mac has received. Early on he told me about revelations he had received from God, I prayed about them because I didn't want Mac going down the wrong road. All along, through the prophecies that came true and the ones that

didn't, I received that it was God talking to him. I desperately wanted to tell him he was off and that he needed to check himself and maybe even get some professional help. I do not believe my friend is sick or off. I even now, in this moment, get, "I am with Him." It has been a stumbling block for me at times. I know as well as anyone that one of the tests of a prophet is that if one doesn't come true...he is not a true prophet. I even pray that we get to take this section out because I do not know if people will be able to look past this and still hear our message of connecting with God. I know if I was in your shoes, I would be wary. The only theory and guidance I have received from God is that we can be faulty radios. The transmission can be true and correct but if the receiving equipment is of poor quality or faulty, it can mess up the intended message. However; this leaves us with the problem of how do we listen to anything God says. I know some will think, "SEE???!!!?? This is why you can only hear God through the Bible." I don't buy it. First, we've shown how even the Bible requires the Holy Spirit to divine correctly. Second, what about the prophecies that have been correct??? Are some from God and others not? How can we trust any of them then?

Is our only option to close ourselves off from trying to hear God? This seems like no option at all. I do believe that if we are wrong that God will forgive the parts that need forgiving. I believe He will see our hearts are for Him 100%. If I received the word today from God that Mac was off or wrong, I would drive to His house and deliver the news. We would be relieved in a way. I wish I could just tell him he's off. Again, if you got an answer that is in line with what we get from God and can solve our catch 22...help some brothers out.

(mac):

I continue to struggle and pray about this, to this day. Part of me thinks that God needed me to back down or away from Him, because I was flying too close to the sun, so to speak. Like if I kept drawing nearer, I might burn up. Another part of me thinks God is purposely messing with me, like the story of Job in the Bible. In there God is making a bet with the devil about how faithful Job can be. So God put Job through hell to test his faith. If this is the case, then I doomed, and things could and definitely will, get worse for me. Part of me thinks that this is all part of

His plan, and He is using these 'false calls' in my life as a way to perfect and purify me. That's my hope. That's the best, most ideal case, out of all of them. Unfortunately I just don't know, or can't tell on my own. All I have to go on is the Source of these impossible 'calls'. It's hard for me to believe either way, because the real results of these 'calls' in my life has been for me to trust Him less, at least to trust the voice less. I now always have in my mind a caveat or asterisk next to every 'call'. Like that's what I'm 'getting' now, but we all know it could turn out to be some strange 'false prophecy'. I also think that maybe God was like, "You want to be close to me, but look how easy it is to shake your faith. Look at what I asked Abraham to do to his son Isaac. Look at the prophets that I sent throughout history. They had to run around for years, naked, telling the world about Me, and nobody listened. Look at Jesus Himself, the pain and suffering He went through. Look at all the apostles after Jesus' death and resurrection. They were thrown to lions, tortured, and killed because of Me! What did you expect?!" I imagine God quoting that movie, "You can't handle the Truth!" It's funny in that nervous laugh humbling before you die kind of way. When I pray I 'get' to stay with Him. I still feel and hear Him, clearly. I still have nowhere else to go. Seriously and honestly, I have no better way to live, or make even the 'smallest' decisions. I still bow down in the face of confusion, chaos, and disarray. I still in my lostness, turn to the only One that has ever given me hope.

It seems counterintuitive to even write this in the book. If God wants people to come to Him, why wouldn't He have me leave theses parts out. They don't seem to make His argument stronger. Even one of the friends that I was ministering to used this as an excuse to walk away from me and Him. He used these 'false calls' to dismantle my claim, that I am hearing God. My friend said during one of our last encounters that, "Your friend's mom didn't die, God said she did. Therefore you aren't hearing God. The end." It's a strong argument. I really don't have an answer, besides those I have laid out. The friend that said this I haven't seen for years, he was one of the 10 that walked away. I hope one day I have more clarity. I don't know why this thorn is in my side, but it is. For now I believe, it's taken me years to get the courage to draw nearer once again to Him. My heart has hardened and is beginning to soften again.

This journey of ours is still unfolding. There is more to it, that I have yet to share, and there is more to come that I have yet to live. I still pray and get that we are all prophets, that we can all get to Him, and that we can all hear Him. That Jesus died, and rose again, to purify us, to pay for our sins. That He sent the Holy Spirit to act as a conduit to Him. As far as the stricter definition of future telling prophecy, that is still a mystery to me. I have experienced both sides, the amazing miracle of it when it turns out to be true, like in the case of my beautiful daughter, and the bitter confusing failings of the 'false calls'. That's all I got for now.

Oswald Chambers and My Utmost for His Highest (mac):
While I was reading the entire Bible, Sanchez was 'called' to give me a book. It was called, "My Utmost for His Highest" by Oswald Chambers. I 'got' the 'call' to read it along with the Bible. I would read a few pages of Oswald's book, and then lots of Biblical pages daily. The book by Oswald was old and raggedy. It was an old printed version, unabridged and in one of it's first publications. The book is set up as a daily devotional. It

has 365 different passages on how to give ourselves over to Jesus. It was amazing. Besides the red letters in the Bible, directly from Jesus Himself, this little book packed the most Truth in it, than anything I had read up until that point, and have read, heard, or seen since. From God when I pray I 'get' that this little book is 'on', like 'really on'. The book in great detail and repetition is all about handing every little and big piece of ourselves, all of us, over to Jesus. The call was to read it through from cover to cover three times. I did. Eventually the call was to send it onto another friend. I did. There are two passages that stand out for different reasons in my mind. One is about the saint. First the saint is the closest representation of any man can get to Jesus. It's the archetypal follower of Jesus Christ. Oswald says says, and I think rightfully so, that the saint often looks like a fool. That stood out then, and since then, as something to hold onto, especially after the 'false prophet calls'. Many 'calls' since then have led me to feel foolish. I was 'called' to sell our house, and to buy one that we couldn't afford. The one that we are currently living in. It daily makes me feel extremely blessed, and at the same time, extremely trapped and foolish. All sorts of tricks and strings were pulled to get us in here. We walked into the open house on its first showing with a full priced offer, site unseen. It was all around strange process, but we were able to get into our dream home following His lead. It has turned out to be a bit of a financial circus, where we're the clowns. Each year we have had to do financial somersaults and acrobats to stay afloat. After a year of living here on credit cards, the 'call' was to file bankruptcy. Yet another example of feeling foolish. Very foolish. Not only was bankruptcy bad enough, but it's the five year plan type, that locks you into to this payment plan. It's strict financial handcuffs for five years. We are currently only into the third year, and it's been hard, but not impossible, we are still just getting by. We are still broke, but still afloat, staying right with Him. I'm not saying this to say that I am a saint by any stretch. What I am saying is that I try and follow Jesus, and in following Him I often feel foolish. Following the voice of God when nobody else seems to, alone is enough to make me feel foolish. Not being able to explain it to many people, makes me feel foolish. Living in a way that seems to at many times fly in the face of reason, and common sense, makes me feel foolish.

Constantly throwing down my pride, makes me feel foolish. Being 'called' to wait, for no clear reason, or rest when I'm not tired, or stay quiet, when awkwardness is in the air, all make me feel foolish.

That passage on foolishness, from Oswald, has brought me comfort many times. Most recently I was 'called' to keep my work keys over the summer, even though my boss told me to turn them in. It caused great anxiety for me, my wife, and Sanchez. The risk of being fired or written up was real. Telling my dad the story, and having him trying to give me advice, without being able to tell him it was the 'call' was hard, and made me feel foolish. Keeping quiet, when the boss was calling me was hard. About a week into the summer, I received a letter in the mail from the boss that said, I wouldn't be paid, unless I turned in my keys. The 'call' changed. Now the 'call' was to turn them in. Bizarre. It made me angry, again it made me feel foolish. I wanted to keep them all summer if I was going to keep them at all. Or turn them in when I was supposed to, if I was going to turn them in at all. But this weird middle ground, of keeping the keys until he threatened to dock my pay, made me feel foolish. Sanchez and I discussed this a lot, we both were relieved when the 'call' was to give them back. But we were equally confused by it as well. I am no saint, but following the voice has definitely brought me to feel like a fool often. I never felt like a fool before Him, not really. I have felt betrayed, or angry, or hurt, but a fool, that never (or at least extremely rare that I can't remember) was a feeling I had before God. I always felt intelligent and reasoned, often guilty, or ashamed, but not foolish. Now I was less angry, guilty, and ashamed, but always foolish, and without reason.

The other passage that stood out in Oswald's book, was the one that explained that the saint would eventually have their own will, united with, His Will. That eventually, after much training and laying it down, that the two wills would unite. They would become one. Now when I read this, each time, and when I pray about it now, I always 'get' the same thing, that this was the one place where Oswald was off. That it was impossible for anyone, except for Jesus, to have their will aligned with the Absolute. I still 'get' that. Out of 365 passages, this one passage was 'off'. Every time I gave this book to someone I was ministering to, they found that one passage and used it as an excuse to not pray. It was like they found the one error, called it true, and the rest of the book they just set aside. Each person (it was only a couple of them) would literally find this one passage, and automatically equate themselves with a saint. They would be like, "See, I don't have to pray, I'm in such relation with God, I'm so close to Him, that my will is in line with His Will"...I was like, what?! Sanchez also said that in all the years of his own ministering to Christians, that many of them would have the book on their shelf, but nobody held it in high esteem. He would ask them about it and they couldn't talk about it. Its as if they never read it. It's like the Christians that are constantly quoting Jeremiah 29:11, ' "For I have plans for you" declares the LORD, "plans to prosper you and not to harm you, plans to give you hope for the future" ', Taken alone to mean your life, here on earth, will be great! But this in no way represents the entire Bible. In fact, most of those who followed God or Jesus had it rough in many ways. This is the cherry picking effect that non truth seekers use to justify their own ends. They use this method to believe what they want, instead of what is real. This is what people were doing with Oswald. It's what non truth seekers do with everything. People use this method to justify all sorts of things. It's a major reason why relying on our own will, just doesn't work. It's a major reason that as foolish as I often feel, and as 'false' as some of the 'calls' turn out to be,I still find it's way better than relying on myself. I have way more evidence against me, my flawed rationalization, and weak reasoning, than I do against any of the 'calls' I've received. It's that old adage, a bad day with God, is better than the best day without Him. That's true even through the pain of being 'wrong' and 'foolish'.

Magically Delicious (sanchez):

1 times out of 5 when I talk to my fellow Christians, they have read most of the New Testament and very little of the Old Testament. The book by Oswald Chambers is on most bookshelves of believers, but again very few have read it all the way through, if at all. Just a short conversation reveals just how little that person has spent learning. It's sad. It's almost like people think their books are totems. As if owning them is the same thing as reading or understanding them. If this is you, I recommend you start with these works and authors:  the Bible,

C.S. Lewis, William Lane Craig, and, G. K. Chesterton. There is no need to recreate the wheel. Stand on the shoulders of giants so you can see further. I want to address another fear. There is something about great works that people have a false humility about. They think they are not worthy or able to understand great works so they don't even try. If you are a normal functioning person, you can eventually understand. I think part of the self disqualification is because we don't really want to know. We think it's like we're at the gym and some muscle bound person was on the machine right before us. We think, "there's no way I can lift this." We don't even try. Now, while this may be prudent at the gym, this is not how it is mentally when it comes to understanding the Truth. All of us are equals when it comes to the potential to understanding and obeying the Truth.

On the other hand, we will spend nearly a lifetime watching TV shows, reading materials that do not bring us closer to Truth, and wasting time on social media. I have done this too. 99% of us have. This doesn't make it right or mean that we can continue now that we know the Truth. We have the time and ability to understand the great secrets of the universe. Maybe it's time to be honest that we don't want to. It's ok. Free Will has always been the only thing that can keep us away from the Truth.

Soft Heart vs. Hard Heart (mac):
Before God, I had an idea about how much my heart mattered, I even had an idea that my heart wasn't always good. Looking back, as is usually the case, the lens that I was using to look at my heart, wasn't nearly focused enough. It wasn't focused closely or clearly enough and it wasn't focused sharp enough on all of me. Once Jesus entered my life, the intensity, intimacy, and sharp focus of my whole heart found it in much worse shape than I had known or realized before. I knew I was lost and broken and I needed Him, so I eventually lept to Him and submitted my will to His. What I discovered once over to the other side was two fold. I didn't know exactly how great He was, and I was really quite clueless about just how broken, bad, and lost, I actually was.

I scratch your back, you scratch mine (sanchez):

I do want to break in here and address what Mac is talking about. I think most people come to God with the strange notion that they are doing God a favor.

Deep in our hearts we think, "God and I have an equal trade here. It's mutually beneficial." If we could really see how low we are and how high God is, we would not try to make decisions without him. Instead of just checking with God on "big" decisions, we would realize we are not fit to decide if we can get out of bed without His direction. Don't be confused. It's not like God says, "Ok...put your right foot in front of the other...now your left...now right...don't forget to breath". It's more like having a walkie talkie that is permanently on and tuned in to God and you check with him or describe your day or what you are thinking and, all the while, you are waiting for him to correct you or guide you. For me, I usually pray about my days in advance. Let's say Mac wants to hang out. First, I pray if we are allowed to. If I get "yes", I see what day is open and I pray, "how about Monday?" (This is to God...not Mac). If I get "no" or silence, I wait and check my heart and mind for anything that may be holding me up from hearing God on my end. Both of us have received "no" before and we have no choice but to obey. Finally, if I get "yes" (and Mac gets "yes"), I pray about a day and time. Sometimes the offer comes from Mac's side or my side, but either way I check with God if the day and time is ok. If I get "yes", then I schedule it. Very rarely, there is the call to cancel. There is a right way to do this and I refer you to another part of this book dealing with how to cancel properly. This call is rare and probably has to do with free will or other considerations beyond my understanding. I know this sounds like a lot, but the more often you do it, the faster the process gets. For Mac and me, it's almost instant. This takes time to develop a finely tuned heart and mind to the Holy Spirit. I still make mistakes. Other times, I believe God makes allowances for my weakness (maybe I'm feeling lazy and just want to rest at home). Either way, I submit to His will.


(mac):

It was as if I was a child who had cleaned their own room, when my Father finally came into see how I did on my own, He simply began showing me how poorly I had done. He showed me where to look how to look and exactly what I needed to do to clean it properly. He shined His light everywhere; Under the carpet, under the bed, on top of the shelves, behind them, around the waste basket, between the cracks in the tile, the gunk on the walls, it went on and on. He didn't show me all at once (for He only gives us exactly the load we can carry, no more no less), but He showed me enough at a time, for me to realize just how gross and off I actually was. I find it fascinating that even with all of the 'real talk' and 'truth seeking' I was doing prior to Him, that it was enough for me to understand I was broke, but not even close to the amount of realness or Truth I would find with Him. He was like you thought you were just broke before, but really you are truly bankrupt. You thought you had a little bit left in your account to redeem, but you have nothing in there, in fact you owe me, you are in debt. You are way filthier than you thought. I needed to know that I was bad in order to find Him, but I couldn't know just how bad, until I found Him. Without Him, if I would've seen my heart in the real light, it would have crushed me. Really, it would have psychologically crushed my heart and soul.

Director's cut (sanchez):

This is why, if we hold on to our sin, we won't be able to stand heaven. Hell is a self imposed prison. Heaven will be the director's cut of our life...including the blooper reel...except instead of all laughing; we will be amazed at the glory of God. His grace and mercy will be infinite ecstasy. Hell will be the absences of these. It will be frustration and mockery at our faults on display. We will own all the sins we committed and have no way out. We will be exposed for the broken and sick individuals we are.


(mac):

I could only hold a very dim light up to my reflection, and vaguely see the evil shape of myself. It was only with Him that I began to see the monster I actually was and am. It makes sense that throughout the Bible God is concerned with our hearts more than anything else. It is no surprise that Jesus speaks over and over about what is in our hearts. It is the thing that is naturally the most corrupt in us. My heart automatically hardens for all sorts of reasons. Selfish desires, hard heart.

Anger, hard heart. Anyone who has stepped on my toes, hard heart. The world and existence, hard heart. God, hard heart. Myself, hard heart. Bitterness, resentment, contempt, anger, revenge, lust, greed, laziness, pride all stem from a hardened heart. To keep my heart soft, it takes constant light shown on it. If I let go of His Light for even a second, my heart, in the darkness, gravitates to hardness. Only with the help of the Supernatural, do I even come close to battling the degradation and atrophy my heart automatically is drawn to. God wants us to hand over every part of ourselves to Him for cleansing and purifying. That means every emotion, every thought, and every idea. He wants every corner of our hearts and minds, and every inch of our being. He wants us to see how disgusting and broken we are without Him. He wants to then lift us up, dust us off, soften our hearts, and fill us with His Love. It's strange and powerful. I'm having trouble putting it into words.

Sanchez and I have used many analogies to describe ourselves. One of them is someone who is trying to quit smoking. Every time they throw their last cigarette down, another one automatically and mysteriously appears lit, and ready to smoke.

It's a strange and surprising and extremely frustrating phenomenon. No matter how fast or often we throw that cigarette down, another one appears in the same instant. We can't on our own quit smoking in the analogy, but in actuality we can't truly stop any sinning. Only by submitting to God, does He help us to put the cigarette or sin down for good. Only recognizing that we are helpless against ourselves, can He come give us help. Another picture of who we are, is that of a dog who throws up, and for unknown reasons returns to lick up their own vomit. It's a really gross way to look at it, but I assure you it's light hearted, compared to how bad we actually are. In our case the vomit is the gross sin that we are ridding ourselves of, we make the mistake of thinking that once it's out, it's gone for good. It's not, it's always close by, the minute we move the light from it, and move onto something else, we return right to it. We start sniffing it, it's as if we forget how gross it is, it's almost comfortable, and if we're not careful, we lap it up, again and again.

Never ending story (sanchez):

Not only do we return to our puke in an effort to find comfort, it makes us sick again from eating the puke. It's gross. It should be. Worse...it's death! It would be like eating cancerous cells tumors that actually caused cancer again. This is something I have struggled with and Mac alluded to earlier. For some reason, humans can know what the problem is, they can suffer tremendously because of sin; and yet, still return to it. This is why God's Grace must be infinite. Unlike humans who may get tired of forgiving the same old sin, God does not. He sees our heart. As long as we are sincerely trying to turn back to Him and sin no more, He will pick us up an infinite amount of times. This is Good News!

(mac):

Yet another comparison is that of an alcoholic. We're much more like alcoholics in the way that they often think; once an alcoholic always an alcoholic. They mean that they are never truly free of that temptation or vice of alcoholism. Sanchez came up with the idea of life's anonymous, because in reality we are all sinoholics. Once a sinner always a sinner, that's just the reality of life.  When we least expect it, something triggers a craving for us to go back and roll in the mud of our sin. The tricks we play on ourselves to pretend that our sin and brokenness aren't 'that bad' are immense. We are constantly trying to minimize our filth. Especially when we are tired, stressed, or hungry, the demons just come raging out. Our defenses against ourselves are down, we get nasty so fast. We give ourselves permission, making excuses of 'we deserve it' or worse 'they deserve it'. We tell ourselves, we were good for so long, a little bad won't hurt anyone or I do so much for these people, I'm done. I quit. "Fuck it." Then things get immediately get worse. As if being tired hungry or stressed wasn't bad enough, we go and make it worse. It's a constant game we all play. Sometimes it's just our knee jerk or natural reaction, we have no excuse in mind, we just react in our true disgusting selves. My three year old son threw a plastic Nerf gun at my head. It hurt, my initial reaction was to throw it back harder and send him running away with a bloody face or worse. I didn't, I prayed, and I forgave, then followed Him in correcting my son, but that person who initially wanted to harm my son, that is who I am. I want revenge on anyone, for anything. It's really quite disturbing actually. I'm quite the monster.

The world tells us that we can do it on our own, that with enough grit or will power, we got this. The sick and broken, who cannot and do not fix themselves on their own, only hide the brokeness. They blindly lead others to their death. 'Self help' gurus, 'self help' books, and the entire 'self help' industry is a big lie. Just the words 'self help' is the myth that Christianity came to destroy. The problem is that a lot of Christianity is actually promoting 'self help'. It's just flat out wrong. Jesus came for sinners. He came for us all. The first step in alcoholics anonymous is to admit you're an alcoholic. The first step in life's anonymous is to admit you're a sinner. Admit you're a fake, phony, broken, dirty, gross ass sinner.

I'm not just a member, I'm the president (sanchez):
The hustle and bustle of life is addicting and destructive apart from God. Again, there are plenty of people that live "good" lives. This is what Mac is trying to explain. It's like functioning addicts who point to their jobs, marriage, or some other thing and think, "see? I'm not that bad." The problem is that if there

is an Absolute power that is personal and wants a relationship with you, then anything "good" you pick separate from Him...in the end, is worthless.

(mac):

I said at the beginning of this section that once I got to the other side that what I discovered was two fold. On the one hand, I needed to know how bad I am, on the other, I needed to know how Great He is.The only other part you need to know besides your own depravity, is to realize just how much God loves you anyway. You need to know and feel just how much he cares for you, how much He cares about you. You need to let it sink in that He made you, that He created you for His Kingdom. You need to understand it personally and deeply that He wants you to share in His Glory, and be in His Light. In order to get to Him, He needs you to see Him, for who He truly is. Let it really sink in, and really see that Jesus gave up His life for you. He sacrificed for you, individually, purposefully, in love and commitment to you. You need to see the Greatness in His life, His death, and His Resurrection. Then and only then can you really submit to Him, not once, but always. Trust that He has your back, that He knows better than you, Trust that the Creator of all things Good and Great is here for you and He is closer than you think. He has been waiting for you, calling you, softening your heart for Him. The Source of Love, loves you, and wants to heal you. He wants to forgive you, if only you would admit defeat. Not defeat to God, not even to some foreign enemy. No, admit defeat to yourself, admit that no matter how hard you try, you still fail to be good on your own. You fail to live properly on your own. You fail to do anything on your own. Admit how lost and lonely you are, and admit how scared, broken, and bad you are. He is right here, He has been waiting for you, just you, for eternity. He has eternal strength, power, and love just for you. He has as much time as you need, He is patient, but this is urgent. He wants your heart. Give it up. Then do it again, and again, and again, then repeat and do it again, and again, and again. Don't worry about the entire process or all the moments you have already wasted, or all the times you will fail. Right now, this moment, lay your tired self down, let His Majesty, the King, Christ your Lord do the work.

I've been talking to me, I'm talking to myself. I need Him every moment. I go out into the wilderness alone, and I get lost and tired. I sin, immediately without Him. I can't do this alone. I've tried. I've tried everything. Nothing worked. Admitting nothing worked, admitting that I'm the problem, and blaming nothing else, blaming nobody else, then and only then do I feel Him making me whole again. Only then am I free. I was never as free as I thought I was. I'm not as good as I once thought I was, or as good as I was told I was. I'm not as brave as I once thought I was. I'm not as smart as I once thought I was. I'm not as interesting or unique as I once thought I was. I'm not as deep or loving as I once thought I was. No, I've been tricked by myself and others, but mostly by myself. I wanted to hear all the good things, I refused the truth. I gladly accepted the false praise. I'm also not a one type or one kind of sinner. I'm not just an alcoholic, or sexoholic, or drug addict. I don't just struggle with one kind of sin. Thats another trick I use to avoid giving all of me to Him. In reality, I run the gamut of sin. I'm an everything-oholic. If it's not sexual desire and lust giving me a problem, then its anger, if it's not anger than it's arrogance, if it's not arrogance than lack of patience, if it's not lack of patience, then it's focusing on everyone else's sins and faults. That's what happens when you see how gross you are, you see it in everyone. If it's not those other sins, it's vanity, if it's not that, it's self-righteousness. It's thinking my sins are justified. My heart gets hard with writing this book. It gets hard that I'm 'hearing' God, that I'm connected. So what? I think I'm so Godly, I'm so saintly, I'm so close to God, and then He shows me how gross that that is. Right when my heart hardens, I can't hear Him anymore, unless it is to show me where exactly I was off. How I am to love Him and love others? I can't do either when my heart swells with pride in finding Him. He shows me, "look how long it took, look how stubborn you were, look how prideful you've become. Now that you found me, look at how much you look down on others. Look at how much higher you put your talent and skills, than they actually are. They aren't even yours, I gave those to you. Look how low you put your kids, even playing with your own kids, you think it unimportant. Look how angry you get at a three year old, a four year old, an eleven year old, or a fourteen year old. Look at you lick your own vomit, look at you smoke your cigarette, look how easy you give up, look how bad you are." I bow I tell Him I'm sorry, and ask for His forgiveness once again. Then I'm back with Him. I submit, I lay it down, I lay it all down. The only reason I pray so often, all day, everyday, trying to stay right with Him, is because I know how easily and quickly I get into sin. It's like letting your untamed dog off the leash, it runs straight out into the street. It runs straight into death. It doesn't know what its running from or toward. It's stupid. So am I. It's not a leash though it's just me choosing to be by His side, I'm free to go at anytime. I often do, I find myself in the middle of the road, staring into oncoming traffic, again.

This simple idea, is a lifelong process, of realizing how bad I am and at the same time realizing how great He is. That's what it all comes down to. But it's not a one time thing. It's a 'way', it's 'The Way', the only Way. It's an everyday, every moment, all the time, laying it down and allowing Him in. The once a week church, or the once in awhile confession, or the once in a lifetime baptism, or the once a day prayer, or the 5 times a day bending of the knees, isn't enough. What about all the gaps in between? Life is full to the brim with moments, and in every moment you're faced with choice. Do you choose your own broken self and will, or do you choose Him? Do you trust the flawed, lost self, or do you turn to the Absolute, the Creator, the source of all Love and Goodness? Do you try to lift yourself, the one that got you in this mess to begin with, or do you let the One who made you, your Father do the lifting? Who do you trust? Who is truly, actually, really looking out for you? You or Him?

My Conscience vs. Him (mac):

Before God I relied heavily on my conscience to do the right thing. Let me just blurt this out now, and then come back to how I got here. The voice of God and the voice of conscience are not one in the same. The voice that I pray to is something quieter, more unique, more personal,more specific, and unemotional. Whereas my conscience is me, it's more blunt, it's a stronger feeling, it's almost solely strong emotional feelings. My conscience supplies me with emotion, the emotion of rightness and wrongness in a loud sort of confused way. The emotion of guilt is supplied directly from my conscience, and without God it supplies a steady surplus of guilt. The emotion of feeling good when helping someone is a result of my conscience; it's the strong feeling of pride when doing good that spills for from my conscience. I had this emotional vehicle, this conscience, that everybody has, without believing in the Supernatural. In fact, my conscience wouldn't allow me to believe. My conscience and my reasoning, albeit flawed, both told me it was better, I was better off remaining separate from God. I couldn't, as the saying goes, in good conscience, submit my will to anyone; natural or Supernatural. My conscience actually screamed not to, my conscience lead my reasoning. The emotion of my conscience lead my reasoning to fight for it. My conscience led my mind to rationalize for it. My conscience felt guilty for lying or stealing in a blunt way, but it felt fine to lie and steal indirectly or covertly. It was only when I began real talk and truth seeking for real that I was able to train my conscience to be more alert to its own flaws and devious ways. I began to manipulate my conscience. I began to mold my conscience. My conscience was able to feel the injustice done to me, but it wasn't able to feel the wrongness in lying by omission. My conscience was proud of my 'heart', but it couldn't feel the wrongness of the pride, or the lie at how good my heart really wasn't.  Real talk led me to realize my conscience could feel guilt free as long as I remained delusional and lied to myself. My conscience had no way of determining a new truth, especially one that was dark. Once the seeking of truth and reality sunk in, my conscience had to learn along with me. My conscience was a guide but it was led by me; it was somehow a part of me and my own learning and experience. It matured and grew along with me, but that meant that my conscience was blind to the unknown, just like me. It was the blind leading the blind or me leading me. What I'm hearing now when I talk of the voice or the 'call' only came after my belief in Jesus. I had to submit my conscience to It, to Him. We can even call the conscience evidence of God, that He uses our conscience as a way to get to us, even when we are reluctant to be with Him. We can say that the conscience is a blunt tool to attempt to get to His will. We have to, at some point, realize that our conscience is flawed, like us; that our conscience is us. We have to admit that we can, in fact, manipulate our conscience. We can avoid feeling bad when doing wrong, by feeding the conscience just enough reason to have it submit to our own desires. Somehow we can convince our conscience into doing horrible things as long as we have trained it step by step. We can remain ignorant to our own hypocrisy, and in good conscience, claim that our conscience is clear. Let me lean on an example, my conscience doesn't want to hurt anybody's feelings. My conscience puts others feelings too high in fact. If I can harm you with a lie, but then make you feel that I was doing you a favor, and in fact protecting you from feeling pain, my conscience can not only not feel bad about the lie, but it can feel good that it did good. The same goes in reverse; if I tell you the truth and it hurts your feelings precisely because it is true. Even if I was telling you a truth that was meant and intended in good conscience to help you. If your feelings are hurt and I know it my conscience feels bad, I feel the guilt of hurting you, I think next time I ought to lie, at least by omission. When it comes to hearing the voice of God, He wants nothing to do with my conscience. He wants me only to obey His Divine Will. He wants me to do the things out of love for Him and others, yet and not care whether I hurt or help their feelings, in the process. He wants me to give others the medicine, His medicine, medicine that they need in the correct dose. Sometimes the 'call' is to be gentle, other times it's not. Sometimes the 'call' is to give them silence, or a quiet ear. Sometimes the 'call' is to get more aggressive, either way the 'call' is to always do it out of love. Love of Him and of them. My conscience tells me none of this, it tells me none of the nuances, and it actually leads me astray. My conscience is like a screaming child compared with the deeply serious, stern and quiet command of God. The Holy Spirit is a highly tuned instrument compared to the blunt dramatic conscience. He has trained me to watch my conscience and to see the flaws in which I trained it. I have to be weary of the guilt on one end, and equally as weary of the pride on the other. My conscience will listen to reason, and change if I can convince it of it's error, God does not. God is steady and still, He asks me to lay my emotions down, to lay the screaming conscience down, then He can get to me.

The fact that I can hear my conscience without being a believer in Christ. The fact that the 'call' often contradicts my conscience. The fact that before God, I felt and acted upon my conscience in a primary way and I still was lost. The fact that I can manipulate my conscience through reason and rationale. The fact that the voice of my conscience is not the same as the voice of the Holy Spirit. The fact that the 'call' is quiet and nuanced, compared to the loud blunt voice of my conscience. The fat that the language of the conscience is emotional feeling, whereas the voice of God is unemotional. These facts taken individually but especially in collection all lead to the same conclusion. They lead to the conclusion that the conscience though works as a good indicator of God existence and even of His echo bouncing off our heart, it isn't a replacement or substitute for Him. Following your conscience in place of Him is wrong. Getting close to the mark is not hitting the mark. It may make remaining in the hands of the devil easier and last longer than if you you missed the mark by a fair margin.

If all we needed was our conscience then we could still live in the subjective world of relativism. My conscience never felt guilty about its own pride. My conscience allowed me to remain blind and ignorant to the simple truth that some things are in fact better than others. My conscience had no problem speaking an opinion that was wrong, as long as it was proudly my own. My conscience doesn't tell me specifics, it communicates in general terms, it bleats out a direction in its loud sheep like cry, but it has no specific language other than its emotion. My conscience changes over time, it matures with me, because of me. The 'call' might change, but not with or because of me. The 'call' will only change because God Willed it to. On my own, I cannot trust myself to consistently follow my conscience. I could, at times hear it banging away at me, but in my flawed nature I would ignore it. The less serious, easier to manipulate, loud bleating sheep like conscience without God would still leave me unable to obey. Only with Him can I have the Supernatural strength to obey Him over my conscience. I feel less guilt following Him rather than my conscience. The 'call' in fact is to feel less guilt, that my guilt is often wrong. I feel way less proud as well. I can no longer be proud of doing good on my own like my conscience once allowed. Now I can only be carefully proud of doing His will. I can be deeply proud when I get the 'call', "well done, I'm proud of you, My son", then I can be carefully, but deeply joyfully proud of myself. Even this pride is buffered by the truth that I'm not on my own, that I have the help of the Divine. In general, He has regulated my emotional conscience and separated me from old emotional self. The conscience deals primarily in emotion, and reason can out maneuver emotion at times. God reigns supreme over both emotion and reason. He has me lay them both down and puts them in their proper place, infinitely second. I feel guilt from my conscience, for not following my flawed and blind reason. God says, "Leave your flawed conscience and flawed reason at my feet. Leave them behind you, and follow Me." The burden of my conscience and my reason, with the help of the Supernatural, get handed over to Him. I can then with a light heart, walk with Him. Him even carrying me, perhaps a piggy back on Jesus is what's really happening. It's hard to tell How much He is carrying and How much I am. It's safer for me to assume that He is doing the heavy lifting while I'm taking only the load that He knows I can handle.

My conscience and reasoning are flawed and off, just like me. My reasoning along with my conscience both get me to Him. Then and only then, He has me lay them both down and trust Him only. Before Him, I had my reasoning and conscience, I still do. I can still turn to them in confusion and weakness, or when I'm 'called' to look at them. I no longer rely on them though, or have them hold the weight of my existence. I can now freely choose to put my life in the hands of the Holy Spirit. It is no longer my conscience that obey. It is more specific, it's the Holy Spirit, it's the Divine Will, it is Jesus Christ. It is here for all of us to grab onto, but we must lay down our old selves. Our old selves rely on our reason, our conscience, and our will. Our old selves rely on what we think, want, and feel. God wants us to lay it all down and be reborn unto Him. He wants us to freely choose Him, over us. It's scary and weird, yet gives me deep comfort below my conscience, below my reasoning, on a more solid foundation, on the Absolute, on the Truth. I can feel Him holding me up from the bottom of my soul directly, the strings of my reason and conscience are there, but fail miserably to hold me afloat in the deep seas of reality. God has me voluntarily lay my vehicle of conscience and ship of reason to rest. He has grabbed my hand and said, "Leave them both here at the banks of your old life. Leave them, and replace them with Me, I will lead to everlasting life. Step away from your old vessels. Yes the ones that got you here to me. Step in Faith to Me. I will carry you the rest of the way, through this narrow gate and beyond." I can freely return to my old vessels, but only knowing that I gave up on Eternity. Returning to the ruins of my conscience and reason, would mean, that I gave up on Him out of weakness and fear. I would be returning to the despair of my sinking ship of rationality and the broken bleating lamb of my conscience. I would be running from the light of Glory, back to the darkness of everything else. I would be running back to myself, back to death.

Running away from home (mac):

When I was young, elementary school aged, I packed a bag and ran away. I ran away because I was angry with my dad. I saw an injustice in one of his parenting decisions. I took my bag out the front door, across the front porch, through our front gate, across our small yard, and into the treehouse, the tree house my dad had built. I sat stubbornly out there, my arms crossed in defiance. I was out there with my bag of clothes, with no food or drink. Eventually my dad came out, after what seemed like hours at the time, but it probably wasn't. He came out and from what I remember he wasn't mad. I think he was lightly laughing at me, but he made the case that I ought to come inside. I obliged easily and immediately. I put up no fight. I plead no case. I was simply grateful to have a reason to come inside. The warm house, my brother and sisters, the safety and security, the food and drink, the entertainment, and the not perfect, but definitely good, parents that loved and cared for me, were all there with open arms. They all welcomed me back and I was entirely grateful to be back. Whatever policy that my dad had implemented that upset me didn't matter anymore, my perspective had changed, I was just glad to be home.

This story really happened, this story in many ways is still happening. I still run away from God to this day. Just as I did when I was a kid, I do it today, I run away when I don't like what my Father is doing. It's not even when I don't like it. It's when I don't trust it because I don't understand it. I can't see what He sees and instead of trusting Him, I cower away and sulk. It happens when I get uncomfortable, when I get fearful, when I get anxiety, especially when I can't see His Reason. What

I do is I begin to get angry with God. I stubbornly and defiantly begin to run away. When I can't justify with my own weak reasons why He is 'calling' me to whatever it is He is 'calling' me to, I begin to question Him. My faith weakens as I weaken. I begin to rationalize, I begin to look for a way out, an excuse not to obey. I begin to focus on me. I begin to focus on the woes and worries of myself. I go inward, I struggle, and I focus on my struggle. I begin to compare myself to others, who seemingly have it easier. It is in these darker times when the 'real' comes out. I look for a way to betray Jesus. I lose the correct perspective, I lose gratitude, I lose site of all the blessing that He has already provided, I lose hope, and faith. I get pessimistic and doubtful. It is only emotion that makes me run away. It isn't reason, not good reason. Reason got me to Him. Reason is what brought me faith. Reason carried me through the emotion of wanting to stay lost, of not wanting to commit. Reason got me home. Reason keeps me coming back. Just like when I was a kid, I run away from Him, I fold my arms in stubborn defiance, and I run to a place that He built. Just like when I was kid, whenever I am ready, my Father allows me back home to His family. I only battle with myself, my limited sight, my limited reason, my limited knowledge, my limited, vulnerable, and finite nature.

He calls us to love others and love Him. There is a reason He doesn't want us focused on ourselves. It's the pride of self import that drives me to commit evil. It's the fear that God won't provide, that drives me to 'take care of myself'. There is a reason He reminds us that He loves us like sons and daughters and will provide and give to His sons and daughters what they want and especially what they need. There is a reason He emphasises faith as a virtue. Over and over Jesus emphasizes the power and goodness of true faith, and equally condemns those with weak or lacking faith. Faith is fundamentally what we act upon. It's staying with Him, when we begin to doubt. Do we trust our own broken selves or do we have Faith in Him? Faith is trusting that your Father, our Father, knows more than us, understands more than us, has got our back, like He always has. Faith is trusting Him more than we trust ourselves. Faith is walking into the unknown with Him, instead of running away into the wilderness without Him.

When I was a kid, it might have, for a second, given me emotional relief to run away out of the range of my dad, but it was short lived. The tree house was lonely, it was cold, it provided weak protection from nature and others. It was, in reality, way scarier than whatever my dad was asking me to do, or not allowing me to do. Obeying my dad would have been better than running away. This is what Jesus emphasized throughout, trust and obey. It's exactly what God, throughout history has sent teachers and prophets to say. "Stay with Me, I love you, I got you. Don't worry about anything, except for trusting and loving Me" That's the message throughout the Scripture. That's the message I get when I pray, as I'm writing this now. We get to faith with His help. We get to faith from goodness. Its weakness that makes us run. We commit to things when we are hopeful and optimistic. We have faith at the beginning of a journey, it's what gets us started. It's only when our feet haven't had to tread the difficulties that we begin to second guess what got us there in the first place. It's the difficulties that make us lose faith. It's irrational to give up on Him, our emotion gets us flustered and irrational. It's our reason, His Reason, that gets us through and keeps us on course. It's the devil that wants us to doubt, the demon within that plants the emotional seeds of excuses to stop. Our fallen nature pulls us away from goodness, not reason, not love, not trust, not faith. It's our pathetic pride, our pride of not wanting to look foolish, our pride of not thinking it's worth the sacrifice of comfort that gets us to fall away. We counted the costs before we set out, but then at first payment we balk. We seek immediate comfort and relief at the first signs of discomfort. Discomfort we knew we would face. We knew there would be waves before we set out, when they come we claim we had no idea just how wavey these waves would be. We are so eager to run out ahead of Him before we set foot on His journey. When we do finally face the dragon of chaos, we immediately cry foul and run and hide.

I wish I would have never left Him when I was younger. I wish I would have found Him sooner. The one blessing I do have from my own twisted journey is that I have perspective. I have the hard fought battle to find truth. I have the hard fought battle to fight my stubborn emotional pride. I have the skills of real talk and those of seeking truth that afford me the ability to see and feel exactly what I'm doing when I lose faith. Just as I did as a kid from my home, I didn't run far or for long, today I don't run far or for long from Him. I know all too well what life without Him is like. I have vivid memories and painful scars of the self inflicted wounds that a life without Him left on my soul. I have plenty of markings and indicators of my old life that still linger like stains on my new life. I know there is no where else to go, I know that I am Home and that my Father has been gracious. He could've and still can close the door on me at anytime. Instead He has left it open. He could've, as I deserve, banished me for eternity, given me death for what I've done. He hasn't though, each and every time I begin to run away, He stays with me, He keeps His arms open and welcomes me Home, where I belong. Where we all belong.

There's a reason that I don't remember why I ran away when I was a kid, but I do remember running away. I do remember how I felt when I ran away. I also remember how I felt returning home. The important details that had an impact on me were the unjustified anger and frustration I had with my father, and the overwhelming relief and joy of returning home. I remember the bitterness of the exit and the sweetness of the return. The specific mechanisms don't matter, I chose to leave and I chose to return. It doesn't matter why I ran away, and it doesn't matter why I returned. It matters that it was wrong of me to run away, and right of me to return. The evil in me that was more concerned with my puffed up pride of feeling slighted, emotionally led me astray. Whereas the good part of me, that actually cared about me and my family, that could see the truth clearly, brought me back. Weakness in spirit and hardness of heart pushed me away, strength in spirit and softening my heart brought me home again. This is in fact the only reason we run away from Him. We fall prey to evil narrow emotion, we falsely justify and rationalize the harm God has done to us, our loved ones or to this world. We don't use truth or reason to avoid goodness, to avoid Him, no we use resentment, revenge and stubborn pride to do evil. We use falsity to keep ourselves from our Creator. Whether you call yourself an Atheist, an Agnostic, a Theist, or Christian matters little, what He is 'calling' you to do is all that matters. There are plenty of self proclaimed religious people that have run away, that are hiding in their own ways, that have built their own tree houses away from Him. They put their faith in false idols and miss the mark. The non religious run away from Him to worship science, they worship health, they worship themselves, they worship nature, or the universe, or a guru or false prophets or they worship ignorance or false humility. The religious run away to the Bible, or Scripture, or church, they hide behind priests, church leaders, pastors, or rabbis, they worship political affiliation, or tradition, law or customs, they hide in culture. Religious or non religious they run and hide somewhere in this world, the one that He created, but is not Him. His existence doesn't depend on how you feel or what you think, it doesn't depend on anything. His existence especially doesn't depend on you. You depend on His existence. He Created you. He has allowed you to choose. He has allowed you to run away. He is also waiting patiently for your return.

We're all sick (mac):
The idea that we are all sick and broken is as powerful is it is true. It does two things simultaneously. It puts limiters on the

high and the low of us in relation to Him. It first humbles me and lowers any other human down to a level that is merely human. No demigods, no super humans. Nobody escapes the Fall. It brings everyone way down from their heights of grandeur, their fame and importance, their place on the pillars. There's an easy slippery slope that happens when we get too comfortable or righteous with our own divinity. We begin to put ourselves above others. It happens naturally, it happens without us even trying. The strange paradox is that the closer we get to God, the easier it is to look around and see how broken the world is, how broken everyone is. The second we begin to compare ourselves to them in a way that puts us higher in the human holiness way, in that same second we fall to our lowest. It's worse to know better and stumble down, than it is to be ignorant of our own pride, pride of humility, is just pride. The closer we are too Him, the more danger we are to falling further back behind the furthest from Him. It's easy to get prideful about our godliness. It's easy to get our heart hard to the world. It's easy to put ourselves in the front and focus of our own heart. It's easy to worship other humans for their success, beauty, holiness, fame or fortune. Admiration quickly turns to idolization. It happens unbeknownst to us. It happens automatically. Our nature is corrupt. We do things automatically, it takes the supernatural power of the Lord to maintain our proper place, the lowest possible place. We only have a chance really to see our own hearts. If we keep a close watch, we can see how desperately low we really are. We can see all the sins spring forth with no effort at all. All of the common sins are common to us all, they all live in all of us. We all puff ourselves up, in some way in pride. The person that emotionally, or otherwise responds, "Not I", is the person that is the most prideful, and furthest from the Truth.

The next limiter is knowing how broken we all are is that of the base. It keeps us not only from putting ourselves and others too high, but it keeps us from putting them too low. No matter where a person is in relation to the Absolute, they are infinitely far, we are all infinitely far. We can't condemn ourselves or others. If we can't know who is going to make it into His kingdom and who isn't. The very idea of focusing on praising someone as definitely going to Heaven or condemning someone as definitely going to Hell, might comfort us, but it most definitely removes our focus from where it ought to be; on God. Who knows who He will send in our path? Who knows who is watching what we do or listening to our words? We know God is watching us closely, we know God will use us in any way He can. We know all His sheep are important to Him. We also know that we're all just sheep. When ministering, we have to allow for Him to do His work on whoever it is, we cannot assume the lost sheep is lost forever, is not in the end findable. God is Supernatural, He turned the biggest Christian persecutor into the biggest Christian evangelist in the wake of Jesus's Sacrifice. He made a man blind, then sent angels to him, then the Holy Spirit to convert his heart. God has his own work to do on each of us. Our job is to do whatever work God has us do, no more or no less. We can't forget that Jesus couldn't convince everyone in person, that God couldn't convince all humans in this life. We don't know what he has planned for each of us in the next. We don't know if the lost souls will have a chance in the afterlife to change their mind and turn to Him. A few minutes in Hell might make a difference. So keeping a soft heart and humble mind toward others is paramount. Keeping His Highest, way up High where He belongs, and us, the lowest, way down low where we all belong, should help us stay open to His Grace and help to tune others toward It. It should help us to not put any of us outside the pack. The tribe of humanity is one tribe, none of us are perfect, we are all sinners. None of us are beyond redemption, or just as importantly, beyond sin. None of us are beyond good and evil. None of us get to claim in arrogance, with certitude, that any of us or going to Hell or vise versa, Heaven. We are allowed the audacity to claim Him as our Lord and Savior, but not the guarantee that we are in the Kingdom. This goes back to what Sanchez told me way back at the beginning of this journey. We will all be surprised at who makes it to Heaven and who does not. Sanchez didn't come to this conclusion lightly or on His own. He used Jesus' own words to realize this Truth. Only God knows, is true in regards to Eternity. This seems extremely important for us all. Keeping the knowledge and faith of Jesus real and alive and close to our heart always, while at the same time keeping the ignorance of exactly what He is up to just as close to our mind. We all need Him. We all could do better.

We're all broken. Nobody has Him all figured out. One of the truisms that I knew before Him, was a smaller incomplete version of this. My dad used to remind me that I was just as 'good' as anybody else, but that at the same time I wasn't any better. Finding God has brought that into the right perspective and proper place to the Higher Truth. In the eyes of God there was only ever one perfect human, His Son, the Son of Man, Jesus of Nazareth, The Christ our Lord. Everyone else on a fundamental level is lost. Our job, as I see it, is to get ourselves to Him, and along the way help anyone else that He 'calls' us to. We are to keep open heart and mind about the ones that He seemingly has us pass by, for He might have us circle back to them for another nudge in the right direction. Those that are lowest or furthest behind, might someday end up ahead of us. Somehow that's what we are to prefer, to put ourselves at the back of the pack, to know that's where we belong. Stay low, keep a servant's heart, stay with Him in Love, and worry not at all, in the slightest, about ourselves. He has in every way made it clear that He has got us. It almost seems like the entire point, that if we would only get out of our own way, that if we would only get out of His way, that everything would be better. Exactly as He wants it to be.

The nature of sin and condemnation (mac):
There is an issue that I need to address of sin and condemnation. Though we're all able to in some way recognize sin in ourselves and therefore in others, there seems to be an easy mistake to make in the judgement or condemnation of others. Knowing when an action or word or behavior is wrong is one thing. The condemnation, judgement, and sentencing of the wrongness, or even understanding the relative wrongness in God's eyes, is an entirely different affair. I'm speaking of this from a moral standpoint only, not in a legal sense. Part of the issue is using God's name to commit acts of hate, violence, or Eternal condemnation on those that sin, even to ourselves, but especially to others, seems wrong in itself. Perhaps this act of putting on the judge, jury, or executioners hat is more wrong than whatever the behavior the sinner is guilty of in the first place. There is such a thing as righteous anger, but there is a line between righteous anger and unrighteous anger. There is an issue with

taking one sin and elevating it above the rest as the 'worst' sin. It might be worse for those using the Bible or God or Jesus as a way to publicly or privately condemn another, then for those their condemnation is pointed at. I'm thinking of the jealous angry ex-wife who condemns her ex-husband for adultery. She holds a grudge with a hardened heart for her ex-husband and maybe even for all men that have ever committed an adulterous act, or maybe simply all men in general, in place of any one that may have harmed her. It's not that I'm saying that adultery is justified, or that it should be forgotten, or even forgiven. It's just that without being connected to the Absolute, how does the woman know how much to forgive or not? How much should she punish him, if at all? How much scorn should she have for her former husband, or should he even be her former husband? Should she go the other way and forgive him completely, the adultery, the lies, and the betrayal, and remained married? What about the repeat offender? What if it was with another man that her husband cheated on her with? What if it were multiple men? My point here is to demonstrate the complexity of not only sin, but the also the complexity in the response to sin.

We are sinners by nature, we even sin in reaction to sin. We need Him so much that we can't even trust ourselves to be a victim in the right way. Our victim status, at some point, turns into perpetrator status without Him. We are ignorant and blind on how to act and treat anyone really, even in the best of life's situations.  In the worst of situations, our worse self gets permission to be free from our normal civility, and our real self gets magnified through retaliation and revenge. We get harmed or worse our innocent loved one gets harmed and we take our free pass to jump into the mud with the pigs. We obviously have a sense of right and wrong. We obviously have reason, instincts, experience, and conscience to guide us in knowing good from evil. This may be the point of this entire book; exactly how, and how much, we react, act, and do in this world is much too difficult to say. The world is simply too complicated, we are too complicated, to know what to do in every moment. It's far too easy to get out ahead of Him, and rely on our flawed nature, or our flawed intellect, or our flawed emotions, or in this case here, our flawed sense of justice. So not just as a sinner, but also as a witness, or a victim of sin, we are equally if not more at risk of missing His Glory. That without leaning on Him, I myself over do my own victimhood and place my will in place of His. This leads to the more difficult and radical realization that all of our actions, words, behaviors, thoughts, and feelings that run outside of His Will, without Him, are in sin. We cannot really do 'good' in the right way without Him. It's hard for me even in writing this to really grasp emotionally the severity of what I'm saying. I understand it I think, intellectually, that everything outside of His will is bad. Therefore feeding the homeless, if we are not 'called' to is bad, because it isn't what He wants us to be doing with our life at that moment. I understand that He might want, and often does want, something else from us. Therefore, in some sense feeding the homeless outside of His will is the same as the rape of a child as far as being outside of His Will in sin is concerned. Literally as I write this I don't buy it fully,I don't trust that it's right, but I 'get' from Him, that it is in fact, correct. As I pray, I 'get' that every human act or thought that is not with Him is 'off', and therefore a sin. And that all acts not with His Will are ultimately against His Will, and are therefore in sin, and wrong, and are leading toward Hell. But to equate emotionally and intellectually, the rape of a child and the misplaced intent and heart of somebody feeding the homeless is wrong. There must be a way that God judges us all fairly, in that He judges how off we are when we do anything, when we think anything, when we feel anything. So that the child rapist and the thief aren't put into the same category of sin against Him. There must, in fact be a range, that He has as to the 'on'-ess or 'off'-ness, the rightness or wrongness of any act in or out of His Will. Since none of us can fulfill His will perfectly, and we all sin in that way, there must be a measuring stick of some sort, a Judge in the truest sense, for the rightness and wrongness of any human endeavor. It must be closer to the Father and son relationship that we all know as a natural, good, and correct relationship between God and us. In that, even though our child does something that is not exactly what we wanted as their parent, an act done in the 'right' heart or intent, and attitude goes a long way in determining the goodness of the said act. When my own son picks the garden flowers to give to me as a gift, even though I wanted him to leave them alone. His ignorant, flawed, but loving gesture is still appreciated, even though it was 'wrong' of him to pick the flowers. I would have rather had him listen and obey, and chose what I wanted him to do, but his heart was in the right place, at least the more right place. This must be how God is looking at each of us. The complexity of each and every other soul is only for Him to judge. For us, our position is to worry solely about our own hearts, and only the hearts specifically of any He calls us to look after, like our fellow believers, children, family, and friends. Not generally, all of their hearts, all of the time, but simply individually, at specific times, while of course continuing to check and keep our hearts and minds pointed at Him. This is the idea that when my older son tries to parent my younger son something becomes corrupted. The relationship is off. It's when my older son puts the parenting hat on that he is worse than whatever sin my youngest has committed. He should be a proper brother and let the fathering be done by me his actual father. This is how it must be with God. When we condemn our brothers and sisters in Christ or in humanity as a whole, God frowns harder on us the 'elders' of the tribe than He does the youth. He is harder in His judgement toward the 'found' sheep of the flock who try and judge His lost. We, the found, ought to brother and sister each other, not parent each other. Leave the parenting to our Father Above. Leave the judging to the Judge. Leave the authority to the Authority. Leave the casting to Hell to the One who does the casting. Leave the gate keeping to the Gatekeeper. Jesus does plenty to knock those who cast stones or who have plank in their own eye. He is clear that in order for us to be first, we must be last. We must stay low. When we're actually humble and low it's impossible to get too 'high and mighty' with each other. It's impossible to get sandwich boarding, soap box shouting, and condemning of others in the world. The evil contempt is hard to garner with a humble heart, and a lowly sinners position. Being righteous really should be left for the purely Righteous One. All of us who fall from His Will sin. Falling from His Will and taking the false authority of the Judge, or the Righteous One, or the King, when we are neither worthy of judging, worthy of righteousness, or worthy of the King, is at least as bad, if not worse, than whoever we are trying to condemn. All sin is bad, it's not entirely clear from the outward observers point of view what exactly constitutes a sin, because it has more to do with one's heart than it does their actual actions. There must be different levels of sin, and therefore levels of goodness, according to God, but again only He knows just how close or far we are. We barely can know our own heart let alone others. So let's focus on drawing nearer Him and be found, and let Him focus on those that choose to wander off and be lost, that is until He 'calls' upon us to go find them. We can't hear the 'call' through the emotion of hate, condemnation, revenge, or contempt. We can only hear Him with our hearts soft, through love.

In this world but not of the world (mac):
Yet another paradoxical occurrence in the Christian Way; the 'call' to be in the world, but at the same time, not to be of it. In the end, this world and this life aren't the final destination. What we do in this world matters for sure, but getting too attached to anything in particular in this world makes us become of or about this world. We as Christians are 'called' to be about one thing, and one thing only; Jesus. When we put Him in His proper place, in our life, we are about Him and His work and His Will. He conquered this world. He defeated temptation, He committed

no evil, and He conquered death. He came into this world, but He was always concerned with getting others to His Father's Kingdom; to the Eternal world. He uses many analogies regarding the importance of this singular focus. He talks about leaving, selling, and abandoning, all worldly things. Including family, friends, funerals, riches, land, and possessions, to follow Him, only and exclusively. When we do this properly, our grip must lighten on everything in this world. Nothing in this world is worth losing our soul over. When we hold too tightly to worldly possessions, people, and ideas, we aren't free to follow Him.

 What this has specifically done for me is create a more bland world in one way, and a more exciting and colorful world in another. I no longer can honestly get as excited about many of the things I once did, because my excitement came from placing those things too high. Identifying myself with objects or activities, being about those things made me excited for them because I valued them like treasures that I found here on Earth. What putting Jesus way up on my list, and therefore God's Kingdom, has done, is raised many things I had dismissed as not worthy of my attention. In that way it has elevated the things I had dismissed into the background of life and brought them up. Lowering some of life's colors, yet at the same time, enhancing and elevating all the rest of life's colors, has overall made the availability of colors available to paint my life, magnificent in depth and range. Instead of self limiting my choices and narrowing my field of view, God has broadened my perspective to the whole of life's variety and choice. While at the same time He has not let any one of them stand in my way as a stumbling block to Him. I am about one thing; and that is to follow the 'call', everything else gets moved way back. This way I can focus on whatever it is I'm 'called' to do, without worrying about whether the 'call' is valuable. Don't let me fool you here, I struggle with this plenty. I am a sinning corrupt person, so my valuation gets brought to the forefront way too often. I can't help making judgements on the import of things and people. This happens naturally without me even trying, I place my own value on all sorts of people, things, and situations. I can't help it. I can however choose to focus on my own sinful natural response to 'calls' or things, or I can pray for a light grip on my own opinions reasons and value judgements, and choose to obey the 'call' in good and honest faith. Trusting in the end that He knows what's best for me and the world. Trusting that I don't. If I get too hung up on this world, I can't be about Him. Trying to be about both is equivalent to obeying two masters, which we can't honestly do. We can obey one master while performing other tasks, but we can't obey two master's. Two masters will ultimately conflict and we are forced to choose. Whatever we choose is the real master we were obeying all along. We all have hierarchies of beliefs, priorities, and values, that we act out and hold as true, deep within. Some of us are aware of them and some of us aren't. This hierarchy is your religion, whether you think you're religious or not. Whatever the thing, that if you had to stop doing in your current life, gives you a negative emotional response, that thing is probably something you are about. That thing is probably part of your religion, your hierarchy of beliefs. We have to give *everything* over to Him, make Him the top of our Hierarchy. Then, and only then, can He re-arrange them in whatever order is best. There are patterns that emerge for an individual, and then for a collection of individuals, that follow God, but we have to be prepared for drastically different 'calls' from our brothers and sisters. We have to be ready for 'calls' that put our worldly affairs into chaos. We have to be willing to lose all of our worldly stock, including our own life. We are 'called' to give up our life, in order to gain Eternal Life, in order to gain in back. The things that we value, that seem to honor Him, are often the hardest to recognize exactly how tight our grip has become on them. It's difficult, until we offer it to Him, and actually lay it down to Him, and He 'calls' us to walk away from it, to tell exactly how attached we are to it. It's in our nature to value and attach ourselves to things, to family, to friends, to careers, to hobbies, to groups, clubs, and ideologies. We all get into habits and rituals, practices that become part of us, part of our world. It seems easy and obvious that He might ask us to stop things that we know to be wrong, like lying, lusting, thieving, gossiping, adultering, or using drugs or alcohol. It's less obvious to understand that He wants *everything*, including the good that we do like, our health and exercise, what we eat, our bedtime routine, prayer, meditation, volunteering, serving the community, entertainment, our career or job, our time, money, and talents, our friendships, relationships, and our loved ones. It might be less obvious, but it's definitely true that he wants all of our hearts, minds, and souls, we have to hand over, our political beliefs, our religious beliefs, our biblical interpretations, our news and information, our *everything*. He is asking us to hand over *everything* to Him, with the knowledge and reality that we might not get them back. We might have our things tweaked and changed from what we want, in fact more than likely He will tweak and change what we think and feel about *everything*. It's hard, but God is Good, not necessarily safe. With the 'good' that he takes away, we argue, "but it's good!", or "but they're mine!" The problem is that they aren't yours, *everything* is His. Your money, toys, tools, home, cars, skills, and talents are all His. He might 'call' you to stop your career or your wealthy lifestyle, or even your 'healthy' lifestyle. You might think that you deserve to be happy, and that these things make you happy. Your happiness is not His aim, your soul is. Besides, you don't deserve anything but death. You're a broken sinner that literally deserves death for your transgressions. Giving up all of your worldly status, power, wealth, love, likability, comfort, and agreeableness, for that of otherworldly, Supernatural Truth and Goodness, might seem easy in the emotional kind of way before you actually make any sacrifices for a cause, but this is exactly what counting the costs of following Him are all about. It's hard to give things up to Him, it's hard to sacrifice for anything. It's especially hard to take ourselves out of the equation. It's hard to take our earthly and worldly stability and security out of the equation. That's what we hold onto in this world; certainty, stability, security, and safety, that's exactly what He doesn't guarantee in this world. Only in the next life, He gives those guarantees. The sacrifice is real and incredibly scary, and therefore difficult. I don't think that it's actually possible to really truly have the kind of faith He is asking for without Him, without His help. You have to want Him more than you want the comforts of this world, and then He can meet you and carry you the rest of the way. You have to want Him more than your dignity, more than being right, or smart, or respected. You have to give all that up for Him; all your pride and self worth. It's actually radical and extreme. In the end, I understand that it's 'good news', but in the meantime the path is narrow, the way is treacherous, and the gate is narrow and easy to miss. Before I entered into Christianity I thought it a sign of weakness, that people had given up on this world, that they had quit. Instead what I found was that they weren't supposed to be giving up, as in quitting, no they were supposed to be freely giving, this world, and this life, to Him; they were sacrificing, not quitting. This sacrifice to Him is what makes us 'salty' as Christians. It's what is supposed to make us stand out in the world. The fact that we are not part of it, makes us go against the current of the world. The fact that we don't care about the same things, or at least not in the same way, as the rest of the world, makes us flavor the world in the right way. We care about pleasing our Lord, not ourselves. We care about building wealth in His kingdom, not wealth on Earth, in this life. There's a reason He talks about camels and eyes of needles in regards to the wealthy. In order to become rich and maintain wealth, you must put your wealth high on your priorities, high on your hierarchy of values, too high. You must spend time and energy protecting your possessions and wealth. You must store things and keep account of them. Your energy, time, and talents get used up by your wealth and possessions.

You're too busy tending to your wealth in this life to care about Him and His 'calls'. Again, He might 'call' you to own things, and have some wealth at times, but there is a huge vast gulf between being 'called' to it and going off on your own to it. The boat God 'calls' you to own is the same boat that He will 'call' you to give away or sell. You can't become attached to it like this world is so used to encouraging. It was never yours, it was always His, you are just stewarding His possessions. The Father analogy that He uses works well here too, *everything* has been given to you by your Father, including the air you breath and the water you drink to sustain it. He might need you to pass along His possessions to someone else. He might need you to hold onto, and cultivate, some new skill or tool. In order to do this, you might need to give up your old skill or tool, the one you've grown good at, and accustomed to. He then might 'call' you to freely pass them on to another. *Everything* needs to be looked at as renting or borrowing from Him, not owning, even our 'own' life isn't owned by us. We owe Him our life, He paid our debts for our sins. So we freely and gladly give it all back to Him. Sometimes He gives things back to us or allows us to keep and steward them for a long time. My wife and children are that way, so far. Remembering that their his children, and not my own, helps me to love them in the proper way. I am human, and it's easy to think this intellectually or in theory, but to put into actual practice, it gets harder. However with His help, when done properly, it allows me to enjoy and love my family in the proper light without weighing too heavily on any of them. Knowing that in the end, my kids are truly His, and that they will eventually have to choose, helps me stay close to Him when parenting them. That way if I get them to Him, as He wants them to, in love, they will be independent of me and dependent on Him alone. In this way I am free of the normal and usual burden of over or under parenting this world puts on us. Parenting is complex, I know I would just mess it up on my own, I've witnessed it, I've done it, I still do. With Him though it's magical, mystical, and miraculous, the work He does through me and through them. The work He has done and continues to do in my family is awe inspiring. My family is special to me, and I am glad that I'm 'called' to them. I have to allow my grip to maintain a loose grip on them as well. All of my relationships are this way, fellow souls that I am either 'called' to minister to, or not. Either way, I am trying and hopefully succeeding to be only on the path toward Him, aiming at His world, and His Kingdom, not anything in particular about this one, including my loved ones. The minute we get too attached to this world, is the same minute our soul is endangered. This is what happens when we put false idols up, we worship them, we place them too high where He belongs. We put our looks, our status, our possessions, our worldly accomplishments in His place. We put our holiness on display, we get proud, and we hold onto things in this world too tightly. Those things or people we place at the altar are the idols that destroy our relationship to Him. It's the same with ideas or platitudes, putting those ideas that are not absolutes, into the Absolutes spot is just as wrong as people and things. We do this with the Bible, the church, sayings, quotes, political ideologies, etc. We do it with those we admire, intellectuals, commentators, politicians, entertainers, famous and successful people, influencers, etc. We turn admiration of their worldly success into mimicry and idolatry. We care too much about what click, brand, store, sport, hobby, pastime, clothes, style, item, group, organization, or club says about us, rather than what God thinks about us. Rather than we can get into the ultimate club, the only one that matters, Heaven. We literally get in our own way. We care about the world way too much. We either try to save it and get behind a cause, or condemn it. Either way, if you're not being 'called' to it, then you are simply off. You are in the way. You need to give up your cause, your agenda, your party's line, or groups identity, and get with Him. With your will, ask Him for His. We each possess the ability to work directly with Him for His cause. It might be vastly different than your Christian brothers or sisters. It might be very similar. That's between you and Him. All worldly stuff gets infinitely far from Him in relative importance. All worldly blessings are gifts from Him, not things you deserve. The gratitude that comes from the right perspective is even hard. The lack of gratitude means we are focused on the wrong things. If He has forgiven us, and sent the Holy Spirit to guide us, then we are already incredibly Blessed, beyond what we deserve. The ability to commune with Jesus through the Holy Spirit and be in His Divine Will is all that we can hope for. The rest is just details.

Deep inner comfort and peace, versus outer discomfort and confusion in the trade off. When we let go of this world, and grab on tight to Him, we are free. Free in a way I had never experienced before Him. When I get it right with His Grace and His Glory, I feel joy, deep and utter joy. I am no longer a slave to this world, or this body, or this mind. I am free to feel the joy of the gifts and the blessings He has provided. I am free to hope and laugh and play, like I never have before. I am free to work, and to relax, in the right way, and the proper amount. I am free to feast guilt free, and to fast joyfully. I am free to be grateful, when I let go of me, my comfort, my mentality, myself. I get in the way because my nature is of this world, it's about itself, it's about the natural, material world. My nature is about the bread of the body, whereas He is concerned with the bread of my soul. The funny thing is, letting go of the physical, natural cares, and worries of this world has given me both. I have been fed deep in my soul since finding Him, I have already been rewarded handsomely for my commitment to Him, and my letting go of this world, and I have gotten bread for my body in bountiful amounts. I have never eaten so well physically, and my soul has never been satisfied. My soul was only ever able to be fed in bits and pieces, tastes really. I was only ever to find scraps for my soul before Him, always in a state of constant hunger. I would randomly get a bit of soul nourishment before God, but not like this, a steady supply of true soul food. Truly deep and continual, never ending, never ceasing, constant, soul ease, soul calming presence of Jesus. He has proven to be the never ending well of life. He is the key that fits the lock of my entire being. I would have never guessed.


Interpretation; the flaw and the solution (mac):
The arrogance and audacity of anyone to say that the Bible is not confusing or not full of mystery and riddle is obnoxious beyond belief. The Bible and especially the New Testament is full of radical events, teachings, words, rebukes, and parables. The amount of seemingly wild contradiction in what to do in any moment if we are to follow our Lord is insane. Do I sell all my possessions, or preach the gospel? Do I become meek as to inherit the earth, or do I become salty as to inherit His Kingdom? The disciples themselves, were right there with Him

yet often found themselves confused by Jesus and what He did and said. Jesus had to explain Himself, seemingly at times even annoyed with their hard hearts or overly dull heads, what exactly He meant. Even after His explanation I still find myself knowing it's true on a very clear level, but also at the same time not exactly knowing why, or realizing the mystery is deeper than my reach. Jesus talks about dividing believers, reaping what has been sewn, not all mercy and love, but judging the wicked and burning the weed. He speaks of separating the grain from the chaff. Then there is love and mercy in the extreme other direction, love our enemy. We know at once this must be true, but just as quickly we ask, how on earth are we to actually hold onto this love for the enemy who is out to harm me? As if this isn't enough to make us pause in our tracks and at the same time cheer for our Lord, all at once forgetting that we could be the chaff He comes to discard. There is also a continual checking and rebuking of every one who assumes they know, know Scripture or anything else. It's only the faithful, the incredibly faithful, that are applauded and encouraged by the Lord. None of the 'know it alls', none of the well reasoned get a thumbs up from Jesus. He Himself out reasons them all, besides the faithful, the ones that quit everything and follow Him and turn from themselves and drop and worship Him. The ones that ask Him for healing and have faith that He will save and heal, those are the ones He shows a bit of praise. It is the ones that admit they're lost and admit their ignorance, they are the ones that turn on a dime to worship and believe. They are the ones Jesus blesses. None of the arguing, so called experts, get any of His praise. They get His overpowering authority seeing through all of their trick questions. He isn't impressed by intellect, He again is only impressed by loyalty and faith. Then there is what seems a contradiction in Jesus telling some people to tell no one about Him or what he had done, and yet at other times He tells us to shine the light and not to cover it. At times He Himself seems to slip in and out of hiding, at times facing the authorities and at others avoiding them. He at times seems an extrovert and at others a lone introvert. He tells us to turn the other cheek, yet whips people for turning His Father's house into a market. He speaks of truth reigning supreme, yet speaks in parable that some will not understand, and at others He is very blunt and direct. He is never fearful, but rather extremely cunning. His claim is to the truth, He values it in a way that is above all else, at least above almost everything, all but His Father and Himself. Either way, He values truth extremely high.

It seems then that if there is ever anything that isn't true, or confusing, false or contradictory anywhere, including, and maybe especially in the Bible, versus a thing that is known to be true or fact in reality, then it's truth that reigns supreme. It cannot be true that something written is more true than Truth Himself. We can't put anything above truth and reality if in fact He is claiming that position. A piece of scripture that may or may not be literal can't be hoisted above Him. No where in the Bible does it say scripture is literal. It's clear that the Bible is true in the sense that it is pointing to God, but even Jesus speaks in metaphor and parable, He Himself isn't speaking in complete literal and technical terms. He often is saying things in reference to, allegory, allusion, and metaphor. He is very often teaching, and as good teachers do, He explains things in ways that relate, that makes sense to the audience. Yet this is the greatest teacher in human history because He is in a way, all of human History.

He is God. He doesn't mean literal sheep, when He speaks of sheep and finding the lost or helping the fallen ones. He doesn't mean actually casting a net to catch men, as they do with fish, when He speaks of fishing for men. He doesn't mean a literal treasure as in gold and jewels when he speaks of Heaven. No where does Jesus speak of the church as a small building, He is always speaking of a body as in a body of believers, not an actual body or even a building. If our Lord needs interpreting, than so does the rest of scripture. If we are flawed men, with flawed intellect, then we can't even trust that we will get all of the Bible's depth and nuance and meaning correct, or that we will pick up all that's there. We can't trust that our interpretation is accurate, or that there is only one specific interpretation that is relevant to us. Like any good truth, there are levels of understanding.

The Bible is mysterious and confusing, it's beautiful and contradictory. The Bible is a literal history but at the same time it is literal in a way that memory is. Memory will tell a story, but will miss the exactness in some ways of all the details, but only because we place emphasis on the point, punchline, or true meaning of the events. Our memory, like the Bible, is flawed and not literal in some sense, but also precise, exact, and meaningful in another. The Bible wasn't meant as a scientific work to find the truth of only the material world, this is not and never was it's intent. It is a story, a real story, a true story, but nonetheless a story that is meant to tell the world about the world, about itself. It's meant to let the reader know God and themselves in relation to Him. It is real and true, but not in a perfect or scientific way, it's a real history, a real telling, but no history is of interest in it's every excruciating detail. It takes a mind to decipher the important data points and discard the unimportant. It takes a mind to observe and then tell a meaningful story. The story, all stories for that matter, have a point and a focus. Some things are highlighted by the storyteller and other things are omitted. Certain events are important for different reasons and certain events are not. I'm not at all here saying the Bible is a myth or that it is untrue, I am saying that it is fallible in the same way any true story is. The breadth and depth of the story or rather stories in the Bible mean some are more true than others. It isn't a math book full of axioms that are then built on to each other, that all fit precisely together. It's not exact in, this is true, therefore this is necessarily true, kind of mathematical way. It's more real and unscripted as reality is. It is messy as the telling of events is. It is real and true just as reality is, but as reality is fallible so to is the book that explains it best.

For anyone, even the great theologian and logician, Thomas Aquinas to claim that they understand every part of the Bible is approaching a level of astonishing obnoxious pride, not witnessed as often as a unicorn. If you are claiming you understand the words and then generally you understand it for the most part then ok. But if you are laying claim that you understand the depths of all knowledge and wisdom and deep layered understanding of God, Jesus, and the Holy Spirit in its entirety as laid out in Scripture, than you are in the same astonishing group of men that claim atheism or claim sainthood or claim super powers on the level of comic book villain. No actual saint ever claimed to be a saint, nor do they claim to be absolutely inline with the Holy One. It's only the simple arrogant village idiot, the high school quarterback, that can make such an insanely ignorant and audacious remark. The high school quarterback just has not a clue as to what they are saying, not any real idea of what they're saying. When they say they are invincible or that they could conquer any woman in the world, it's simply the ignorance of youth, the utter lack of experience or challenge, coupled with the complete lack of reality or truth seeking that gives them the sense that they are in the right. The world just hasn't kicked back yet, undoubtedly it will. When an older man makes the same claim as the younger man in the same regard, they are worse than the younger, for they haven't the same excuse. The older man hasn't their youth to blame, they aren't ignorant in the same way as in their youth. They are willfully ignorant in old age, stubborn in a prideful way. The old man has ignored all the kicks and checks life has given him. They are the youth that purposefully never grew up, never grasped reality, never faced the truth. They spent their whole life looking away, now it's too hard to face the years they have wasted.

The man who claims the entire Bible is entirely understandable, doesn't understand their own words. They don't understand the weight they are placing upon their flimsy intellect. If you aren't connected to God when reading the Bible, you are bound to error, just as you are bound to error when doing anything without Him. If you can't be trusted, then why are you so trusting that you can interpret the scriptures? Jesus made many a fool when correcting so called scripture experts. I am not claiming here that we can't read and understand some of the Bible, even a lot of it. I'm not laying claim that some men understand more than others. Even the same man can read something twice and gain more understanding a second time around. This can and does happen often and can be iterated over time. I'm making the claim that nobody can know it all. I'm simply making the claim that with something as vast and with as much depth as the Holy Scriptures all men are bound to misunderstanding or misinterpretation or simply missing something. The fact there are so many branches of Christianity, and that they differ in emphasis or interpretation proves my point. Real scripture experts are men that have spent their lifetime studying, and have not reached the end of their study, they know like we all do that the more you study the infinite depth of a subject, the farther away the end gets. Yet you the layman, or the 'educated' fool, will look upon the scripture and be certain it is completely knowable, and that you are in the know. As if it were an easy read, a perfect, easy story, that you have mastered. Even if you had the words memorized, the complexity of even the smallest verses meaning and application would have you still reaching for their bottom. Where and when to apply your new knowledge, in any given situation, increases the level of intellectual claim that you are making by an exponential degree. Thats equivalent to laying claim that you alone can take every tool man has ever made and not only know it, but know exactly how and when to use it in every moment. I mean for every repair and new build of all of mankind throughout space and time. Besides the complexity of Scripture, it isn't written as a manual is, it isn't written to be lived with as a flip through guide to life. It isn't a stack of platitudes to be picked at random for all of the convenient easy to use answers to life. It's a story to lead to the answer, to Jesus. It's a guide to Him, it isn't a guide through each and every current moment in your life. It's meant to be put down in awe, and turn to our God in awe. Nowhere in the Bible will you find an answer to whether you should continue reading this book, the one you're reading this very moment, or whether you should've started in the first place. No where in the Bible does it tell you how often you ought to read, or refer to scripture throughout the day or your life.

Besides what are we to do when a fact from our world, collides with a claim in scripture? The answer seems to be, follow truth, follow the facts. The validity of scripture doesn't prove or disprove God, it only proves the flaw of men to make it into something it's not. It only proves that either the authors or the readers have made an error in interpretation. The Bible points us to the Truth, it isn't the Truth. There is no conflict in Him. He is pure. If there is a conflict in anything you thought, or read, and the Absolute, then the Absolute wins, that point is settled. Truth wins, God wins, nothing else. Especially not scripture, God and scripture are not equal in any sense, they are not one in the same. Just because I tell you of the Holy Trinity doesn't in anyway make me a part of the Holy Trinity. Nobody owns the Truth, we all have access, He gave you access, it's only you in the way of getting it, let go of any book, even this one, rather especially this one, and get with Him. Put all of your questions into the one true God. He is the answer to everything, simply ask Him if what we're saying is true. Ask Him, with anything ask Him. More importantly ask Him what you can do for His Highest, ask how you ought to spend your next moments. If it's to continue reading then great, read on, but if it is to serve in another way, love in another way, bring goodness and order in another way, rebuke yourself or your neighbor, who is knee deep in absurd worship of a book, then by all means get to it.

I suppose what we are doing in this book is laying claim to yet another way, what we think the correct way to be a Christian is. In a way it is completely audacious, in another we're not claiming it's ours at all. We found this way, we have discovered it, we did it in the same way we have found any truth. We did it in the same way anybody has ever discovered the truth. We laid it out as clearly as possible in this book. In the end we are only pointing everyone including ourselves to God, to His way, to the way. Not even because that is what we want, we are laying claim to something more audacious than that, it's what He wants. We are saying that God Himself wants you, He wants us all to be in communion with Him. We are simply messengers, but not because we are special, but because we realize we're not.


Reading Signs (mac):

If interpreting the Bible is difficult, then interpreting reality in real time is on a level of difficulty that puts Bible interpreting in the plane of nursery rhymes while real world sign interpreting in the realm of Shakespeare. Does God work in mysterious ways? Yes. Can you read the signs He presents without Him? No. I don't have much to say here other than trusting yourself to read the world and determine its meaning, using your intellect alone, seems like wishful naive thinking in the very best most generous light on one end, and just categorically incomprehensibly wrong and evil on the other end. The same can be said about dream interpretation. The level of complexity and personal intimate knowledge of dream interpretation it takes to get it right is vast. God definitely speaks to us through dreams, signs, wonders, and miracles. This I'm certain of. The chasm between Him speaking to us in this way, external signs and dreams, and us on our own figuring out what it means, is a much larger break than the sign reader wants to believe.  Unless we get connected to Him through the Holy Spirit and Jesus, how are we to know the mind and intention of God in the world, or if it is even Him creating a sign? I guess it's two fold; one, is it even a sign from Him, and two, if it is, what does it mean? Without going back to the Source of the message, how can we be confident in our answer to either question? Here is an example of what I mean; let's say you are driving on your way to play golf with your friend in the car. Suddenly you get hit by a drunk driver. Let's say you survive, but are unable to walk as a result of your injuries, and the passenger, you're friend dies. Let's also throw in that the drunk driver is unharmed. If you're a disconnected sign reader you can interpret these events in various ways. You can claim God wanted this to happen and that it was a sign from Him that golf is evil. You can also read it that God needed another angel for His army so He took your friend. You could also read it as God is punishing your friend for their sins. You could claim the same about the loss of the use of your legs. You could read it all as a test of your faith. You could read it as a test of your ability to love your enemy and forgive the drunk driver. You could read it as a sign that now you must travel the country fighting the evils of alcohol. You could read it as a sign that you need to fight for the rights of the disabled people in America or even around the world. You could read it as a sign that your entire life needed to be overhauled and that now you need to suddenly move to a 3rd world country and open a foster center for the disabled youth of that country. You could read is as a sign that God is making a deal with the devil and seeing how bad He can make your life before you break. You could read is at a sign that you are to save the drunk driver's soul and personally help them to find Jesus. You could read it as any combination of the aforementioned or none of the above. I could go on, I won't, I'm sure I've made my point. The sign reader doesn't stop to consider that maybe God had nothing to do with it. Maybe He didn't want any of it. Maybe He is just as sad and disappointed at the results of the car crash as you are. Maybe he is more devastated. Maybe He is equally as disappointed that you still have not asked Him directly what it meant if anything at all, or even what to do next. Maybe you weren't supposed to play golf that day? Maybe either was your friend, maybe the 'call' would have been to do yard work or take a nap or any of the thousand other things that He could've wanted from you? Maybe He gave you a sign not to go golfing that day and you missed it?

This goes back to a section of this book that Sanchez wrote, that people want to believe everything happens for a reason. Sanchez spoke about freewill and how powerful of a force for evil it is when we are out of His will. We all know the universe is a causal one and that there are in fact reasons for everything. The problem is that we assume to know the reason, or that it is a good reason, or that the reason a thing occurred is that it is a sign from God, and that we know what the sign means. The problem is us projecting our own reason onto an event and calling it His reason. Unless we are in His will and He chooses to let us in on His reasoning, we have to accept that we are in the dark. We are in the unknown. Being in the unknown is scary. It's equivalent to hearing a noise come from the dark, we automatically start to imagine a reason for it. We can't help it. We automatically want to know the unknown, we automatically want to understand the cause for the noise. We want to know so bad that we make up the cause for the noise rather than investigating or admitting we can't know. The truth is we often don't get to know what the reason is that something happened. The truth is we often don't even get to know the reason why we ourselves do a certain thing, or feel a certain way. We are complex creatures beyond understanding and comprehension on some level. The world jumps in such a degree of complexity in comparison to ourselves, that there is a very small chance in comprehending many of the reasons or causes in it. When we move our attention to the Creator, the depth of complexity grows infinitely large, so that our guessing and claiming to know His mind become foolishly arrogant.

There is plenty we do know and can know, I think there is a danger in the skeptic to take this lack of knowing and understanding to the level of an absolute. We can't go too far in the other direction in claiming nothing is knowable. The skeptic argues that since the level of unknown is so vast and so great that it means somehow that what we do know is diminished. To claim that there is no way of knowing anything, just goes back to cutting off the branch you are sitting on. The statement you made about not knowing is therefore part of what you can't possibly know. Therefore we must be able to know some things. My only claim is that what we can claim to know is limited, especially when it comes to reading and interpreting signs from above. When we get connected to the Creator the amount we can know grows to the appropriate level, the level He wants us to know, not the level we want to know. Again, His will, not ours.


A word on existence (mac):

I've actually struggled with existence in general for most of my adult life. In my search for truth I found what is called existential boredom; the very point of existing at all and the feeling of being stuck. Either in that nothing matters so what's the point kind of way, or the extreme opposite in that everything matters so much that I'm stuck not being able to decide what to do next. I'm paralyzed in fear that I will make the wrong step. Fear of the wrong step gets me stuck into not making any step, which is in fact a step, at least a choice, and this leads to no movement, and eventual existential boredom. Something like that, I'm pretty sure it's a fairly broad wide ranging field of philosophical and psychological study. Whatever it is, it fit for me. I wasn't bored in the micro or typical way, but rather on the macro or existential way. I was really stuck with, what's the point of even being? I have often felt like I didn't belong. Not only locally, like in my family or neighborhood or school, but globally like I didn't really fit into the world at all. I would get urges to just leave. Leave the planet, leave the area I'm in, leave the universe, or just leave the damn meeting. Especially a meeting, but that's for quite a different reason, or at least an exaggerated sense of the same reason. The sense that whatever this place is, whatever these people are up to, it's not for me. Not in a superior, holier, or better than thou sort of way either (though to be fair I have been guilty of that too); no I mean in a way that is more like, this doesn't resonate with me. This thing you all seem so into, doesn't move my soul. Whatever you all are up to isn't what I want to be up too. When I would try and explain we would just get to an impasse or a point of confusion. I came to the conclusion that the world just isn't quite right and neither am I. Without God the conclusion was pretty unbearable. Without God I was full of despair, longing, and hopelessness. Without God the sensation made no sense, and was deeply disturbing; it would flare up often and would never really go away. I would think that I was truly too sensitive for the world; or the world was too harsh for me. I have explained my conversion to Christianity and finding God in great detail and the miraculous nature of the entire journey, there is no need to re explain the awe inspiring life changing goodness that that really was and has been. With Him the act of existing became easier, way easier, but something has always been a struggle even through the amazing grace I have been given. The full scope and depth of understanding that existence was in fact good had still not sunk in. With God existing was better and bearable, even good, comforting, peaceful, less lonely etc. ; but it was still hard. It has been difficult to be deeply grateful for existing at all. Don't get me wrong, what was once unexplained chaos and confusion was now at least understood. Where I was once deeply lonely and alone, I now had supernatural help and guidance. The load is definitely lighter. The balance and peace that I so desperately was fighting for has come in unexpected ways. However I was (and still very much am) still broken and so was the world. I was kind of like, really, just throw me in this broken place in a flawed body with a flawed nature, to struggle endlessly and fight my way through until I die, and then maybe I will get through the narrow gate? Gratitude is not my first response to this reality. I understand that imperfect me plus imperfect world means that there is no nirvana, no perfect place or state of existence that I get to float around in, in pure bliss. No it's more like instead of feeling crushed by the waves of the ocean in swirling turbulence I am now actually swimming. I can now float at least, barely, but still way better than drowning. I am now, with a lot of help, going with the ocean, rather than fighting it. It's not easy, but it's easier. I'm still broken though, and so is the world, it's just now I understand so I can reach out for help, and I actually get it; which by the way is completely miraculous, strange and amazing. Still, with all the goodness, I wasn't satisfied with existing. I was walking around the world as if it were an amusement park before God, when really it was a battlefield. Understanding it's a war, makes stepping on landmines less likely, but why did God make existence a such a warzone? I'm no longer surprised at being shot at, I am way better equipped to defend myself. The tools I was using were like garden tools, when what I really needed were weapons; mystical supernatural weapons. Now that I have said weapons, I feel deeply comforted and at peace; but let's not forget that I exist in a world where I need weapons. Understanding that I am broken helps, but I'm broken. Understanding that I can't help being broken is in a way comforting, but isn't there a better way? Knowing that God is here for me always at every moment makes walking into battle easier, but war still sucks. This is where me and existence have had a difficult relationship. Even knowing how free will and the Fall played a roll still left me wanting. Something just wasn't fully clicking when it came to existence. I understood mentally, but not deeply. My knowledge of the good of existence had always been an issue, and it had gotten better, but I still could not convince myself of it's goodness. It seems like such a bad way to live; always at war. But it's not absolutely true is it? The war analogy is just more true than an amusement park one; for there still is amusement in this life. I would get pessimistic with reality because optimism seemed foolish, and the hope for heaven has just always seemed ridiculous; it's just too far off, too vague and uncertain as far as details and time.

Heaven went from this completely far fetched fantasy before belief, to a more plausible and quite possibly real reality, but it lacked the urgency of the present, and there still lingers the wishfulness of fantasy. It was as if my faith wasn't strong enough in Heaven, maybe it still isn't. I felt like the crazy people lived only for the hope of Heaven, the naive longed for Heaven while stumbling around in this actual world. There is still something I find off about forsaking the present for the future. Even in sacrificing the now for tomorrow has always seemed like a high stakes gamble. There is a paradox here. This isn't our home, but we're to love it as if... as if it were; or treat it as a training ground for our 'real home'. Immortality and eternity are intellectual realities that are part of the package deal when it comes to God, but they're not as real as Him right here right now. In my own life, trapped in time and space, knowing we have to die, immortality and eternity seem somehow less important. It seems unfair, the good news is good no doubt, but the cost of entry seems high... that is until GK Chesterton gave me this powerful and subtle idea that seemed to creep into my soul and paint the whole picture with something that finally clicked. It reminded me of how many of the conversations with Sanchez would go. I would get some nugget truth, big or small it did not matter, and over the next days and weeks and even years it would work its way through me like billiard ball, rattling around every part of me. Eventually it would settle down into my very bones as true. Like a nugget of gold sinking below the rest of the less valuable rubble and debris. There it would lie with the rest of the gold highlighting the Truth of it all, in all its Glory. It was simply this; the ability to complain about existence makes existing better than not. It didn't hit me at first, but now I cannot shake its profound truth. It's very similar to the old idea that it's better to have loved and lost than to never have loved at all. That truth I have known for a long time. If you've ever lost a loved one then the pain of loss is precisely because of the goodness of their existence in your life to begin with. Like lots of truths I have experienced it seems obvious to me once I see the truth in it, like how did I not know that? But I didn't, not about existence, not really, deeply, truly. I knew it had to be better to exist than not because God is good, and therefore whatever He brings into existence is good, but it's a tough sell when everything seems like such a struggle and everything is so imperfect. The fact that anything *is* at all, is where the blessing comes unexpectedly for me. Suffering through the struggle is better than no ability to struggle at all. What Sanchez had said long ago that "something was better than nothing" really hadn't hit me. There is a reason suicide, murder, and even death seem so wrong, it's because they are. We know it in our bones, but only because we know that life or rather existence is good. GK puts it another way; that the minimum good of life, is worth it. Not even counting the higher good, or the best good, or the better good; no it's the least good, the lowest minimum good that makes existing worth it. The idea that being able to know that something is in fact not good is paradoxically good. And this is the missing piece that I needed to make me finally get it deeply. The simple ability to say this sucks, makes the suckiness of life worth it. The alternative is nothing, no ability to even gripe. There is joy in the ability to know how unenjoyable life can be. I'm sure I will doubt this new found truth the next time I am in actual pain. My toe will be freshly stubbed and I'm sure I will be thanking the Lord for the ability to feel the pain of my stubbing.

When I am tired and grumpy and joy seems like a distance and absurd childish mood, I'm convinced the subtle joy of the ability to be a curmudgeon will fail to crack even a faint draw of a smile on my heart; but at least it makes me smile now. Thinking of my grumpy future self cursing my present self, in the naive subtle optimism of youth is a higher pleasure that I have no trouble being grateful for. The thing is, even in the great Fall there is good to be had. The knowledge of good and evil is good; it's not as good as God wanted, but it's still minimally good. That's what I've been missing in my heart; that the act of knowing I'm broken is good. The ability to see my brokenness, makes the absurdity of being broken worth it. Again the next time I have to swallow a difficult truth of my depravity, or even when I'm laying on the ground with my leg broken, or worse my heart broken, I'm sure I won't be able to recognize this truth; that it is in fact good to be able to see my fragility, my brokenness, and general filth. I have wrestled with existence for a long time, even sadly once I found God. 'Existence is good', was never something I could convince anyone else of because I couldn't convinced myself. I was being too greedy with the mark in which

I measured. I had to lower the bar. Just in case you're confused I'm not saying evil is good, let's celebrate. No that would be absurd and that's exactly what positive thinking and popular optimism has always seems to do. Like let's call this pile of dog shit between two slices of bread a good gourmet meal. Let's call this shit sandwich a blessing. I have always had a problem with this approach, namely because it's categorically false and simply ridiculous. Besides its very often the person who created the shit and is now giving you the sandwich for which he is claiming is really the next best thing if you would just look at it in the right way. It's the kind of mentality that causes harm and angers me at its obvious flaws. Let's just call it what it is, period, especially when it's a pile of shit. Let's call the shit sandwich that life or you or your boss or neighbor or 'friend' has given you exactly what it is; a sloppy disgusting shit sandwich. Please let's not dress it up, let's not put lipstick on a pig (the more subtle version of the same picture). What I was doing with existence was this; I was getting the ability to recognize the shit sandwich confused with the existence of the shit sandwich itself. Thank you Mr. GK Chesterton for separating the small good from the enormous bad. In reality this small good is in fact the gift of life that I for the life of me couldn't see, and it is in its truth much more magnificent than all the shit sandwiches life has served me thus far. I guess I found out it's better to be able to taste the shit sandwich than it is to have never tasted it all.

Object permanence (sanchez):

One of the reasons life is so hard is because we think we are the purpose of life (or our family, job, or cause). If this were true, then the despair of life would just be a matter of time. I would be climbing a mountain for no reason but to climb (even mountain climbers are not climbing just to climb. They climb for glory, self improvement, the challenge.) If there is not a permanent objective goal I am moving towards, then all movement would be meaningless. I could not make progress unless my objective is fixed. If my destination was simply wherever I happen to be standing, then there's no point in moving. The Absolute Object would need to be fixed in space so that I could in fact be closer or further away from It. This is why existential boredom is so prevalent and destructive.

The Way (mac):

What we're claiming here in this book is radical. It's extreme and audacious. We are purposely leaving you or us without wiggle room. There might be depths of the Holy Spirit. We each are obviously different containers. So the gifts, talents, and amount of the Holy Spirit we each receive must vary accordingly. Even in the Bible there were degrees of power of the Holy Spirit. There was Jesus the ultimate most connected to the Holy Spirit, then there was a varied of amount power and Spirit received by those that followed Him, after the Resurrection. The Apostles were able to raise the dead and perform miracles, but not everyone who received the Holy Spirit in the early Church were doing so. Lots of members were simply filled by the Spirit and lived in what seemed peaceful and rather ordinary lives. In fact I would say the majority of those committed to the Holy Spirit did just that. Their lives, no less significant, were lived as they should have been in harmony with each other, raising families, and looking out for each other. Most of us don't seem to be called to die for our beliefs in some romantic or heroic fashion, though I'm sure there are some. It seems more true that we are called to live in a radically committed way and yet be a hero in ordinary and simple service to others. It wouldn't seem to work if everyone was called to die; who then would raise the kids or love their neighbor? I know for me the calls have not all been to conquer the world and shake the worlds foundations. I'm not wandering the earth slaying dragons or performing miracles (at least not yet). The call has often seemed mundane, perhaps even boring. There seems to be an emphasis on my immediate family; my wife and children. There have been some strange calls and tough calls, but often it's to just be with Him and love my family, correct, guide and cherish. The call to adventure, not so much. The call to go to work and go to the grocery store and pay bills are regular occurrences. Everyone is healthy and we are taken care of. In a way we are just moving along in our day to day life, living with Him and being grateful. Some seasons the call has been to minister to friends and extended family, then another season to physically work and build and minister less. It's always been the call to be a good husband, father and friend. Lately, I have been called to read, and now write. I don't even get to call myself a writer, I'm just a

Christian; a follower of Christ; of the Way. I get to change diapers, cook dinner, work on my families vehicles, and listen often. Nonetheless, what we are claiming is in fact extreme and radical. We are claiming in the most clear way possible that there is, simply put, only one way to live, at least to live properly and truly; that is, by committing whole heartily to the Holy Trinity. We are to choose to jump into the deep end with Him and leave ourselves behind. Rather to kill our former selves, our fallen natural selves, at least in spirit, and allow for the Holy Spirit to fill our mind body and soul. There seem to be a lot of Christians claiming that they are swimming, but in reality they are firmly planted on the side of the pool with only the tips of their toes in the water, claiming that they are all in. Just because the calls from the Holy Spirit might be ordinary or mundane or subtle, the extreme nature of fully committing and throwing ourselves at the feet of Jesus, leaves no room to for partial commitment. It doesn't work that way. Partial commitment is no commitment. There is an excluded middle, an either or situation. Either you're all in or you're not in at all. The person on the side of the pool is not in. Only those out in the deep end not touching the bottom or the sides is counted as all in. He wants us all in the deep end relying solely upon Him for everything, relying on nothing else at all. It's extreme, it really is. Early Christians would say they were following the Way, before the term Christian become more prevalent. They didn't say a way, no, it was the Way; it still very much is. The cost of entry is your literal life; we must give it up in order to get it back. We must freely choose to submit our entire life in order to become truly free. The costs are great. If you find yourself waivering at the gate, then chances are you find yourself at the correct gate. If you find yourself strolling through without any cost or sacrifice, or saying that was easy, then you probably haven't counted the costs, and are more than likely you missed the gate. You're probably sitting at the edge of the pool in lukewarm water with only your toes dangly in, not fully understanding or committing. You still rely on you. You are still holding onto this world, to the old you, and don't trust that He has you or will have you if actually let go. You don't trust, or have faith, that this is the only way, that He is the Way. We must jump into the pool to be baptized with the Holy Spirit, and then maybe He will call us to be baptized in water. We must fully commit, we must be completely submerged.

After my conversion the call was to ask my brother for help in building a tabernacle of sorts to get married in. While we were working in my backyard the call was to confront Him with a question. I asked him if he thought I was crazy or did he believe me that I was actually hearing God. He replied with, "That's good for you, but not for me." I pushed back as gently as I could with, "That's not how Truth works." I continued following God and said, "Either I am hearing God, and He wants everyone to hear and follow Him, or I'm not, and I'm badly mistaken, I'm crazy and I need help." My brother's mood changed, he got defensive. He said, "I think we're just animals, we're just like dolphins." That threw me off, it was not only a confusing response, but it was never something I had held as a serious argument against God. It threw me off, not in a way that doubted my beliefs, but more in a way that surprised me with exactly where my brother was at in his own journey. I responded with, "That's not true that we're *just* animals, and it doesn't answer the question of whether or not you think I'm crazy for claiming to hear God right now as we speak or not." He said, "I know you man, I grew up with you, what is this?" He was upset, he threw his tools down and left. He didn't like the push, ever since then there has been a gap between us. The call for me is to love him without bringing up the subject. His heart is hard for the truth. Your turn. We're either right or we're wrong. There is no middle ground. There is either one way to live and we have found it or we haven't. If there is more than one way to live then we are wrong. If there is only one way to live but this isn't it, then we're wrong. You have a choice, we all do, it's an extreme choice, it means the death of you. You either give it all up to Him, or you hold on tight and do it some other way. Jesus or not? Do you live by the Holy Spirit or by something else? You have to be prepared to sacrifice it all, your most prized and cherished possessions. You have to give up your way of doing things, your way of believing, your way of thinking; you have to give it all up to Him, lay it all down to Him, and ask Him for help. Then listen and obey, that is the only way. Jesus is radical, He asks the impossible, He is the good news, He is the Way. If we're wrong then we're sorry, really we are, we obviously need help. If we're right, then this might be the only chance you have, right now to turn toward Him and follow the Truth, the Way. In this moment and every moment the choice is yours, it always has been. You've been given that honor, the honor to choose the wrong way, your own way; or the right way, the True way, the only real way... His way... good luck.

CPSIA information can be obtained
at www.ICGtesting.com
Printed in the USA
FSHW010501300320
68613FS